7.95

HANDBOOK OF

CONCEPTS FOR LIVING

by
BILL BRIGHT

D1600525

HANDBOOK OF
CONCEPTS FOR LIVING

by
BILL BRIGHT

A Compilation
of the
Nine Transferable Concepts

Campus Crusade for Christ Incorporated

San Bernardino, California 92414

HANDBOOK OF CONCEPTS FOR LIVING
A Compilation of the Nine Transferable Concepts

A Campus Crusade for Christ Book
Published by
HERE'S LIFE PUBLISHERS, INC.
P. O. Box 1576
San Bernardino, CA 92402

Library of Congress Catalogue Card 81-67818
ISBN 0-86605-011-6
HLP Product No. 35-140-3

Manufactured in the United States of America.

WHAT IS A TRANSFERABLE CONCEPT?

When our Lord commanded the 11 men to whom He had most shared His earthly ministry to go into all the world and make disciples of all nations, He told them to teach these new disciples all that He had taught them (Matthew 28:18-20).

Later the apostle Paul gave the same instructions to Timothy: ". . . .and the things which you have heard from me . . . these entrust to faithful men, who will be able to teach others also" (II Timothy 2:2).

In the process of counseling and interacting with tens of thousands of students, laymen and staff have discovered that many church members, including people from churches which honor our Lord and faithfully teach His Word, are not sure of their salvation, that the average Christian is living a defeated and frustrated life and that the average Christian does not know how to share his faith effectively with others.

In our endeavor to help meet these three basic needs and to build Christian disciples, Campus Crusade for Christ, Inc. has developed a series of "how to's" — or "transferable concepts" — in which we discuss many of the basic truths that Jesus and His disciples taught.

A "transferable concept" may be defined as an idea or a truth which can be transferred or communicated from one person to another and then to another, spiritual generation after generation, without distorting or diluting its original meaning.

As these basic truths — "transferable concepts" — of the Christian life are made available through the printed word, films, tapes and cassettes in every major language of the world, they could well be used of God to help transform the lives of tens of millions all over the world.

We encourage you to master each of these concepts until you are personally prepared to communicate them to others "who will be able to teach others also."

To share these vital truths with others, use the brief outline at the beginning of each chapter, the amplified outline at the end, or tape recordings of the Concepts. Share as often as you can. If possible, give a book and perhaps a tape or cassette to those with whom you share the Concepts so that they, too, can study the material in depth and pass it on to others.

In so doing, many millions of men and women can be reached and discipled for Christ. They can then make a significant contribution toward the fulfillment of the Great Commission in our generation.

CONTENTS

What Is a Transferable Concept? 5
General Study Guide 9
Notes For Teachers................................ 11
Chapter 1: How To Be Sure You Are a Christian 13
    Study 1. Intellectual Commitment.................. 17
    Study 2. Emotional Commitment 26
    Study 3. Volitional Commitment 33
    Chapter Study Guide 44
    Amplified Outline 45
Chapter 2. How To Experience
       God's Love and Forgiveness 49
    Study 1. Adventure and Challenge 49
    Study 2. The Great Problem........................ 57
    Study 3. The Great Solution...................... 66
    Chapter Study Guide 78
    Amplified Outline 78
Chapter 3: How To Be Filled With the Spirit.............. 83
    Study 1. Who? Why? What?........................ 83
    Study 2. Appropriating the Fullness................ 95
    Chapter Study Guide 111
    Amplified Outline 111
Chapter 4: How To Walk In the Spirit.....................117
    Study 1. Spiritual Breathing 117
    Study 2. Be Sure You Are Filled With the Spirit.......128
        Be Prepared For Spiritual Conflict...........131
    Study 3. Know Your Rights.........................137
        Live By Faith.............................144
    Chapter Study Guide 153
    Amplified Outline 153
Chapter 5: How To Witness In the Spirit 159
    Study 1. First, Be Sure You Are a Christian 163
    Study 2. Second, Be Sure There Is No Unconfessed
        Sin in Your Life 174
        Third, Be Sure You Are Filled With
        the Holy Spirit............................176

   Fourth, Be Prepared to Share Your Faith
     in Christ. 179
   Fifth, Pray 180
  Study 3. Sixth, Go 187
   Seventh, Talk About Jesus 188
   Finally, Expect Results. 191
  Chapter Study Guide 197
  Amplified Outline 198

Chapter 6: How To Introduce Others To Christ. 203
  Study 1. Why Witness? 205
  Study 2. How To Witness 210
  Study 3. Conflict — Assurance 225
  Chapter Study Guide 235
  Amplified Outline 236

Chapter 7: How To Help Fulfill the Great Commission. 241
  Study 1. Who? What? 241
  Study 2. Why? When? Where? 251
  Study 3. How? 261
  Chapter Study Guide 279
  Amplified Outline 280

Chapter 8: How To Love By Faith. 285
  Study 1. God Loves Us 285
  Study 2. Command To Love. 297
   Our Inability To Love 304
  Study 3. We Love With God's Love. 307
   We Love By Faith 307
  Chapter Study Guide 317
  Amplified Outline 318

Chapter 9: How To Pray 321
  Study 1. What Is Prayer? 324
   Who Can Pray? 325
  Study 2. Why Are We To Pray? 330
   To Whom Do We Pray? 332
  Study 3. When Should We Pray? 336
   What Should Be Included In Prayer? 338
   How Can We Pray With Confidence? 343
  Chapter Study Guide 355
  Amplified Outline 355

Addendum. 359

GENERAL STUDY GUIDE

1. Read each chapter in HANDBOOK OF CONCEPTS FOR LIVING and/or listen to the cassette tape* of each Concept for six consecutive days. Educational research has shown that it is necessary to read or hear a concept six to ten times to understand it thoroughly. Think through the Review and Thought Questions at the end of each study section each time you read the Concept. The application of the principles outlined will enable you to live a consistent Spirit-controlled life.

2. Memorize the verses and references indicated for each chapter. Your memory work will be easier and more lasting if you review it for an entire week rather than try to complete it in just one day.

3. Answer the questions at the end of each study section, looking up the Scripture references and filling in the blanks.

4. Participate in a group that is studying the Transferable Concepts, or form your own group by inviting others to join you in a Bible study program. As you discuss the study question, share what God is teaching you about each Concept, and how you plan to apply the principles to your life and how you plan to share them with others.

*For current catalog or more information, write:
Cassette Tape Services
Campus Crusade For Christ
Arrowhead Springs
San Bernardino CA 92414

NOTES FOR TEACHERS

A Transferable Concept. Here at your fingertips is a tool that can be used to make disciples of each one in your group. A disciple? Yes. Someone who knows the principles Christ taught in His earthly ministry and has "transferred" or incorporated them into his or her own life. Thus, he has not only grown in the Lord himself, but he is capable of transferring that concept (or principle) to another and helping him to grow also.

Growth is exciting. It's stimulating. The questions will provide you a place to start discussion and stimulate personal growth. This "how to" essential of the Christian life presents tremendous opportunities for teacher and students alike to revitalize their witness, reconsider their priorities and change their world.

Each study should take about 40-50 minutes of teaching time. But this is a general guideline. You can also tailor each lesson to the needs of the group. Students may want to incorporate their own thought questions and delve into even deeper Bible studies.

Christians at all stages of maturity in the faith struggle at times. A clearer focus on what's really involved in the Christian walk encourages those who are growing weary in well-doing (often an indication of trying to live the Christian life by self-effort) and excites those who haven't really started walking wholeheartedly with the Lord. This book reaches those at all levels of Christian maturity and in every walk of life.

Renewing one's purpose or kindling the fires of faith — these studies can do either or both.

CHAPTER 1
HOW TO BE SURE YOU ARE A CHRISTIAN

Study 1. Intellectual Commitment
Study 2. Emotional Commitment
Study 3. Volitional Commitment

STUDY 1.

My experience in counseling thousands of students and laymen through the years since I met Christ personally has convinced me that literally tens of thousands of good, faithful church-goers have received Christ in prayer but are not sure of their salvation. Regardless of how hard they try and how disciplined their efforts to please God, they are still uncertain of their relationship with Him.

A dynamic young businessman sat across from me in my office. By almost every standard of human measure, this man was an outstanding success in both his business and his religion. One of the world's leading men in his field, he was a highly moral, religious person and very active in his church; yet, he was not sure that he was a Christian. He wanted desperately, more than anything in the world, to be sure, but did not know how to go about obtaining such assurance.

Doubt Of Salvation

Many pastors and other Christian leaders, I have discovered, have this same gnawing doubt about their salvation. One pastor who had preached the gospel for 40 years told me that he was still unsure of his salvation. The wife of an evangelist confided, "During the past 30 years, my husband and I have introduced thousands of people to Christ, but I have never been sure of my own salvation. I have never before shared this concern with anyone, but now I am so desperate that I have come to seek your help."

A student who had prayed to receive Christ after hearing my message on "The Uniqueness of Jesus" stood to his feet after we had prayed together and, with a puzzled and troubled look on his face, said, "I don't feel any different. I guess God didn't hear my prayer. How can I be sure that Christ has come into my life?

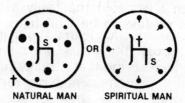

SELF-DIRECTED LIFE
S - Self is on the throne
† - Christ is outside the life
• - Interests are directed
by self, often resulting in
discord and frustration

CHRIST-DIRECTED LIFE
† - Christ is in the life
and on the throne
S - Self is yielding to Christ
• - Interests are directed
by Christ, resulting in
harmony with God's plan

NATURAL MAN   SPIRITUAL MAN

Why does this heartbreaking uncertainty exist among so many students and older adults who genuinely want to know God and have sought Him for years? I am persuaded personally that the lack of assurance is due either to misinformation or to a lack of information regarding who God is, the true meaning of the crucifixion and the resurrection and what is involved in receiving Jesus Christ as Savior.

They Did Not Know How

Since its beginning on the University of California at Los Angeles (UCLA) campus in 1951, Campus Crusade for Christ has conducted surveys of literally thousands of students on hundreds of college campuses across the United States and around the world. In these surveys, the response to the question, "In your opinion, how does one become a Christian?" revealed that 89% of the students polled did not know how.

Hunger For God

The fact that men and women are hungry for God is dramatically illustrated by the thousands of students and older adults who, each week through this ministry alone, actually sign decision cards and receive Christ into their lives through prayer as an act of faith. Of course, only God knows how many actually experience the new birth and become true followers of Christ, though their real desire to know God is apparent to all who work with them, from the youngest child to the oldest adult.

This hunger is not limited to people in the United States, but is experienced by people throughout the world. While in Paris recently, I was informed of a religious survey taken among many of the 400,000 students in France. Though I am told that only a few hundred of these students profess to be Christians, more than 60% indicated a desire to know God personally.

In Korea, approximately 10,000 students, laymen and pastors participating in a week-long Campus Crusade for Christ leadership training institute interviewed more than 42,000 people. They presented to them the gospel as contained in the Four Spiritual Laws booklet, which is a simple presentation of God's love and forgiveness made possible through Jesus Christ. Of those interviewed, 16,352 prayed with them to receive Christ, and an additional 3,800 expressed a desire to be filled with the Holy Spirit by faith. In Haiti, more than 1,000 students and laymen prayed to receive Christ when approximately 500 pastors and lay leaders shared the gospel through the use of the Four Spiritual Laws booklet. In the Watts area of Los Angeles, 1,600 staff and students, largely white, prayed with an estimated 3,000 blacks who expressed their desire to know our Savior.

Lack Of Information

Basically, I believe that millions of people are unsure of their relationship with God because they simply lack information. They need to know that Christianity is not a philosophy, not a code of ethics, not a standard of performance; it is a personal relationship with God as He has revealed Himself to man through the Lord Jesus Christ. Because of this, the historical facts concerning the birth, life, death, resurrection and coming again of the Lord Jesus assume tremendous importance. Take Buddha out of Buddhism, Mohammed out of Islam, and, in like manner, the founders of other religions out of their religions, and little would be changed. But take Christ out of Christianity, and there would be nothing left — for Christianity is a personal relationship with the living Christ!

Could it be that you yourself are still unsure of your relationship with God even though you may have been reared in a Christian environment and have "believed" in Him and in His Son for years? If you were to die this very moment, do you know where you would spend eternity? Do you have the assurance right now that the Lord Jesus is in your life and that you are a child of God?

Or perhaps you have only recently "received" Christ and are still not sure that anything has really happened — you have no assurance of your salvation and have serious misgivings about where you will go when you die.

Of the tens of thousands of students, laymen and pastors who attend our various training institutes, an average of 10-25% indicate in the course of the training that they are not sure of their relationship with God. They may have previously "received" Christ in prayer, but they are not sure of their salvation.

Threefold Commitment

If you are among that vast multitude who are still looking for God, the next few moments could well be the most important ones of your entire life.

Becoming a Christian involves receiving the Lord Jesus Christ — the gift of God's love and forgiveness — by faith (John 1:12; Ephesians 2:8, 9). It results in a threefold

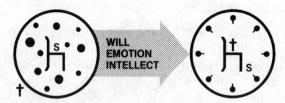

commitment to a person, the person of the Lord Jesus Christ. It is a commitment to Him of one's intellect, emotions and will.

Our relationship with Christ can well be illustrated by the requirements for a marriage relationship, which ideally must contain these same three ingredients: the intellect, the emotions and the will.

For example, a man may be convinced intellectually

that the woman who is his intended bride is the "right" one for him. He may be involved emotionally and love her with all his heart, but marriage requires more than the intellect and the emotions. It also involves the will. It is not until the man and the woman, as an act of the will, commit themselves to each other before a minister or another person of authority that they become husband and wife. The two words "I do" make the difference. So it is in our relationship with Jesus Christ. It is not enough to believe intellectually in Christ, nor is it enough to have an emotional experience. Though both are valid, one does not become a Christian until, as an act of the will, he receives Christ into his life as Savior and Lord.

INTELLECTUAL COMMITMENT

Let us examine more clearly, one by one, each of the three elements of Christian commitment. First of all, in order to become a Christian, or to be sure that you are a Christian, you must have a clear, intellectual understanding of what is involved. Christianity is not "a blind leap of faith." It is built upon historical fact, documented by centuries of scholarship and research. Many leading scholars have dedicated their lives to investigating the life, teachings, death, resurrection and influence of Jesus of Nazareth. As a result, we have more historical evidence proving His resurrection than we have of the fact that Napoleon was defeated at Waterloo.

Professor Edwin Selwyn, in his work, *The Approach to Christianity*, said, "The fact that Christ rose from the dead on the third day in full continuity of body and soul, and passed into a mode of new relationships with those who knew Him on earth — that fact seems as secure as historical evidence can make it."

That good news was the message of the revolutionary New Testament Church. It is a revolutionary message today. It is a fact of history.

Greatest Person

For many years, in many countries of the world, I have asked thousands of people — Muslims, Hindus, Buddhists, atheists, communists — "Who is the greatest person who has ever lived? Who has done the greatest good for mankind?" Every knowledgeable person I have ever encountered who has had the opportunity to investigate the evidence has answered, "Jesus of Nazareth." Not all have received Him as their Savior, but the problem has been one of the will rather than of the intellect, for the facts concerning who the Lord Jesus is and what He has accomplished are clear for all men to see.

While visiting one of America's leading universities, I was invited to interview a well-known communist and professing atheist.

"Who, in your opinion," I asked, "is the greatest person the world has ever known?" Who has accomplished the most good for mankind throughout the centuries?"

From the expression and response it was obvious that such a question had never been considered before. After several moments of deliberation, "I guess I would have to say Jesus" was the reluctant reply.

God's Plan

Paul writes: "Praise be to the God and Father of our Lord Jesus Christ for giving us through Christ every possible spiritual benefit as citizens of Heaven! For consider what He has done: before the foundation of the world He chose us to become, in Christ, His holy and blameless children living within His constant care.

"He planned, in His purpose of love, that we should be adopted as His own children through Jesus Christ — that we might learn to praise that glorious generosity of His which has made us welcome in the everlasting love He bears toward the beloved. It is through Him, at the cost of His own blood, that we are redeemed, freely forgiven through that full and generous grace which has over-flowed into our lives and opened our eyes to the truth.

"For God has allowed us to know the secret of His plan, and it is this: He proposes in His sovereign will that all human history shall be consummated in Christ, that everything that exists in Heaven or earth shall find its perfection and fulfillment in Him. And here is the staggering thing — that in all which will one day belong to Him we have been promised a share (since we were long ago destined for this by the One who achieves His purposes by His sovereign will), so that we, as the first to put our confidence in Christ, may bring praise to His glory!" (Ephesians 1:3-11, Phillips)

The Great Commission

Shortly before Jesus physically ascended into heaven, He gave to His followers the Great Commission: "Go therefore, and teach all nations..." (Matthew 28:19). Beginning in Jerusalem, the early Christians took His message to the ends of the then-known world, so that before many years had passed, even the enemies of the faith admitted that these men had "turned the world upside down" (Acts 17:6, Phillips).

Greatest Influence

The British scholar, W. H. Griffith Thomas, said, "The testimony to the present work of Jesus Christ is no less real today than it has been in the past. In the case of all the other great names of the world's history, the inevitable and invariable experience has been that the particular man is first a power, then only a name, and last of all a mere memory. Of Jesus Christ the exact opposite is true. He died on a cross of shame, His name gradually become more and more powerful, and He is the greatest influence in the world today."

George Romanes, British physicist, agrees, "It is on all sides worth considering (blatant ignorance or base vulgarity alone excepted) that the revolution effected by Christianity in human life is immeasureable and unparalleled by any other movement in history."

Kenneth Scott Latourette, director of the department of religion in Yale's graduate school, historian and author of a set of well-known works, comments, "Measured by its fruits in the human race, that short life (referring to Jesus Christ) has been the most influential ever lived on this planet. As we have been at pains to point out, the impress of that life, far from fading with the passing centuries, has deepened. Through Him millions of individuals have been transformed and have begun to live the kind of life which He exemplified. Gauged by the consequences which have followed, the birth, life, death and resurrection of Jesus have been the most important events in the history of man. Measured by His influence, Jesus is central in the human story."

Who Is He?

Now who is this person Jesus Christ, whose great influence is so universally recognized? By way of review, Jesus of Nazareth was conceived by the Holy Spirit and was born of the Virgin Mary almost 2,000 years ago. Hundreds of years before, the great prophets of Israel had foretold His coming. The Old Testament, which was written by many individuals over a period of 1,500 years, contains more than 300 references to His coming.

The life Jesus led, the miracles He performed, the words He spoke, His death on the cross, His resurrection,

His ascent to heaven — all point to the fact that He was not mere man, but more than man. Mohammed was merely a prophet; Buddha from his own admission was an agnostic; Confucius was an ethical teacher — but Jesus claimed to be God. He asserted His deity when He

said, "I and the Father are one" (John 10:30); "He who has seen Me has seen the Father" (John 14:9).

Miraculous Power

John the apostle, after he had recorded the changing of water into wine, the healing of the centurion's servant and of a man paralyzed for 38 years, the giving of sight to a man born blind and the raising of Lazarus from the dead, wrote, "These things I have written to you who believe in the name of the Son of God, in order that you may know that you have eternal life" (I John 5:13). Jesus' miracles were not capricious demonstrations of brute power, but were acts of a loving God who was anxious to reveal His benevolent character to man.

Imagine anyone predicting accurately his own death and resurrection. And yet this is exactly what Jesus Christ did. He foretold, "The Son of Man must suffer many things, and be rejected of the elders and chief priests and scribes, and be killed, and after three days rise again" (Mark 8:31).

The priests and scribes knew of this prediction and attempted to prevent its fulfillment by placing guards at the tomb. But no human effort could prevent what God had planned.

Why Did He Come?

You may ask, "If Jesus Christ is, in fact, the Son of God, why did He come to earth?" Why Jesus rather than someone else?

In the Old Testament, the Israelites periodically brought animals to the priest to be sacrificed. The priest then slew the animal and sprinkled its blood on the altar as a temporary covering for the sins of the individual making the sacrifice. These animals had to be perfect, without spot or blemish, in order for the sin of the one making the sacrifice to be transferred to the innocent offering.

This was the picture of the coming of God's one special Lamb, the One whose blood would not just cover man's sins temporarily, but would wash them away forever.

"Without the shedding of blood," we are told in the Scriptures, "there is no forgiveness of sins" (Hebrews 9:22). That is why God sent His only Son, Jesus Christ, who was without sin, without spot or blemish, to shed His blood upon the cross for the forgiveness of our sins.

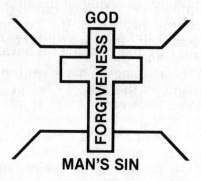

As one studies the religions of the world, he becomes aware that no provision is made for the forgiveness of sin apart from the cross of Jesus Christ.

There is no more precious truth in the Word of God than this, that Christ died for our sins (I Corinthians 15:3).

Born To Die

Not only were the death and resurrection of Jesus remarkable, but so also was the purpose for which they occurred. Jesus Christ was born to die. By dying on the cross in our place, He willingly took upon Himself the death that each individual person deserves.

At the conclusion of one of my lectures on "The Uniqueness of Jesus," a young Hindu professor from India approached me. He was very angry and impatient. "I resent you Christians," he said. "I resent the arrogance with which you say that you have the only way to God. I believe that Christianity is one way. Hinduism is another. Buddhism, Shintoism, and other religions are all ways to God."

He was an unusually brilliant young man, completing double doctorates — one in physics and one in chemistry — at the same time. As we talked, he began to see that Christianity is uniquely different, that it is not just another man-made religion or philosophy, but that it makes provision for man's basic need, the forgiveness of sin. He admitted that although he was a devout follower of his religion — diligently reading the sacred Hindu writings and dutifully observing all the rites and rituals — he had never found God. Finally, we got down on our knees together, and this young Hindu prayed that Jesus would forgive his sins and become his Savior.

In order to become a Christian, then, you must honestly and squarely face the claims of Jesus Christ and believe intellectually that He is God, that He died for your sins and was buried, that He rose again, and that He wants to come into your life and be your Savior and Lord.

Review and Thought Questions

1. According to the following passages, who is Jesus Christ?

   Mark 1:1 _____

   _____

   John 1:1, 14 _____

   _____

   John 10:30 _____

   _____

   John 14:6 _____

   _____

2. What does knowing who Jesus Christ is mean to you?

   _____

   _____

   _____

3. Why did Jesus have to die?

   _____

   _____

   Hebrews 9:22 _____

   _____

   I Peter 1:18, 19 _____

   _____

   I Corinthians 15:3 _____

   _____

4. a) What do you believe intellectually about Christ?

   _____

   _____

b) By what evidence do you know these beliefs to be true?

_____

_____

5. Why were Jesus' miracles recorded for us? See John 20:30, 31.

_____

_____

_____

6. In I John 1:12, what is the relation between the words "receive" and "believe"?

_____

_____

7. Why is Christianity different from all other religions?

_____

_____

_____

8. What does this difference mean to you personally?

_____

_____

_____

_____

Questions 2, 4, 7 and 8, can be used to stimulate effective group discussions.

STUDY 2.

EMOTIONAL COMMITMENT

Second, being sure that you are a Christian involves the emotions. An emotion is a feeling or a reaction to a specific act, event or experience. The failure to distinguish between different types of emotions has caused many people to be confused in their relationship with God. Probably no one thing has caused more people to lack the assurance of a vital personal relationship with God through Jesus Christ than the wrong emphasis on emotions.

Man is an emotional creature by nature, and everything he does, from the time he arises in the morning until he goes to bed at night, involves his emotions. The way he responds to other people in his office or on the campus, even the selection of the tie he wears or the food he eats involves his emotions.

Different Responses

One person may be aggressively extroverted and highly emotional, while another may be calm, reserved and introspective. Viewing the same act or participating in the same experience, these two may respond quite differently — one with great joy and the other calmly.

Failure to understand personality differences as they relate to becoming a Christian has caused many people to become confused. The apostle Paul, for example, had an unusually dramatic experience with God. He had dedicated his life to the annihilation of the followers of Jesus Christ and was actively pursuing his goal when the Lord met him on the road to Damascus. The dramatic experience changed the course of Paul's life, caused him to become a mighty apostle, a man whom God used as He has used few others, to take His message of love and forgiveness to the world.

On the other hand, Timothy, Paul's son in the faith, learned about the Lord from his mother and grandmother. He grew up believing that Jesus Christ was the Son of God and knew that Christ was living in his life.

Dramatic Encounter

Frequently one hears Christians enthusiastically sharing how their dramatic encounter with Christ resulted in their being healed of drug addiction, gross immorality or some other distressing problem. The fact that their lives were indeed changed validates their claims. On the other hand, there are many who, like myself, have knelt quietly in the privacy of their homes, at a mountain retreat, or in a church sanctuary, and there received Christ into their lives with no dramatic emotional experience at that time.

I remember well the night I knelt beside my bed and prayed, "God, what do you want me to do?" It was a simple prayer, nothing profoundly theological about it, and there was no dramatic emotional experience. But I meant what I prayed, and God heard me.

My life began to change with the passing of the days and weeks and months as I studied the Scriptures and met with other Christians in the fellowship of a local church. I began to experience the quiet assurance of God's love and forgiveness, and my relationship with the Lord Jesus Christ became the most real, the most vital force in my life. The better I know Him, the more I love Him and the more enthusiastic I am about sharing Him with others.

Emotions Can Deceive

Emotions have come and gone through the years — I have had moments of great joy, times of great enthusiasm and spiritual awareness, and I have also experienced moments of sorrow and disappointment — but I do not depend upon these feelings, for they can be deceiving.

The Bible says, "The just shall live by faith" (Romans 1:17), and "... without faith it is impossible to please

Him" (Hebrews 11:6). "Whatever is not from faith," it continues, "is sin" (Romans 14:23).

The very act of seeking an emotional experience, therefore, contradicts the very thing that pleases God. Faith is another word for trust, and our faith must be placed in the person of God and in His holy, inspired Word, rather than in our feelings.

An acquaintance brought his friend to see me, hoping that he might receive Christ, which he did. But in the course of our conversation, it became apparent that my friend, despite his concern for his friend, was himself not a Christian. So I asked him,

"When did you become a Christian?"

"I'm not really sure that I am a Christian."

"Do you believe that Jesus Christ is the Son of God?"

"Yes."

"Do you believe that He died on the cross for your sins?"

"Yes."

"Do you believe that if you receive Jesus Christ as your Savior, He will come into your life and make you a child of God?"

"Yes."

"You would like to receive Him, wouldn't you?"

"Yes, I would. But I'm waiting for an experience. When my mother became a Christian, she had a dramatic emotional experience, and I've been waiting all these years for God to give me such an experience."

Though he was a professing Christian and active in his church, the thing that kept him from assurance of salvation was the wrong emphasis on emotions. I was able to explain to him that he did not have to look for an emotional experience, but could believe God's Word. Finally we bowed in prayer, and as a simple expression of faith, he received Jesus Christ as his Savior and Lord and rejoiced in the certainty that Christ was in his life.

Threefold Confirmation

How, then, can one be sure that he is a Christian? Is

there not some kind of confirmation that God gives to the man who sincerely receives Christ? I believe there is a threefold confirmation that Jesus Christ is in our lives.

TRUSTWORTHY WORD
CONFIRMING HOLY SPIRIT   = ASSURANCE
CHANGED LIFE

Trustworthiness Of God

First we have the external witness, or evidence, of the Word of God. Assurance is based on the authority of God's Word. When you meet God's conditions, as revealed in His Word, you can be assured that you are a child of God.

"We believe men who witness in our courts, and so surely we can believe whatever God declares. And God declares that Jesus is His Son. All who believe this know in their hearts that it is true. If anyone doesn't believe this, he is actually calling God a liar because he doesn't believe what God has said about His Son.

"And what is it that God has said? That He has given us eternal life and that this life is in His Son. So whoever has God's Son has life; whoever does not have God's Son does not have life. I have written this to you who believe in the Son of God so that you may know you have eternal life" (I John 5:9-13, Living Bible).

Holy Spirit

Second, there is the internal witness, or evidence, of the Holy Spirit. Paul writes to the the Romans, "For His Holy Spirit speaks to us deep in our hearts and tells us that we really are God's children" (Romans 8:16, Living Bible). Paul emphasized the validity of this inner source of assurance to the Thessalonian converts: "For when we brought you the good news, it was not just meaningless chatter to you; no, you listened with great interest. What we told you produced a powerful effect on you, for the Holy Spirit gave you great and full assurance that what we said was true" (I Thessalonians 1:5, Living Bible).

Changed Lives

Our changed lives are a third witness to the fact that we are Christians. Jesus explained to Nicodemus, a devout religious leader of the Jews. "You must be born again or you cannot see the kingdom of God." This was the experience of the Colossians as Paul explains, "The same good news that came to you (Colossians) is going out all over the world and changing lives everywhere just as it changed yours that very first day you heard it and understood about God's great kindness to sinners" (Colossians 1:6, Living Bible). The proof that we have experienced a new birth and have become children of God will be demonstrated by our changed lives:

"And how can we be sure that we belong to Him? By looking within ourselves; are we really trying to do what He wants us to do? Someone may say, 'I am a Christian; I am on my way to heaven; I belong to Christ.' But if he doesn't do what Christ tells him to, he is a liar. But those who do what Christ tells them to will learn to love God more and more. That is the way to know whether or not you are a Christian. Anyone who says he is a Christian should live as Christ did" (I John 2:3-6, Living Bible).

Unless there is a genuine desire to obey and please the Lord Jesus, one has a right to question his salvation.

Jesus said, "He who has My commandments, and keepeth them, he it is who loves Me; and he who loves Me shall be loved by My Father, and I will love him, and will disclose Myself to him" (John 14:21). Jesus is saying here that He will make Himself known to all who obey Him in such a way that they will experience the reality of His presence in their lives. Such a manifestation will differ, however, according to the individual and the circumstances.

There is a place for emotions in the Christian experience, though we should not seek them nor attempt to recapture them from the past.

We are not to ignore the value of legitimate emotions. It is more important, however, to remember that we are to live by faith . . . in God and in His promises . . . and not by seeking an emotional experience.

Review and Thought Questions

1. a) What is an emotion?

_____

_____

b) How and when can emotions be wrong?

_____

_____

c) What place does emotion have in your Christian life?

_____

_____

2. What scriptural assurances do we have that our salvation is more than emotion (based on these verses)?

Romans 8:16 _____

_____

Ephesians 1:3-11 _____

_____

I John 5:11-13 _____

_____

3. a) What emphasis do you think Christ placed on emotions during His earthly ministry?

_____

_____

_____

b) What do these two Scripture passages show?

Mark 8:12 _____

_____

Luke 10:21 _____

_____

4. Why can emotions deceive you?

_____

_____

_____

5. What happens as you begin to know God better?

_____

_____

_____

6. What does God's Word say about faith?

Romans 1:17 _____

_____

Romans 14:23 _____

_____

Hebrews 11:6 _____

_____

7. What threefold confirmation is there that Christ is in your life?

_____

_____

_____

_____

_____

_____

_____

Discussion questions: 1, 3a, 4, 5.

STUDY 3.

VOLITIONAL COMMITMENT

In addition to the intellect and the emotions, becoming a Christian and being sure that you are a Christian involves the will.

Christ emphasized the importance of man's will in relation to the assurance of salvation. He said, "If any of you really determines to do God's will, then you will certainly know whether My teaching is from God or is merely My own" (John 7:17, Living Bible).

According to these words of Christ, unless you are willing to obey the truth, you will never know the truth; unless you are willing to walk in the light, you will never see the light.

He Loves Us Perfectly

Occasionally I counsel with individuals who are reluctant to receive Christ and commit their lives to Him for fear that He will change their plans and take all the fun out of life.

But when you commit yourself to Christ, you can be absolutely confident that He will fill your whole life with what is best for you, because he loves you. He is more interested in your good than you are yourself! God's Word assures us, "We need have no fear of someone who loves us perfectly; His perfect love for us eliminates all dread of what He might do to us. If we are afraid, it is for fear of what He might do to us, and shows that we are not fully convinced that He really loves us" (John 4:18, Living Bible).

A Matter Of The Will

Another reason why people are reluctant to receive Christ is pride or self-will.

For more than 20 years I have worked with the so-called intelligentsia and yet, in all those years, I have not met one single person who has said, "I have considered all the historical evidence and the claims of Christ, and I cannot believe that He is the Son of God." Rejection of Christ has always proved to be a matter of the heart, not the head; a matter of the will, not the intellect. Intellectual issues are usually only a smokescreen to cover deeper issues of the heart!

A Good Man

This was illustrated through the life of a famous professor at one of our nation's leading seminaries. He did not believe in the deity of Christ, yet he had taught thousands of young students to become ministers. One day I was invited to visit this great scholar by a friend who was getting his doctorate under his supervision. My friend explained, "He does not believe that the Bible is the Word of God, but he is a good man. I like him. He is personable and warm-hearted, and I think you might be able to communicate with him."

After we were introduced, his first words to me were, "Mr. Bright, when you talk to college students about becoming a Christian, what do you tell them?" Knowing his reputation, I wanted to weigh my words carefully, but before I could reply, he asked a second question, "Better still, what would you tell me? I would like to become a Christian."

Control Of The Throne

Taking him at his word, I drew a circle on a sheet of paper and explained that it represented his life. In the circle I drew a throne, and on the throne I placed the letter "S" for "self." I explained, "In order to become a Christian you must receive Christ into your life as God's gift. And when He comes in, He will want to be your Lord and take control of the throne of your life."

"That's my problem," he replied. "Intellectual pride has kept me from doing this. Many honors have come to me in the academic world and I haven't been willing to humble myself before God. For years I have denied the deity of Christ and have taught thousands of young men to do the same.

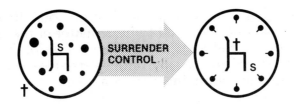

"Recently I have been reading the Word of God with a new understanding, together with the writings of the church fathers and the biographies of great men of God such as John Wesley and St. Augustine. And now I am convinced intellectually that Jesus is the Son of God, but I do not know Him as my personal Savior."

A Prepared Heart

At that moment we were interrupted by a telephone call, and due to other scheduled appointments we were unable to finish our conversation. He asked us to return two days later. When we returned, he took us into an office with no phones and, locking the door behind us, said, "I want you to know that I went this morning to one of the local churches, took communion and prepared my heart for your coming. I have been meditating on the third chapter of John, and I want you to pray for me that I may know Jesus as my personal Savior."

First I prayed, then he prayed and then my friend prayed, and that day this man of international renown, like a little child, received Christ and his whole life was changed. His teachings changed, his philosophy of life changed and he became a new creature in Christ. Basically his problem was not intellectual; it was a problem of pride and self-will.

Fear Of Consequences

Many students who may be intellectually and emotionally convinced that Jesus Christ is the Son of God fail to receive Him as their Savior because they believe that doing so will take all the fun out of life. They are afraid of the consequences.

I counseled with one student who hesitated to receive

Christ because he enjoyed a life of drinking and sex and all of the "rah-rah" of collegiate life. He resisted God, condemned the Christians and was known as the campus atheist. Then one day, in response to the prayers of many of his fraternity brothers and of a godly missionary, I had the privilege of praying with this young man as he received Christ.

Soon after, he became one of the most vital, dynamic Christians on the entire campus, and he is today one of America's leading theologians. He had known that Jesus Christ was the Son of God, but had fought against Him and against God's will for his life until the working of the Holy Spirit caused him to realize the truth of the Scripture, "What will a man be profited if he gains the whole world and forfeits his soul?" (Matthew 16:26). And the promise of Jesus, "I came that they might have life and might have it more abundantly" (John 10:10). He soon discovered that what he thought was an exciting life was nothing compared to the abundant life which the Lord Jesus gives.

Sell Their Possessions

Many successful business and professional leaders have refused to receive Christ as their Savior because they have been led to believe that they would have to sell their possessions and give everything to the poor, as Jesus advised the rich young ruler to do (Mark 10:21). Though God does lead some to do this today, others are led to use their influence for Christ in other ways.

Unwilling To Trust

There are others who have received Christ but who do not have the assurance of their salvation because they are afraid to trust God completely with their lives. One of the leading athletic coaches of America, a man held in high esteem by millions of people, a man of sterling character and tremendous ability, shared with me his reluctance to surrender his life fully to Christ for fear that He would ask him to become a minister and give up the joy and love of his life, which was coaching.

As we walk in obedience to God and allow Him to change our lives, we will have an increased assurance because it will be evident that God is at work in our lives enabling us to do that which we could never have done on our own. If our attitude is resistance to God's will, we will usually have doubt regarding our salvation.

Willful Sin

Also, if willful sin is allowed to continue in our lives, we will begin to doubt the validity of our faith in Christ. These doubts, however, will spring from the will rather than from the intellect. Intellectually, we only rationalize them into arguments for not believing as a camouflage for our disobedience.

Occasionally, when I talk to men about Christ and about God's wonderful love and plan for the lives of all who receive Him, they do not respond at all. When this happens, I know that their failure to respond is usually the result of one of two things. First, they may not have sufficient information about who the Lord Jesus is, why He came and about all the benefits that belong to those who are children of God; or, second, they may have been deceived by Satan, the enemy of their souls.

Some time ago, I was counseling with a student in England who wanted to receive Christ, but could not do so for some reason. Apparently the student had lived a life of immorality and disobedience, a life that was very self-centered. And yet in the depths of his heart he had a longing to know God.

Deceived By Satan

When we knelt to pray, no words came, and finally the plea, "I can't pray. I want to, but I can't!" "Pray after me," I suggested and began to pray. Still my friend could not pray.

Then I began to pray in behalf of this student, asking God to liberate him from the darkness and gloom of Satan's kingdom into the wonderful kingdom of the Lord Jesus Christ as Paul explained in Colossians 1:13, 14.

Again I asked the student to pray, and immediately

there was a joyful response and a warm invitation for Christ to take control. With this invitation came the joyful assurance of salvation.

If you want to receive Christ, but something is holding you back, it is because you, too, are in bondage. If so, Christ is waiting to liberate you.

Source Of Assurance

In conclusion, we have discussed how you can be sure you are a Christian in terms of the intellect, the emotions and the will.

We have likened becoming a Christian to getting married. However, in these two experiences there is a definite difference in sequence.

In marriage, the sequence of commitment is: first, intellect; then emotions; and, finally, will. But in commitment to Christ the sequence is: first, the intellect, then the will; and, finally, as a by-product, or result, the emotions or feelings.

Basic Truths

To be sure that you are a Christian you must be aware, intellectually, of certain basic truths:

First, God loves you and has a wonderful plan for your life.

Second, man is sinful and separated from God; thus he cannot know and experience God's love and plan.

Third, Jesus Christ is God's only provision for man's sin. Through Him you can know and experience God's love and plan.

And fourth, we must individually receive Jesus Christ as Savior and Lord; then we can know and experience God's love and plan.

Christ said, "Behold, I stand at the door, and knock; if anyone hears My voice and opens the door, I will come in to him, and will sup with him, and he with Me" (Revelation 3:20).

In John's Gospel we are told, "But as many as received Him, to them He gave the right to become children of God, even to those who believe in His name" (John 1:12).

Saved Through Faith

But it is not enough to merely ask the Lord Jesus Christ into your life. You must have faith, you must believe that He will enter according to His promise. We read in Ephesians, "For by grace you have been saved through faith; and that not of yourselves, it is the gift of God; not as a result of works, that no one should boast" (Ephesians 2:8, 9).

Most people ask Jesus into their lives again and again in times of emotional crises or in response to a moving presentation of the gospel. Yet nothing seems to happen in their lives. Why? There are two possible reasons.

Not Just A Man

First, some ask Jesus into their lives without realizing that He is not just a mere man, a historical figure, Jesus of Nazareth, but He is the God-Man — both God and man, the Savior, the promised Messiah, who died for our sins and was buried and on the third day was raised from the dead. He is the living Lord of life and history and has the power to change the life of any and all who receive Him. When one "receives" Him superficially just because others are receiving Him, without understanding who He is, nothing is likely to happen.

For example, an alcoholic asked Jesus into his heart for years, but nothing happened. Then one day he was asked, "Are you asking Jesus, the man, into your life or Jesus, the omnipotent Son of God?" He replied, "Jesus, the man," whereupon a careful explanation of who the Lord Jesus is and why He came was given. This time the alcoholic received the living Christ into his life with understanding and was immediately changed. He has not had a drink since.

Ask Him Once

Second, some people do not ask the Lord Jesus to come into their lives as an expression of faith. They insult Him by asking Him in again and again. Ask Him to be your Savior once and thereafter thank Him daily as an expression of faith that He is in your life, for He has promised never to leave or forsake you.

Does all that I have shared with you make sense? Have you ever personally received the Lord Jesus Christ as your Savior? If you have received Him, do you have the assurance of your salvation? Are you sure that if you died right now, you would spend eternity with God in heaven?

If you cannot answer "yes" to these questions, may I suggest that you find a quiet place where you can be alone or with the friend who shared this information with you, and receive the Lord Jesus as your Savior.

If you have never received Christ by a definite, deliberate act of your will, you can do so **now** in prayer. And if you are not sure you are a Christian, you can make sure now. In either case, may I suggest that you pray this or a similar prayer of faith, making it your very own.

"Lord Jesus, I need You. I thank You for dying for my sins. I open the door of my life and receive You as my Lord and Savior. Thank You for forgiving my sins. Take control of the throne of my life. Make me the kind of person You want me to be. Amen."

Where Is He Now?

Did you just ask Christ into your heart? Then where is He right now in relation to you? You can be sure, if you prayed that prayer sincerely, that the living Christ now indwells you and that you have eternal life. That is His promise, and He will not deceive you.

But, again, the question may arise, "What about feelings?" Do not depend on feelings. The integrity and trustworthiness of God and His Word, not our feelings, is our authority.

Several logs burn brightly together; put one log aside on the cold hearth and it will cease to burn. So it is with you and your relationship to other Christians.

If you do not belong to a local church, do not wait to be invited. Take the initiative; call the pastor of a nearby church where Christ is honored and the Bible is preached. Make plans to start this week and to attend regularly.

The decision to receive Jesus Christ as your Lord and Savior is absolutely the most important one you will ever make in your entire life. Now that you are sure you are a Christian, share your faith and assurance with others as a way of life!

Review and Thought Questions

1. Why does becoming a Christian involve an act of the will?

   _____

   _____

   _____

2. a) Why are some people reluctant to accept Christ? (See also II Corinthians 4:2-4).

   _____

   _____

   _____

   b) What are some consequences of becoming a Christian?

   _____

   _____

   _____

3. How can you give God control of your life?

   _____

   _____

   _____

4. From Matthew 16:26, Mark 10:21 and John 3:1-21, explain Christ's advice and promises to those who hesitate to accept Him as Savior.

   _____

   _____

   _____

   _____

5. How can you be sure of your salvation and position in Christ?

   John 3:16 _____

   _____

   John 10:28, 29 _____

   _____

   I John 5:11-13 _____

   _____

6. Why do some Christians lack the assurance of their salvation?

   _____

   _____

   _____

7. How would you relate Matthew 21:22 to salvation and a Christian's assurance of his salvation?

   _____

   _____

   _____

Discussion questions: 1, 3, 6, 7.

CHAPTER STUDY GUIDE

1. The application of the principles outlined in this Concept will help you to put your faith in Christ as your Savior if you have not done so, and will help you come to an assurance of your salvation if you have no such assurance at present.

2. Memorize the following verses and references:

Revelation 3:20: "Behold, I stand at the door and knock; if any one hears My voice and opens the door, I will come in to him, and dine with him, and he with Me."

I John 5:11-13: "And the witness is this, that God has given us eternal life, and this life is in His Son. He who has the Son has the life; he who does not have the Son of God does not have the life. These things have I written to you who believe in the name of the Son of God, in order that you may know that you have eternal life."

3. Make the Concept, "How To Be Sure You Are A Christian," a way of life.

a. Make sure that you are a Christian. If you are not sure that Jesus Christ has come into your life, make sure. By a deliberate act of your will, invite Christ to come into your life to be your Lord and Savior. Review the prayer on page 40 and make it your own. Once you have received Christ by faith, begin to thank Him daily that He is in your life. If you still have a problem with the matter of assurance, talk with some vital Christian friend and ask him to help you.

b. Once you are sure that Christ is in your life, share the fact with someone. Share it with the members of the Bible Study group or action group to which you belong. Begin to share it with your friends. The act of sharing your faith will cause you to make it a matter of public knowledge. This will serve as a stimulant to your growth.

c. Begin to spend some time each day in Bible study and prayer. It is best to set aside a particular time each day to do this and to make it a habit. You may want to begin studying through this series of Transferable Concepts.

d. Become associated with vital Christians. Become a

part of some small group study where you can discuss the Bible and where you can learn from other Christians. If you are not already doing so, begin attending a nearby church regularly where Christ is honored and His Word is preached. If you have not already been baptized, plan to be baptized as an outward expression of your identification with Christ.

AMPLIFIED OUTLINE

Study 1.

I. There are many good, faithful churchgoers who have received Christ in prayer but who, because of a lack of proper information, are not sure they are Christians.

II. Being sure you are a Christian, like the experience of marriage, involves a commitment of the total individual — the intellect, the emotions and the will.

    A. Being sure you are a Christian involves the intellect.

       1. Christianity is not "a blind leap of faith."

       2. Christianity is built upon historical fact documented by centuries of scholarship and research.

       3. Jesus Christ is the greatest person the world has ever known.

       4. The life Jesus led, the miracles He performed, the words He spoke, His death on the cross, His resurrection, His ascent into heaven all point to the fact that He was not mere man, but God.

       5. Jesus came to die on the cross for our sins as was pictured centuries ago in the sacrifices of the Old Testament (Hebrews 9:9).

Study 2.

    B. Being sure you are a Christian involves the emotions.

       1. An emotion is a reaction to a specific act, event or experience.

       2. The wrong emphasis on emotions has kept

many from being assured of a vital, personal relationship with God.

3. Man is an emotional creature by nature, and everything he does involves his emotions.

4. Because of personality differences, not everyone who receives Christ will have the same kind of emotional experience.

   a. Some, like the apostle Paul, may have a dramatic experience.

   b. Others, like Timothy, may become Christians in a very quiet way.

5. The Christian life is to be received and lived on the basis of faith, not emotions.

6. Assurance is based upon:

   a. First, external witness, the authority of God's Word (John 5:9-13).

   b. Second, the internal witness, or evidence, of the Holy Spirit (Romans 8:16).

   c. Third, the change that results in a person's life after he receives Christ (I John 2:3-6).

7. There is a place for emotions in the Christian experience, but we should not seek them, nor attempt to recapture them from the past.

Study 3.

C. Being sure you are a Christian involves the will.

1. Unless you are willing to obey the truth, you will never know the truth; unless you are willing to walk in the light, you will never see the light. (John 7:17).

2. There are several reasons why some are reluctant to commit their lives to Christ as an act of the will.

   a. Some fear He will change their plans and take all the fun out of their lives, not realizing how much he loves them and wants to do what is best for them.

      b. Some have the barrier of intellectual pride or self-will.

      c. Some are afraid they may have to give up all their possessions.

      d. Some are afraid to trust God with their lives.

    3. Willfull sin will cause a person to doubt the validity of his faith in Christ.

    4. Satan can also deceive a person and hold his will in bondage.

III. In summary, how then can you receive Christ or know with assurance that Christ is in your life?

  A. First, you must recognize certain basic truths:

    1. God loves you and has a wonderful plan for your life (John 3:16; 10:10b).

    2. Man is sinful and separated from God; thus he cannot know and experience God's love and plan (Romans 3:23; 6:23).

    3. Jesus Christ is God's only provision for man's sin. Through Him you can know and experience God's love and plan (Romans 5:8; I Corinthians 15:3-6; John 14:6).

    4. We individually receive Jesus Christ as Savior and Lord; then we can know and experience God's love and plan (John 1:12; Ephesians 2:8, 9; Revelation 3:20).

  B. It is not enough simply to ask the Lord Jesus Christ into your life. You must have faith; you must believe that He will enter according to His promise (Ephesians 2:8, 9).

    1. Remember that the One you are inviting into your life is not just a mere man; He is God.

    2. Once you have asked Christ in, don't ask Him to come into your life again and again, for this insults Him and repudiates the principle of faith.

  C. Finally, do not depend upon feelings; the promise of God's Word, not our feelings, is our authority.

CHAPTER 2
HOW TO EXPERIENCE GOD'S LOVE AND FORGIVENESS

Study 1. Adventure and Challenge
Study 2. The Great Problem
Study 3. The Great Solution

STUDY 1.

To know Jesus Christ personally as Savior and Lord is the greatest privilege and adventure that man can ever experience.

Jesus of Nazareth is invariably recognized as the most remarkable, the most powerful and the most attractive personality of all the centuries. The date on your morning newspaper gives witness to the fact of His influence in history — A.D., meaning Anno Domini, in the year of our Lord, and B.C., meaning "before Christ." No other life since the beginning of time has so influenced for the good the lives of so many multitudes of men and women.

Hundreds of years before His birth, prophets of Israel had foretold His coming. These prophecies were fulfilled in the life of Jesus down to the very last detail, including His miraculous birth (Isaiah 7:14; Matthew 1:18-25), His life, His teachings, His miracles, His death on the cross for the sins of man (Isaiah 53:4-6; II Corinthians 5:21), and His resurrection (Psalms 16:9, 10; Luke 24:46). He claimed to be the promised Messiah, the Son of God, and most of those who knew Him best died as martyrs — executed for telling the good news of God's visit to this planet through Jesus of Nazareth.

ADVENTURE AND CHALLENGE

Jesus meant for the Christian life to be an exciting, abundant adventure. He said, "I came that they may have and enjoy life, and have it in abundance — (to the full, till it overflows)" (John 10:10). When we walk in the fullness and the control of God's Holy Spirit, every day is filled with wonder, meaning, purpose and fruitfulness. A rich and satisfying life is the heritage of every Christian, "For the fruit of the Spirit is love, joy, peace, patience, good-

ness, kindness, faithfulness, gentleness, and self-control"
(Galatians 5:22, 23).

Love	Christ centered
Joy	Empowered by H.S.
Peace	Introduces others to Christ
Patience	Effective prayer life
Kindness	Understands God's Word
Faithfulness	Trusts God
Goodness	Obeys God

But most Christians do not know anything about this kind of life — a life of victory, joy and abundant fruitfulness for our Savior. On the contrary, to many people the Christian life is a burden, a chore, a terrible cross to bear. They emphasize the Savior's infamous trial, brutal beatings and humiliating death on a cruel Roman cross, as well as the tens of thousands — even millions — of Christian martyrs throughout the centuries.

An Abundant Life

To many, Christianity is something to be endured in anticipation of heaven. This is not the way our Lord intended it. I would remind all men that Jesus had more to say about peace, love, joy and victory in the last few hours of His life on earth than in all the rest of His recorded teaching.

The apostle Paul, who endured all kinds of suffering, beatings, imprisonment and finally martyrdom for our Lord, said, "We can rejoice, too, when we run into

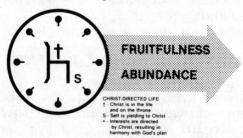

CHRIST-DIRECTED LIFE
† - Christ is in the life
 and on the throne
S - Self is yielding to Christ
• - Interests are directed
 by Christ, resulting in
 harmony with God's plan

problems" (Romans 5:3), "Rejoice always" (I Thessalonians 5:16), "In everything give thanks" (I Thessalonians 5:18). Whatever our circumstances — in joy or in sorrow, in abundance or in need, in health or in sickness, in freedom or in persecution — we are assured by our Lord, "Peace I leave with you" (John 14:27), "I have overcome the world" (John 16:33), "I will never desert you, nor will I ever forsake you" (Hebrews 13:5), "I am with you always" (Matthew 28:20), "Ask Me anything in My name, (and) I will do it" (John 14:14).

Further, our Lord has called us to a life of fruitfulness in terms of introducing others to Him as Savior. In Matthew 4:19, He said, "Follow Me and I will make you to become fishers of men." In John 15:8, He said, "You prove that you are truly following Me when you bear much fruit. In this way My Father is honored and glorified."

Proof of Discipleship

The average Christian is not fruitful. Being fruitful, however, according to Christ's own words, is the best way to prove that we are His disciples. It is not enough to live a good life. Those who subscribe to other religions and cults which deny the deity of our Lord often live exemplary lives.

An atheist can memorize prayers and wear a pious facade and do everything that the average Christian does — as has been dramatically demonstrated in certain countries where Christianity is discouraged or banned and informers have infiltrated into positions of leadership in the church for the purpose of spying.

It is here that we discern a vast difference between the church of the New Testament, and the church of today. The book of the Acts of the Apostles tells the thrilling story of what God did through those first-generation Christians as they went door to door sharing their faith and, constrained by the love of Christ, often in the face of death and martyrdom, went everywhere, as the apostle Paul said, telling everyone about Christ. This is seldom the experience of twentieth-century Christians.

In his preface to *The Young Church in Action,* J. B. Phillips writes, "No one can read this book (Acts) without being convinced that there is Someone here at work besides mere human beings. Perhaps because of their very simplicity, perhaps because of their readiness to believe, to obey, to give, to suffer, and if need be to die, the Spirit of God found what surely He must always be seeking — a fellowship of men and women so united in love and faith that He can work in them and through them with a minimum of . . . hindrance.

"Consequently, it is a matter of sober historical fact that never before has any small body of ordinary people so moved the world that their enemies could say, with tears of rage in their eyes, that these men 'have turned the world upside down!' " (Acts 17:6).

Christians of that first century, filled with the Spirit, constrained by the love of God, took the good news of God's love and forgiveness in Christ to the entire then-known world.

Influence of Spiritual Christians

Why was that first-century church able to make an impact for God upon a wicked Roman Empire? The only logical explanation is that the church was composed largely of spiritual Christians, men and women filled with and controlled by the Holy Spirit. They knew that, before they could experience fellowship with God and be used of Him to help fulfill His purpose in the world and build His kingdom, they needed to be filled with His Holy Spirit, they needed to be forgiven and cleansed of their sins.

Moral Detergents

Many people today are trying all kinds of moral detergents, but the stains and blotches are all a part of their nature. Moral reform, social adjustment, therapeutic psychology, sensitivity seminars — all these have failed to produce a "new person." The only hope for sinful man is a supernatural cleansing, and only Jesus Christ, through His death on the cross, makes it possible for us to be forgiven. This cleansed life can be experienced only by God's power, not by our own will power. The living Christ dwelling within us makes the difference.

The psalmist King David understood the need for cleansing and forgiveness of sin. Listen to his heartwarming prayer, "Wash me thoroughly from mine iniquity, and cleanse me from my sin. For I acknowledge my transgressions: and my sin is ever before me ... Create in me a clean heart, O God; and renew a right spirit within me ... Restore unto me the joy of Thy salvation; and uphold me with Thy free Spirit. Then will I teach transgressors Thy ways; and sinners shall be converted unto Thee" (Psalms 51:2, 3, 10, 12, 13). Cleansing from our sins is a prerequisite for the abundant and fruitful life to which Christ has called us.

The Great Challenge

The opportunity for presenting the claims of Christ is greater today than at any previous time in recorded history. The Spirit of God has created an unprecedented hunger in the hearts of the multitudes of the earth. What an exciting hour to be alive to serve the King of kings and Lord of lords. Both students and adults are turning to Christ in ever-increasing numbers. Even so, this great harvest is being accomplished by relatively few Christians.

The vast majority of Christians still live in defeat and spiritual sterility. The average layman and many pastors seldom, if ever, introduce another person to Christ.

What has happened to the Christians of our generation? Former President Woodrow Wilson said, "Our nation was born as a Christian nation, established on Christian principles."

Review and Thought Questions

1. Prophecy is a foretelling. From the following Scriptures, tell what prophecy was fulfilled in Christ's birth, life, death and resurrection.

   Micah 5:2/Matthew 2:1 _____

   _____

   Isaiah 7:14/Luke 1:26-35 _____

   _____

   Hosea 11:1/Matthew 2:14, 15 _____

   _____

   Zechariah 11:12/Matthew 26:14, 15 _____

   _____

   Isaiah 53:7/Matthew 27: 12, 14 _____

   _____

   Isaiah 53:12/Mark 15: 27, 28 _____

   _____

   Psalm 22:1/Matthew 27:46 _____

   _____

   Psalm 16:10/Mark 16:6 _____

   _____

2. a) What does John 10:10 mean to you personally?

   _____

   b) How should it affect your Christian walk?

   _____

   _____

3. a) In what ways can you be fruitful for Christ?

   _____

   _____

b) In what areas of your life now can others see the fruit of the Spirit?

_____

_____

_____

4. a) God's Word says that our sins have already been forgiven. Why, then, do we confess sins?

_____

_____

_____

b) What does each of the following verses tell you about God's view of sin?

Ephesians 2:1 _____

_____

Psalm 107:17 _____

_____

Isaiah 59:2 _____

_____

Habakkuk 1:13 _____

_____

c) What do these verses assure you regarding God's cleansing from sin?

Psalm 103:3, 9-12 _____

_____

Psalm 86:5 _____

_____

Matthew 12:31 _____

_____

I John 1:9 _____

_____

5. How would you influence someone else to believe in the vitality and excitement of living for Christ?

_____

_____

6. What do the following verses teach us about our attitude toward suffering?

Romans 5:3 _____

_____

I Thessalonians 5:16, 18 _____

_____

John 16:33 _____

_____

Philippians 4:4, 11, 19 _____

_____

7. Have you confessed every known sin to God and made right every wrong done to others as far as it lies within your ability to do so (read Matthew 5:23, 24)?

_____

_____

If not, what further action do you need to take?

_____

_____

_____

_____

Questions 2, 3, 4a and 5 can be used to stimulate effective group discussions.

STUDY 2.
THE GREAT PROBLEM

Even today, more than half of our nation's population of more than 220 million people profess to be Christians. More than 97% of one large cross-section interviewed said that they believe in God. Yet, our attitudes and actions prove that our nation has become a materialistic nation — morally and spiritually decadent. Many Christians have become more a part of the problems of our society than a part of the solution. Non-Christians see little or no difference between their quality of life and that of the average Christian.

A Christian friend, a pillar of his church, once confided, "I used to encourage my neighbor to go to church with me. He always refused, but I persisted. One day he said to me, 'Herb, don't pester me any more about going to your church. Obviously it hasn't done you any good. I see nothing about your life that is any different from mine. We live basically the same kind of lives. Frankly, I don't want your religion and I don't want to hear any more about it.' "

Many young people have left the church because they feel that their parents and other adults are hypocrites, professing something with their lips that they do not demonstrate in their lives.

Wrong Way

Yet, I have found, as I have had the privilege of speaking to hundreds of Christians around the world in many lands, that the average defeated, frustrated, fruitless Christian is not happy with his spiritual condition. He would like to change but he does not know what to do. This kind of person does not need to be rebuked or criticized and condemned. He needs to be loved and helped.

Some time ago when I was driving in a strange city in Mexico, I made a wrong turn. I found myself driving against traffic on a one-way street. The people along the sidewalk began to tell me that I was going in the wrong direction. But I had already realized this in the split second after I turned. My problem was not to determine whether or not I was going in the wrong direction; it was how to get turned around! I soon succeeded in changing my direction through the help of a friendly policeman and I went on my way rejoicing, driving with the traffic.

So it is in the Christian life. One does not need to be told that he is a hypocrite or that his life is not honoring to our Lord if he is a defeated Christian. He needs to be shown how to get turned around. He needs to understand the nature of his problem and how to find a solution to it. This is exactly what the Word of God does for us.

Three Kinds of People

In I Corinthians 2 and 3, the apostle Paul, writing under the inspiration of the Holy Spirit, correctly diagnoses the problem when he tells us there are three kinds of people in the world — the natural man, the spiritual man and the carnal man.

If you are a defeated, frustrated, fruitless, impotent Christian, I have good news for you. Observe carefully what Paul has to say. You and every person alive on this planet can be identified in one of these three categories.

Natural Man

The natural man is not a Christian. He depends upon his own resources and lives in his own strength. He cannot understand or accept the truths of God's Word.

SELF-DIRECTED LIFE
S · Self is on the throne
† · Christ is outside the life
• · Interests are directed
    by self, often resulting in
    discord and frustration

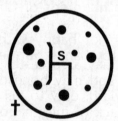

His interests and ambitions are centered around fleshly and worldly things. Spiritually, he is dead to God — separated from God because of his sin.

Spiritual Man

The spiritual man, however, is a Christian who is controlled and empowered by the Holy Spirit of God. He draws upon the unlimited resources of God's love and power and lives in the strength of the living Christ. He understands and believes God's Word, and his interests and ambitions are centered around and subject to the

CHRIST-DIRECTED LIFE
† · Christ is in the life
   and on the throne
S · Self is yielding to Christ
• · Interests are directed
   by Christ, resulting in
   harmony with God's plan

perfect will of God. Spiritually, he is alive. He is rejoicing in the Lord and bearing fruit for our Savior because he is allowing the Holy Spirit to have unhindered control of his life.

Carnal Man

The carnal man, described by Paul in I Corinthians 3, is a defeated and fruitless Christian. He is living in the energy of the flesh instead of drawing upon the inexhaustible resources of the Holy Spirit. He may be a Sunday school teacher, a salesman, a student, or even a minister or missionary who, even though he is a Christian, is in control of his own life — wanting to be his own master and hoping to please Christ at the same time. He desires and sometimes attempts to set his affection on the things of God but still holds onto the things of this world. He may assume that he knows what God wants him to be and may honestly try to live up to that self-made standard, only to fail again and again, because of rebellion, lack of information, or lack of faith. He never allows the Holy Spirit to mold him into the person that God created him to be. Thus, in endless frustration, he lives outside the perfect will of God.

'Somebody Else'

Most Christians, whether or not they realize it, are in this carnal category. One man said to me, "I didn't know I was carnal. I have heard my pastor talk about carnal Christians, but I always thought he meant somebody else, who, I hoped, was hearing the pastor's message. Now after hearing your message I realize that I, too, am carnal."

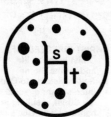

SELF-DIRECTED LIFE
S · Self is on the throne
† · Christ dethroned and
    not allowed to direct
    the life
• · Interests are directed
    by self, often resulting in
    discord and frustration

A businessman came to see me one day, greatly distressed because his church was splitting. "Half of our members are going to move out and start another church," he said. This distressed me, too. I cannot think of anything more tragic than for a body of Christians to be divided.

As we talked, the man admitted that he was a carnal Christian. I began to explain that God had made a provision for him to be a spiritual person. He did not need to continue to live as a carnal Christian. Finally we knelt together and prayed. He asked forgiveness for his sins and asked God to fill and control his life by the Holy Spirit. As we were rejoicing over what God had done, he said, "You know, there won't be any problems in my church now. You see, I am the one who has been causing all the trouble."

I Do What I Hate

Paul tells us more about the carnal Christian when he writes, "The law is good, then, and the trouble is not there but with me, because I am sold into slavery with sin as my owner. I don't understand myself at all, for I really want to do what is right, but I can't. I do what I don't want to — what I hate. I know perfectly well that what I am doing is wrong, and my bad conscience proves that I agree with these laws I am breaking.

"But I can't help myself, because I'm no longer doing it. It is sin inside me that is stronger than I am that makes me do these evil things. I know I am rotten through and through so far as my old sinful nature is concerned. No matter which way I turn I can't make myself do right. I want to but I can't. When I want to do good, I don't; and when I try not to do wrong, I do it anyway" (Romans 7:14-19). Does this passage of Scripture describe your present relationship to God?

A gifted young educator with his doctorate, a successful career and an even brighter future came for counsel. "I became a Christian years ago when I was a young boy," he said. "But through the years I gradually took back the control of my life. I was still active in the church — in fact, in the biggest church in the city. Yet, I am ashamed to say that I have been more interested in promoting my own business and social position than I have been in serving the Lord and getting to know Him better. I have compromised my business and professional standards, and have not always been honest and ethical in my dealings with others.

"God has shown me that I am a carnal Christian and has reminded me of the many years I have wasted living selfishly for my own interests. I have come," he said, "to confess my sins to God and surrender my life completely and irrevocably to Christ. Please pray for me that I may be a man of God — a spiritual Christian — and not the carnal Christian that I have been all of these years. Now I want to help evangelize the world for Christ."

Living By The Book

Another friend, one of the most dedicated men I have ever known, lived by a little black book. This book told the story of a life of extreme discipline. In this book he kept a careful record of all of his activities — past, present and future. In it he recorded the time he was to get up every morning, how long he should have his devotions, and to how many people he should witness. I was very impressed; I wanted to be like him.

However, one day he had a mental breakdown. After

he was released from the hospital, he said to me, "I was unable to live the Christian life. I tried to be a man of God by imposing upon myself certain rigid spiritual disciplines. Before they took me to the hospital, my last conscious act was to throw that little black book, which had become my god, into the corner. I never wanted to see it again." My friend had been trying to live for God in the energy of the flesh.

A Changed Attitude

A minister of a large church came to one of our institutes for evangelism at Arrowhead Springs. After my message on "How to Experience God's Love and Forgiveness," he came to talk to me. He was filled with hatred and resentment for the lay leaders of a church where he had formerly served as pastor.

"These people did me great harm," he said. "They tried to destroy me. I tried to get even with them and as a result I now realize that I have become a mean, critical, carnal Christian. I must either get right with God or get out of the ministry. Every time I preach the gospel, my words come back to condemn me. Pray for me that God will deliver me from this hatred, this cancerous carnality that is destroying my life and ministry."

Tears of repentance were followed by tears of joy as we knelt together to claim the love and forgiveness of God. The man who stood to his feet was a far different man from the one with whom I had knelt such a brief few minutes before. A few days later he went to visit these "hated" church leaders. He told them that he loved them and asked them to forgive him.

These leaders responded to him with love and forgiveness, and they embraced each other with joy and Christian love. This dear pastor returned to his church with a heart of love that burned with zeal for the Lord. His ministry was revolutionized.

War Within

Paul continues his description of the carnal Christian: "Now if I am doing what I don't want to, it is plain where the trouble is: sin still has me in its evil grasp. It seems to be a fact of life that when I want to do what is right, I inevitably do what is wrong. I love to do God's will so far as my new nature is concerned; but there is something else deep within me, in my lower nature, that is at war with my mind and wins the fight and makes me a slave to the sin that is still within me."

"In my mind I want to be God's willing servant, but instead I find myself still enslaved to sin. So you see how it is; my new life tells me to do right, but the old nature that is still inside me loves to sin. Oh, what a terrible predicament I'm in! Who will free me from my slavery to this deadly lower nature?" (Romans 7:20-24)

Upon reading this, one of my friends said, "That's my biography — the story of my life." Have *you* ever asked this question in your own words, "Who will free me from my slavery to this deadly lower nature?" Listen to the good news of Paul's answer: "Thank God! It has been done by Jesus Christ our Lord. He has set me free" (Romans 7:25).

Review and Thought Questions

1. a) How would you describe
     — the natural man _____

   _____

     — the spiritual man _____

   _____

     — the carnal man _____

   _____

   b) Which of these characterizes your life?

   _____

   _____

   c) What would you like to change in your life?

   _____

   _____

   d) How will you do that?

   _____

   _____

2. How do I Corinthians 3 and Romans 1 describe the carnal man?

   _____

   _____

3. What place do pride and humility have in the Christian life?

   _____

   _____

   _____

   _____

4. In your own words, explain how Romans 7:14-19 relates to your life.

_____

_____

_____

5. Christ offers true freedom. From the following verses, explain the freedom Christ gives.

Romans 8:21 _____

_____

Galatians 5:1, 13, 14 _____

_____

I Corinthians 8:6, 9-13 _____

_____

6. How do these verses describe a spiritual man?

Romans 14:22-15:3 _____

_____

Galatians 5:22-6:2 _____

_____

7. Why does God care if there is sin in your life?

_____

_____

_____

_____

_____

_____

Discussion questions: 3, 4, 7.

STUDY 3.

THE GREAT SOLUTION

Every Christian has this same problem until he makes the discovery that Paul made — that Jesus Christ our Lord has set him free: "So there is now no condemnation awaiting those who belong to Christ Jesus. For the power of the life-giving Spirit — and this power is mine through Christ Jesus — has freed me from the vicious circle of sin and death."

"We aren't saved from sin's grasp by knowing the commandments of God, because we can't and don't keep them, but God put into effect a different plan to save us. He sent His own Son in a human body like ours — except that ours are sinful — and destroyed sin's control over us by giving Himself as a sacrifice for our sins" (Romans 8:1-3).

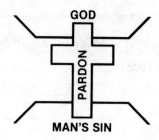

GOD

PARDON

MAN'S SIN

How well I remember the years that I sought God with all my heart. I resorted to all kinds of self-imposed discipline, begging God for His power. The more I tried, the more defeated and frustrated I became. Then one day as I was studying the book of Romans, I read chapter 8, verse 7 (Living), "The old sinful nature within us is against God. It never did obey God's laws and it never will."

What a relief it was to me to discover that I would never be able to live the Christian life through my own efforts, but I could trust Christ to live His resurrection life in and through me. He alone could enable me to live the Christian life (Colossians 3:10). It is faith, not effort, that pleases Him (I Peter 1:7; Hebrews 11:6).

Object Of Faith

What is faith? Faith is another word for trust. Faith must have an object. The Christian's object of faith is God and His Word. And His Word tells us that we need not continue to be defeated, carnal, fruitless and impotent Christians. We can be fruitful witnesses for Christ, and that is what He has called us to be (John 15:16). The Lord Jesus gave the incredible but reliable promise that if we believe on Him we will be able to do greater works than He did (John 14:12). He assured us that whatsoever we ask in His name, He will do it (John 14:14).

It is important that we recognize that it is our Lord and Savior, Jesus Christ, the object of our faith, who has both the power and the willingness to deliver us from carnality.

We do not have faith in faith itself. For example, a person could have great faith that the ice on a pond would support his weight. He may boldly walk out on thin ice through his faith and get very wet! On the other hand, a person who may have a very weak faith may move slowly out onto a pond of very thick ice. As he walks on the ice and realizes its ability to support his weight, his faith in the ice increases.

So it is in the Christian life. We place our faith, even a faith that may be very weak, in a trustworthy God and His Word. The better we know God, the more we can trust Him, and the more we trust Him, the more we experience the reality of His love, grace and power. Faith is like a muscle — it grows with exercise.

Practical Atheists

A man booked passage on a ship with just enough money to buy a ticket, a block of cheese and some crackers for the long voyage. The first few days at sea the crackers and cheese tasted good, but eventually they became stale. Each day as he watched the porters carry large steaks, lobsters, chicken and many other delicious foods to the other guests, he became very hungry. In fact, he became so hungry that he finally stopped one of the porters.

"I'll do anything to get one of those steaks," he said. "I'll wash dishes, clean rooms, even mop the deck." The porter replied, "You bought a ticket didn't you? The meals come with the ticket." Too many people today are, ignorantly, cheese-and-cracker Christians — missing out on all of God's steak dinners.

It is tragically true that the average Christian is a practical atheist. He professes to believe in God, yet he acts as though God either does not exist or is unwilling to help him. He has all the resources of God available, yet he lives in self-imposed spiritual poverty. He fails to act as a child of the King or live as one who has been adopted into royalty from a state of poverty and illiteracy. How can the carnal man get off and stay off this emotional, roller coaster-type of existence and overcome his inconsistent way of life?

PERSONAL APPROPRIATION

"Spiritual breathing" is a principle which enables the believer to live a consistent Christian life. Just as we exhale and inhale physically, so we can also exhale and inhale spiritually.

Exhale and Inhale

We exhale when we confess our sins, and we inhale when we appropriate the fulness of God's Spirit by faith. The Bible promises, according to I John 1:9, "If we confess our sins He (God) is faithful and righteous to forgive us our sins and to cleanse us from all unrighteousness."*

Confession (homologeo in the Greek) suggests agreement with God concerning our sins. Such agreement involves at least three considerations. First, I acknowledge that my sin or sins, which should be named specifically, are wrong and therefore are grievous to God. Second, I acknowledge that God has already forgiven my sins — past, present, and future — because of Christ's death on the cross. It is essential to realize that there is nothing I can do that will add anything to what He has already done for me. Third, I repent, which means that I change my attitude toward my sins.

Through the enabling power of the Holy Spirit, this will result in a change in my conduct. Instead of doing what my old sinful nature — my fleshly self — wants to do, I now do what God wants me to do.

God loves us unconditionally — whether we are good or bad — as Jesus illustrates so movingly in the story of the prodigal son. The father, at the insistence of his younger son, gave him his share of the family estate. This

the son wasted on parties and prostitutes. Yet, when he returned home in hunger and defeat, professing his unworthiness as a son, his father ran to meet him, embraced and kissed him, put a ring on his finger and shoes on his feet and held a banquet in his honor.

Unconditional Love

God loves us with an inexhaustible love. He loves us not "when" or "if" we deserve His love, but even when we are disobedient. One of my most moving discoveries

---

* This chapter deals with exhaling. Chapter 3, "How to Be Filled With the Spirit," deals with inhaling. The concept of spiritual breathing — both exhaling and inhaling — is found in Chapter 4, "How to Walk in the Spirit."

in my study of the Scriptures was the statement of our Lord in His high priestly prayer to God the Father as recorded in John 17:23: "So that the world will know You sent me and will understand that You love them as much as You love Me" (L.B.).

Think of it. God loves you and me as much as he loves the Lord Jesus Christ, His only begotten Son. Incredible but true! Though God hates sin and will discipline His children when we are disobedient, He never ceases to love us. "Whom the Lord loves, He disciplines" (Hebrews 12:6). In fact He disciplines us because He loves us, not because He hates us. He hates only our sin.

When I truly confess my sins, I first recognize that any act of disobedience in attitude or action which is contrary to God's Word or will is wrong. On the basis of His promise (I John 1:9) I then receive His forgiveness and cleansing by faith.

This is what repentance is all about: determining to do what God wants me to do. In other words, we do not confess our sins with our fingers crossed. There must be a genuine desire to be different, followed by a willingness for God to control our lives, before we can realize that God has forgiven and cleansed us from our sins.

Perfect Sacrifice

Now, what is the basis for our forgiveness? The writer of Hebrews answers this question beautifully in the tenth chapter: "For the Law, since it has only a shadow of the good things to come and not the very form of things, can never by the same sacrifices year by year, which they offer continually, make perfect those who draw near . . . Therefore, when He comes into the world, He says, 'Sacrifice and offering Thou hast not desired, but a body Thou hast prepared for Me.' "

"Then I said, 'Behold, I have come (in the roll of the book it is written of Me) to do Thy will, O God' . . . And every priest stands daily ministering and offering time after time the same sacrifices, which can never take away sins; but He, having offered one sacrifice for sins for all time, sat down at the right hand of God . . . For by one offering He has perfected for all time those who are sanctified . . . Now where there is forgiveness of these things, there is no longer any offering for sin" (Hebrews 10:1, 5, 7, 11, 12, 14, 18).

Confession And Forgiveness

If you are a Christian, your sins — past, present and future — have been forgiven. Pleadings, tears, personal efforts and religious ritual cannot provide reconciliation with God. They are not needed. Faith is simply believing and claiming as truth what Jesus Christ has said and what He has already done for us.

Faith enables us to view ourselves as God views us as His children — loved, forgiven and cleansed. Faith motivates us to repent. Repentance, which in the original Greek means "a change of mind," results, through the enabling of the Holy Spirit, in a change of action. It will cause us to turn from doing what displeases God to doing what God wants us to do.

In Hebrews 10, we discovered that what man tried to do concerning his sins, Christ did for him by His death on the cross and by shedding His blood. We cannot add anything to what Christ has already done. We simply accept His forgiveness and cleansing by faith.

Why Confess?

You may wonder why, as a Christian, you need to confess if Christ has already paid the penalty for your sin. It should be understood that confession does not result in another forgiveness, since Christ has forgiven us once and for all, according to Hebrews 10. Confession is necessary as an expression of faith and as an act of obedience to claim God's promise.

When you confess your sins, confession makes real in your own experience what God has done for you through the death of His Son. The benefits are not simply psychological but are real and valid, based upon the Word of God. If you refuse to be honest with God in confessing your sins, you become carnal and walk in the shadows instead of walking in God's light.

The Bible says, "But if we are living in the light of God's presence, just as Christ does, then we have wonderful fellowship and joy with each other, and the blood of Jesus, His Son, cleanses us from every sin" (I John 1:7).

Perhaps you have committed sins, and have not experienced God's forgiveness. You may feel some resentments toward friends or members of your family. You may have lost the joy of your relationship with Christ. You pray, but there is no response. You read the Bible, but get little joy or help from it. You witness for Christ, but no one responds.

Short-Circuiting God's Power

One day, as I was operating the controls of my sons' electric train, the train suddenly stopped running. I could not figure out what was wrong. I took the train apart, and put it back together. I pushed the plug in and out of the socket; nothing happened. Then I discovered that a little piece of metal which had fallen across the tracks was

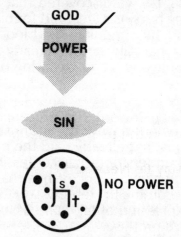

causing the problem. Just a tiny piece of metal — a "no left turn" sign — had fallen across the negative and positive rails of the track, short-circuiting all of the electrical power, so that the train would not run.

In like manner, sin short-circuits the power of God. God is holy and will have nothing to do with sin. But God loves us even though we may have unconfessed sins in our lives. He has forgiven us. All that we need to do to experience afresh the wonder of His love and the joy of His promises is to confess our sins — exhale spiritually — and experience the reality of His cleansing power.

List Your Sins

Ask the Holy Spirit to reveal to you every sin in your life. As he does so, write them down on a sheet of paper. Your list may include jealousy, pride, selfishness, lust, indifference to things of God, unbelief, lukewarmness, loss of love for God, and many other items. After you have completed your list, write out this wonderful promise in I John 1:9: "If we confess our sins, He is faithful and righteous to forgive us our sins, and to cleanse us from all unrighteousness."

Realize that this list is just between you and God, so be completely honest. Tell God everything that is wrong. When you have completed your time of prayer, destroy the list. Before you do so, however, express your gratitude to the Lord that He has forgiven you through Christ's death on the cross 2,000 years ago.

Remember that faith — not tears, pleading or any other self-imposed spiritual discipline — lays hold of God's promise to forgive and cleanse us from all sin. This is not a new or second forgiveness. You are simply realizing in your experience the once-and-for-all forgiveness which we read about in the tenth chapter of Hebrews.

Restitution May Be Necessary

For some, confession will also involve restitution — returning something that you have stolen or asking another to forgive you for a wrong you committed against him. This is vitally important because you cannot maintain a clear conscience before God if you still have a guilty conscience before your fellowman.

At the conclusion of a Christian medical meeting at Arrowhead Springs, where I had spoken on this subject of forgiveness, a doctor accepted my challenge to go alone and make his list. He was very excited when he came to see me early the next morning. "Last night about midnight," he said, "a doctor friend of mine came to my room and told me that he had hated me for years, while pretending to be my friend. As he was making his list, God told him that he should come and tell me, and ask me to forgive him."

"We had the most wonderful time of prayer, and God met us in a special way. I wanted to tell you this in order to encourage you to keep telling Christians to confess their sins to God and, if necessary, to ask forgiveness of those whom they have wronged, as the Holy Spirit leads them."

Facing The Problem

God has a wonderful, abundant and fruitful life planned for us. But He will not bless us, He will not use us, until we face up to this problem of sin. God is holy and righteous, eternally aflame with the glory of His perfection, and wants us in our experience to be all that He has created us to be. His plan is that we be changed into the image of His dear Son. This can never be our experience if we refuse to acknowledge and confess our sins.

A young man once said to me after an evening meeting, "I didn't believe I needed to make a list. I couldn't think of anything seriously wrong in my life. But when I saw others making their lists, the Spirit of God told me to do the same."

"Well," he concluded, "while there were no serious problems, there were a lot of little things, and the sum total of the little things had dulled the cutting edge of my witness for Christ. If ever you speak on this subject again, be sure to insist that everyone, including those who think there is no sin in their lives, make a list of their sins. Had I not made my list, I would have missed a blessing from God."

You Can Be Cleansed Now

It may be that there are no gross sins in your life, but if your heart is cold toward God; if you lack faith; if you are not fruitful; if, like the churches of Ephesus and Laodicea referred to in Revelation 3, you have lost your first love for the Lord, or are lukewarm, there is something wrong. Tell God about it.

May I suggest that you pause right now — take a pencil and paper and list every sin in your life which the Holy Spirit calls to your remembrance. Take plenty of time; humble yourself before the Lord. Give God time to reveal to you those areas of your life which need to be corrected.

When you have written down all that is shown to you, write across the list the wonderful promise of I John 1:9: "If we confess our sins, He is faithful and righteous to forgive us our sins, and to cleanse us from all un-righteousness." Now thank God for His forgiveness and cleansing through the shedding of His Son's precious blood for your sins.

Guilt Is Gone

If you have confessed all your known sins, any guilt complex remaining will be from Satan, not God, for God has forgiven you all your sins on the basis of Christ's death on the cross for you (Hebrews 10:1-17). Now, thank God that, as He promised, your sins have been removed as far as east is from west (Psalm 103:12) — they are buried in the deepest sea. God doesn't remember them any more. Think of it! God has forgiven you! God loves you! You can be assured without question that today you can experience forgiveness and cleansing for all the sins of the past. Through the principle of spiritual breathing you can get off the spiritual roller coaster and stay off for the rest of your life.

Christ came to seek and to save the lost. He has com-missioned us to go and bring forth fruit, but He will not bless us and use us to bring others to Himself if there is unconfessed sin in our lives. Trust Christ Jesus now for a supernatural forgiveness and cleansing of all your sins and enter into the great adventure for which he created you.

Review and Thought Questions

1. What does the great promise of Romans 8:1 mean to you?

   _____

   _____

2. Name one real difference you can see in your life as a result of having Christ in your life.

   _____

   _____

3. Why can't you live the Christian life through your own efforts?

   _____

   _____

4. How does Hebrews 11:1 describe faith?

   _____

   _____

5. How would you apply that verse in your life on a day-to-day basis?

   _____

   _____

6. What do the following verses tell you about exercising or increasing your faith?

   I Corinthians 2:1-5 _____

   _____

   Galatians 5:6 _____

   _____

   _____

I Corinthians 12:1-8a _____

_____

II Corinthians 4:13-18 _____

_____

James 2:14-26 _____

_____

7. From the following examples, describe the results of faith.

Daniel 3:16-18 _____

_____

Genesis 6:9, 13, 14, 18, 22 (cf. Hebrews 11:7)

_____

_____

Joshua 6:1-5, 12, 16, 20 (cf. Hebrews 11:30)

_____

_____

Acts 8:34-37 _____

_____

_____

8. If a person has confessed all known sin in his life and has claimed the forgiveness of God, but still has guilt feelings, what should he do?

_____

_____

_____

_____

Discussion questions: 1, 2, 3, 5, 8.

CHAPTER STUDY GUIDE

1. As you apply the principles presented in this Concept, the joy of experiencing God's love and forgiveness will become a way of life for you. A thorough understanding of this Concept will enable you to communicate it more effectively to others.

2. Memorize the following verses and references:

John 10:10b: "I came that they might have life, and might have it abundantly."

I John 1:9: "If we confess our sins, He is faithful and righteous to forgive us our sins and to cleanse us from all unrighteousness."

3. Make this Concept, "How to Experience God's Love and Forgiveness," a way of life through practicing the following:

a. Set aside 20 to 30 minutes to be alone with God. Prayerfully ask Him to reveal to you any sinful attitudes or actions of your life that are displeasing to Him and make a written list of them. Confess these sins (agree with God concerning them), according to His promise in I John 1:9. Write out the verse, I John 1:9, across the list. Thank God that He has cleansed and forgiven you according to His promise. Then destroy the list.

b. Ask God daily to make you sensitive to anything in your life which would be displeasing to Him. Then, throughout the day, as you become aware of such an area, immediately pray and claim God's forgiveness, according to His promise (I John 1:9).

AMPLIFIED OUTLINE

Study 1.

I. Knowing Jesus Christ personally is the greatest adventure man can experience.

A. Jesus of Nazareth is the most remarkable, powerful attractive personality of all the centuries (Isaiah 7:14; 53:4-6).

B. Jesus meant for the Christian life to be an exciting, abundant adventure (John 10:10; Galatians 5:22, 23).

C. Unfortunately, most Christians are not experiencing a life of joy and victory as taught in the Bible by the apostle Paul and the Lord (Romans 5:3, I Thessalonians 5:18, John 15:8).
   1. The average Christian is not fruitful.
   2. There is a vast difference between the Christianity of the New Testament and the Christianity evidenced in the lives of many Christians today.

D. The first century church made a mighty impact for God upon the world (Acts 17:6).
   1. They knew the reality of being filled with the Spirit.
   2. They had met God's requirement of supernatural cleansing of their sins (Psalms 51:2, 3, 10, 12, 13).

II. Today we are greatly challenged as we face the most desperate hour of all human history.

A. The entire world is filled with anxiety, fear and frustration.

B. Never before in recorded history has there been such an ideal opportunity for presenting the claims of Christ.

C. In the midst of these tremendous problems and opportunities, most Christians have become a part of the problem rather than a part of the solution.
   1. They do not evidence a quality of life which causes others to want to know the Lord.
   2. They do not know how to appropriate God's power and resources for making an impact upon the world.

Study 2.

III. The fact that many Christians are part of the problem rather than part of the solution can best be understood if we realize that there are three kinds of people in the world (I Corinthians 2:14-3:3).

A. There is the natural man, who is not a Christian.
   1. He depends solely upon his own resources.

2. Spiritually, he is dead to God — separated from God because of his sin.

B. There is the spiritual man, who is a Christian and who is controlled and empowered by the Holy Spirit of God.

1. He draws continually upon the unlimited resources of God's love and power.

2. Spiritually, he is alive to God, for the Son of God is living in and through Him.

3. He brings glory to God because of his fruitful life.

C. There is the carnal man, who, though he is a Christian, is trying to live in his own strength (I Corinthians 3).

1. He is a defeated and fruitless Christian.

2. He never allows the Holy Spirit to mold him into the kind of person God created him to be.

3. He lives in endless frustration.

4. Sadly, he is often a person who does not realize that he is in the carnal category (Romans 7:14-19).

5. He lives in slavery to sin (Romans 7:20-25).

Study 3.

IV. God has provided the solution for the carnal Christian through the power of the Holy Spirit, who is able to liberate him from the vicious power of sin and death (Romans 7:25-8:3).

A. Self-imposed religious disciplines lead only to defeat and frustration.

B. By faith we can experience Christ's resurrection power and life in and through us (Colossians 3:10; I Peter 1:7; Hebrews 11:6).

1. Faith is another word for trust, but trust must have an object.

2. The object of the Christian's faith is God and His Word (John 14:14).

3. It is tragic that the average Christian is a practical atheist, professing to believe in God yet acting as though God either does not exist or is unwilling to help him.

V. The carnal man can appropriate God's solution, get off the spiritual roller coaster and become a spiritual Christian by practicing "spiritual breathing."

   A. We exhale when we confess our sins (agree with God concerning our sins), according to God's promise in I John 1:9.

      1. We acknowledge that our sin or sins are wrong and are grievous to God.

      2. We acknowledge that God has forgiven our sins — past, present and future — on the basis of Christ's death on the cross for our sins.

      3. Through the enabling power of the Holy Spirit we repent or change our attitude toward our sin, which results in a change in our conduct.

   B. Exhaling — or confessing our sins — is a prerequisite for inhaling — or appropriating the power of God's Spirit by faith. Inhaling is the subject of the Concept on "How To Be Filled With The Spirit."

   C. The basis for our forgiveness is Christ's substitutionary death on the cross for our sins. (Hebrews 10:1-7, 11, 12, 14).

      1. If you are a Christian, your sins — past, present and future — have been forgiven.

      2. You cannot add one iota to what Christ has already done for you on the cross.

      3. You must simply accept God's forgiveness and cleansing by faith (I John 1:9).

   D. Why do we confess sin?

      1. Confession does not result in more forgiveness, since Christ has already forgiven us once and for all, according to Hebrews 10.

      2. However, confession is an expression of faith and an act of obedience, which results in God making real in our experience what he has already done for us through the death of His Son.

      3. If we refuse to confess our sins, we become carnal and walk in the shadows instead of in the light of God's love and forgiveness (I John 1:7).

E. Making a list of your sins is a tangible aid to confessing your sins and experiencing God's forgiveness.

1. First, you should prayerfully ask the Holy Spirit to reveal every sin in your life.

2. Then you should write each one specifically on a sheet of paper.

3. Next, across the list you should write out God's promise of I John 1:9.

4. Finally, you should destroy the list and thank God that he has forgiven you every sin.

5. It may be necessary for you to make restitution in areas where you have wronged someone.

6. Although God has a wonderful, abundant and fruitful life planned for us, He will not bless us and will not use us until we deal with the problem of sin.

7. You can be cleansed now.

8. After you have confessed all your known sins, any guilt feelings which remain will come from Satan, not from God, for God's forgiveness is complete (Hebrews 10:1-17, Psalms 103:12).

CHAPTER 3

HOW TO BE FILLED WITH THE SPIRIT

Study 1. Who? Why? What?
Study 2. Appropriating the Fullness

STUDY 1.

WHO? WHY? WHAT?

"My life will never be the same after tonight." commented the senior pastor of one of America's leading churches after he heard my message on "How to Be Filled With the Spirit." "I have been a pastor for more than 20

CHRIST-DIRECTED LIFE
† · Christ is in the life
and on the throne
S - Self is yielding to Christ
• · Interests are directed
by Christ, resulting in
harmony with God's plan

years," he said, "but have never understood how to be empowered and controlled by the Holy Spirit as a way of life until now. I can hardly wait to share this with my church members."

A retired businessman and his wife who had come to my office from halfway across the continent said, "Our lives were changed when we learned how to be filled with the Holy Spirit as a result of your ministry. Now we are sharing Christ with others wherever we go. We have come to ask you to share on television how to be filled with the Holy Spirit. Your simple approach reached us, and we want to help you reach multitudes of others."

Thousands of similar stories could be told of students, pastors and laymen who have made the exciting Scriptural discovery of how to be filled with the Holy Spirit by faith.

An Important Discovery

If you have not already done so, learning how to be filled with (controlled and empowered by) the Holy Spirit by faith will be the most important discovery of your Christian life.

Consider carefully the very last words of the Lord as He met with His disciples on the Mount of Olives only moments before He ascended into heaven. Jesus had commissioned His disciples to go into all the world and preach the gospel and to make disciples of all nations.

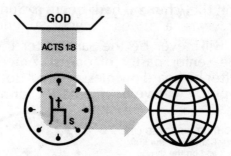

But He had told them not to leave Jerusalem *until they were filled with the power of the Holy Spirit.* "You shall receive power," He said, "when the Holy Spirit has come upon you; and you shall be My witnesses both in Jerusalem, and in all Judea and Samaria, and even to the remotest part of the earth" (Acts 1:8).

By these words, Jesus was suggesting, "Though you have been with Me for three years and more, it is not enough that you have heard Me teach the multitudes, and have seen Me heal the sick and even raise the dead. You need to be empowered with the Holy Spirit if you are to be effective and fruitful as My witnesses throughout the world."

Power To Share

A very discouraged student came to me for counsel after one of my messages. For some months he had spent at least three hours each day reading his Bible, praying and sharing his faith with others. Yet, he had never introduced anyone to Christ. After a time of discussion, his problem became apparent — he was not controlled and empowered by the Holy Spirit, although he wanted to be.

So we prayed together, and by faith he appropriated

the power of the Holy Spirit on the authority of God's Word. That very day he had his first experience of introducing a person to Christ. The next day he saw another come to Christ, and he has since introduced hundreds of people to the Lord. Obviously, his life was transformed.

A very successful businessman came to Arrowhead Springs, our International Headquarters, for training. The son of a minister, he had been reared under the good influence of the church, had been a Sunday school teacher for years, a Sunday school superintendent, a deacon, a member of the board of trustees of one of America's leading theological seminaries, and the president of all the laymen for his denomination for an entire state. Yet, he had never to his knowledge introduced anyone to Christ.

Multiplied Ministry

During the training he learned how to be filled with the Holy Spirit by faith and how to introduce others to Christ. Since that time, he has personally introduced hundreds of people to Christ and has trained thousands of laymen and pastors through our Lay Institutes for Evangelism. Thousands of others have been introduced to Christ through those whom he has trained.

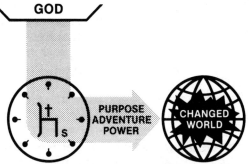

The pastor of a 1,500-member church appropriated the fullness of the Holy Spirit at a Pastor's Institute for Evangelism at Arrowhead Springs and learned how to introduce others to Christ. During one afternoon of witnessing for Christ, 14 of the 15 people whom this pastor interviewed received Christ.

Never before had he had such an experience. He returned to his pulpit a changed man. Soon hundreds of his church members, like their pastor, had appropriated the fullness of the Holy Spirit by faith. Now they are sharing their enthusiasm for Christ, and through their witness many more are responding to the Savior.

A Great Adventure

The Christian life is a great adventure. It is a life of purpose and power. Christ has given the almost unbelievable promise, "He who believes in Me, the works that I do shall he do also; and greater works than these shall he do; because I go to the Father. And whatever you ask in My name, that will I do . . ." (John 14:12, 13).

Obviously, we cannot, in our own energy, accomplish these great works which He has promised we can do. It is Christ Himself — living within us, in all of His resurrection power, walking around in our bodies, thinking with our minds, loving with our hearts, speaking with our lips — who will empower us with the Holy Spirit to do these great works. It is not our wisdom, our eloquence, our logic, our good personalities, or our persuasiveness which brings men to the Savior.

It is the Son of Man, who came to seek and to save the lost. Jesus said, "Follow Me and I will make you fishers of men" (Matthew 4:19). It is our responsibility to follow Him, and it is His responsibility to make us fishers of men. First-century Christians, controlled and empowered by the Holy Spirit and filled with His love, turned the world upside down.

As the disciples were filled with the Holy Spirit, they received a divine, supernatural power that changed them from fearful men into radiant witnesses for Christ. They were used of God to change the course of history.

Ignorance Of The Holy Spirit

Yet, tragedy of tragedies, there are multitudes of Christians who do not even know who the Holy Spirit is, or, if they do, they do not know how to appropriate His power, Consequently, they go through life without ever experiencing the abundant and fruitful life which Christ promised to all who trust Him.

Again and again I am reminded of the great contrast between Christ's church today and His church in the first century. In J. B. Phillips' introduction to the *Letters to the Young Churches,* he states:

"The great difference between present-day Christians and that of which we read in these letters (New Testament epistles), is that to us it is primarily a performance; to them it was a real experience. We are apt to reduce the Christian religion to a code, or, at best, a rule of heart and life. To these men it is quite plainly the invasion of their lives by a new quality of life altogether. They do not hesitate to describe this as Christ living in them."

First-Century Power

This same first-century power — the power of the risen, living, indwelling Christ made known through the Holy Spirit — is still available to us today. Do you know this power in your life? Are you a victorious, fruitful witness for Christ? If not, you can be.

For this reason, I believe the most important message that I could give to Christians is the wonderful news of the Spirit-filled life. I have shared these truths around the world with tens of thousand of Christians, old and young. No other message that I have shared has been used more by God to transform the lives of multitudes.

If you are not already experiencing the abundant life which Jesus promised and which is your heritage as a Christian, if you are not already introducing others to Christ as a way of life and you sincerely desire to do so, I have good news for you!

WHO? WHY? WHAT?

The answers to the following questions will lead you to a knowledge and experience of the Spirit-filled life: First, who is the Holy Spirit? Second, why did He come? Third, what does it mean to be filled with the Holy Spirit? Fourth, why is the average Christian not filled with the Holy Spirit?

Fifth, how can one be filled with the Holy Spirit?

Who Is The Holy Spirit?

The Holy Spirit is God. He is not an "it." He is not a divine influence, nor a fleecy white cloud, not a ghost nor a concept. He is God — with all the attributes of deity. He is the third person of the Trinity — co-equal with God the Father and God the Son. There is only one God, but He manifests Himself in three persons.

I cannot define the Trinity. No one can. One of my seminary professors once said, "The man who denies the Trinity will lose his soul. The man who tries to understand the Trinity will lose his mind." We who are finite cannot comprehend the infinite God.

We try to illustrate the concept of the Trinity, but the attempt is wholly inadequate. For example, I could say that a man has a body, a mind and a spirit — which one is the man? Or I could describe H_2O as a liquid, a solid or a vapor, depending on whether it was water, ice or steam. Which one is H_2O? Or a man is a husband, a father and a son — yet, he is one man. No illustration is adequate. At best, it can only suggest what the Trinity is like.

Why Did The Holy Spirit Come?

The Holy Spirit came to this earth to glorify Christ and to lead believers into all truth. On the eve of His crucifixion the Lord Jesus said to the disciples, "It is to your advantage that I go away; for if I do not go away, the Helper shall not come to you; but if I go, I will send Him to you. But when He, the Spirit of truth, comes He will guide you into all the truth . . . and He will disclose to you what is to come. He shall glorify me; for He shall take of mine and shall disclose it to you" (John 16:7, 13, 14).

The Holy Spirit came to enable us to know Christ, through the new birth, and to give us the power to live and share the abundant life which Jesus promised to all who trust Him.

The Holy Spirit inspired men to write the Holy Scriptures. As we read the Bible, He reveals its truth to us. I read passages of Scripture that I have read many times before, and suddenly, at the moment I need a particular truth, a certain passage comes alive to me. Why? Because the Holy Spirit makes the Word of God relevant and meaningful when I need it. It is a living Book inspired by the Spirit, and only the person who is controlled by the Spirit can understand the Bible (I Corinthians 2:10).

I pray, and — except for the prayer of confession — I cannot expect God to answer my prayer unless I am walking in the Spirit. I witness, and no one responds unless I am controlled by the Spirit.

A minister friend said to me, "I don't like all of this talk about the Holy Spirit. I want to talk about Jesus Christ." I reminded him that that was the reason the Holy Spirit came — to exalt and glorify Christ (John 16:1-15).

It is impossible even to know Christ apart from the regenerating ministry of the Spirit. It was Jesus of Nazareth Himself who said, "Unless one is born of water and the Spirit, he cannot enter into the kingdom of God" (John 3:5). It is impossible for us to pray, to live holy lives, to witness — there is nothing that we can do for the Lord Jesus and there is nothing that He can do for us — apart from the Holy Spirit of God.

What Does It mean To Be Filled With The Holy Spirit?

To be filled with the Holy Spirit is to be filled with Christ. Therefore, if I am filled with the Spirit, I am abiding in Christ. I am walking in the light as He is in the light (I John 1:7), and the blood of Jesus Christ will cleanse and keep on cleansing me from all unrighteousness (I John 1:9). I am controlled by Christ, because the word "filling" means to be controlled — not as a robot but as one who is led and empowered by the Spirit. And if I am controlled and empowered by Christ, He will be walking around in my body, living His resurrection life in and through me.

This amazing fact — that Christ lives in us and expresses His love through us — is one of the most important truths in the Word of God. The standards of the Christian life are so high and so impossible to achieve, according to the Word of God, that only one person has been able to succeed. That person is Jesus Christ. Now, through His indwelling presence, He wants to enable all who will place their trust in Him to live this same supernatural life.

Bearing Spiritual Fruit

If we are willing to have Christ live His resurrection life in and through us, we will bear spiritual fruit — which includes the fruit of the Spirit and souls won to Him — as naturally as a healthy vine will bear an abundance of fruit. Jesus said in Mark 1:17, "Follow Me and I will make you become fishers of men." It is our responsibility to follow Christ — to abide in Him. It is His responsibility to make us fishers of men.

In John 15:8, He said, "By this is My Father glorified, that you bear much fruit, and so prove to be My disciples." One can be a great preacher, a Christian scholar, a deacon or elder, attend church meetings daily, live a clean, moral life, memorize hundreds of verses of Scripture, direct a church choir and teach Sunday school, but if he is not bearing fruit — if he is not introducing others to Christ as well as living a holy life, he is not filled with and controlled by the Holy Spirit, according to the Word of God.

There are those who say, "I witness for Christ by living a good life." But, it is not enough to live a good life. Many non-Christians live fine, moral, ethical lives. According to the Lord Jesus, the only way that we can demonstrate that we are truly following Him is to produce fruit, which includes introducing others to our Savior as well as living holy lives. And the only way we can produce fruit is through the power of the Holy Spirit.

Some time ago I asked a leading theologian and dean of faculty for a renowned theological seminary if he felt that one could be a Spirit-filled person without sharing Christ as a way of life. His answer was an emphatic, "No!"

On what basis could he make such a strong statement? The answer is obvious. Our Savior came to "seek and to save the lost" (Luke 19:10), and He has "chosen and ordained" (John 15:16) us to share the good news of His love and forgiveness with everyone, everywhere. To be unwilling to witness for Christ with our lips is to disobey this command just as much as to be unwilling to witness for Him by living holy lives is to disobey His command. In neither case can the disobedient Christian expect God to control and empower his life.

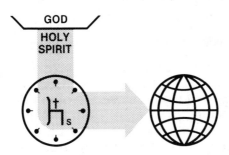

"I have been witnessing for years," a young man once said to me, "but have had no success. What is wrong with me?" After I explained how he could be filled with (controlled and empowered by) the Holy Spirit, we bowed to pray. By faith, he appropriated the fullness of God's Spirit, and immediately God began to use him to introduce others to the Savior.

Not only do we receive a natural power for witnessing when we are filled with the Spirit, but our personalities also begin to change. As we continue to walk in the control and power of the Holy Spirit, the fruit of the Spirit becomes increasingly obvious in our lives. In Galatians 5:22, 23, Paul explains, "When the Holy Spirit controls our lives He will produce this kind of fruit in us: love, joy, peace, patience, kindness, goodness, faithfulness, gentleness and self control . . ." (Living Bible).

The Word of God Is More Meaningful

A word of caution is in order. Do not seek an emotional or mystical experience. Do not depend on mystical impressions. The Word of God must be the basis of our spiritual growth. There is an interesting parallel between the passage of Ephesians 5:18, which admonishes us to be constantly and continually directed and empowered by the Holy Spirit, and Colossians 3:16, which admonishes us to "let the Word of Christ richly dwell within you . . ."

The result of letting the Word of Christ dwell in us and being filled with the Holy Spirit will be our talking much about the Lord, quoting psalms and hymns and making music in our hearts to the Lord (Ephesians 5:19).

Balance Between The Word and The Spirit

It is very important that we recognize the importance of the balance between the Word of God and the Spirit of God. The Word of God is closed to our understanding and has little meaning to us apart from the illumination given by the Holy Spirit, and the Holy Spirit is hindered in speaking clear and life-changing truth apart from the Word of God.

When the emphasis on the ministry of the Holy Spirit and the Word of God is in proper balance in the believer's life, the result is a life of power and great fruitfulness in which our Savior, the Lord Jesus Christ, is wonderfully honored and glorified.

As we continue then to allow the Holy Spirit to control and empower us, and as we meditate upon the Word of God and hide it in our hearts, our lives express more and more the beauty of Christ and the fruit of the Spirit listed in Galatians 5:22, 23. These attributes of our Lord Jesus Himself, plus fruitful witnessing, indicate that the Lord is actually living His life in and through us!

An Abundant Life

Obviously, then, being filled with the Spirit results in an abundant and overflowing life. Jesus of Nazareth once cried out to the multitudes, "If any man is thirsty, let him come to Me and drink. He who believes in Me, as the Scripture said, 'From his innermost being shall flow rivers of living water' " (John 7:37, 38). John adds, "But this He spoke of the Spirit, whom those who believed in Him were to receive . . ." (John 7:39).

Truly, this is "the abundant life," yet most Christians are experiencing little of it.

Review and Thought Questions

1. What command does God give in Ephesians 5:18 and what does it mean?

   _____

   _____

   _____

2. a) What characterizes the life of a Christian who is empowered by the Holy Spirit?

   _____

   _____

   b) How is the Holy Spirit's power evident in your own life?

   _____

   _____

3. Why did the Holy Spirit come?

   John 16:7, 13, 14 _____

   _____

   John 14:16, 17, 27 _____

   _____

4. How can you be filled with the Holy Spirit?

   _____

   _____

5. What does "fruit" mean in John 15:8?

   _____

   _____

   _____

   _____

6. If you were arrested for being a Christian, what evidence would there be to convict you?

_____

_____

_____

7. What does "the abundant life in Christ" mean to you?

_____

_____

_____

8. How do you witness to others?

_____

_____

_____

_____

_____

_____

Questions 2, 4, 6 and 7 can be used to stimulate effective group discussions.

STUDY 2.
APPROPRIATING THE FULLNESS

The average Christian continues to live in disobedience to God and is not filled with the Spirit for two reasons: first, a lack of knowledge; and second, unbelief.

Lack Of Knowledge

I am persuaded that most non-Christians, if they knew how to become Christians and if they understood the exciting, adventurous life which the Lord gives to all who trust and obey Him, would become Christians. Can you conceive of an intelligent person saying "No" to Christ if he fully understood how much God loves him and that when he receives Christ his sins are all forgiven, he is given eternal life, and he receives a whole new life of meaning and purpose? A child of God is a person of dignity and destiny, and for him life is no longer a matter of mere existence.

But the non-Christian who lacks this knowledge continues to live in disobedience, rejecting God's love and forgiveness because he does not understand it. So it is with the carnal Christian. He continues to live a frustrated, fruitless life because he does not understand who the Holy Spirit is and what the rich, abundant and fruitful Christian life is all about — the life which awaits him when he invites the Holy Spirit to control and empower him.

From the moment of our spiritual birth, we have the power to go on growing toward maturity in Christ. And yet, the average person, not understanding how to live by faith, finds himself on a spiritual roller coaster, living from one emotional experience to another.

SELF-DIRECTED LIFE
S - Self is on the throne
† - Christ dethroned and not allowed to direct the life
• - Interests are directed by self, often resulting in discord and frustration

Legalistic attitude
Impure thoughts
Jealousy
Guilt
Worry
Discouragement
Critical Spirit
Frustration
Aimlessness

Ignorance of his spiritual heritage

Unbelief
Disobedience
Loss of love for God and for others

Poor prayer life
No desire for Bible study

In Romans 7, Paul describes the predicament of the carnal Christian, "For that which I am doing, I do not understand; for I am not practicing what I would like to do, but I am doing the very thing I hate . . . Wretched man that I am! Who will set me free from the body of this death?" (Romans 7:15, 24).

The Carnal Christian

In I Corinthians 3, Paul describes a carnal Christian. Such a Christian is usually a miserable person — even more miserable than the non-believer. Having experienced the joy and blessing of fellowship with God, he has lost present contact and does not know how to recapture that lost fellowship. Yet, he can never be satisfied with that old way of life again, and in his search for happiness and fulfillment he has become self-centered instead of Christ-centered.

As a result, he has become increasingly confused and frustrated and does not know what to do about it. He does not know how to live by faith — he lives by feelings. He *tries* rather than *trusts*. He does not know how to stop being carnal, nor how to become a spiritual Christian. The only one who can enable him to change is, of course, the Holy Spirit.

Remember, the Lord Jesus said that we will do greater things than he did while he was here on this earth in His physical body. How is this to be accomplished? By the enabling power of the Holy Spirit.

Think of it! The Christian life is a miraculous life, a supernatural life. Christianity is not what we do for God, but what He does for us. Apart from faith in Christ, we cannot become Christians, and apart from moment-by-moment faith in dependence upon Him, we cannot live the Christian life. When we are filled with the Holy Spirit, Christ lives His supernatural life in and through us.

Living In Spiritual Poverty

But the average Christian does not understand how to draw upon the resurrection resources of Christ by faith. As a result he lives in spiritual poverty, not knowing or experiencing his great riches and resources in Christ.

In west Texas is a famous oil field known as the Yates Pool. During the depression, this field was a sheep ranch owned by a man named Yates. Mr. Yates was not able to make enough money on his ranching operation to pay the principal and interest on the mortgage, so he was in danger of losing his ranch. With little money for clothes or food, his family, like many others had to live on government subsidy.

Day after day, as he grazed his sheep over those rolling west Texas hills, he was no doubt greatly troubled about how he would be able to pay his bills. Then a seismographic crew from an oil company came into the area and told Mr. Yates that there might be oil on his land. They asked permission to drill a wildcat well, and he signed a lease contract.

Resources Available

At 1,115 feet they struck a huge oil reserve. The first well came in at 80,000 barrels a day. Many subsequent wells were more than twice as large. In fact, 30 years after the discovery, a government test on one of the wells showed that it still had the potential flow of 125,000 barrels of oil a day. And Mr. Yates owned it all! The day he purchased the land he received the oil and mineral rights. yet, he was living on relief. A multi-millionaire living in poverty! The problem? He did not know the oil was there. He owned it, but he did not possess it.

I do not know of a better illustration of the Christian life than this. The moment we become children of God through faith in Christ, we become heirs of God, and all of His resources are made available to us. Everything we need — including wisdom, love, power — to be men and women of God and to be fruitful witnesses for Christ — is available to us. But most Christians continue to live in self-imposed spiritual poverty, because they do not know how to appropriate from God those spiritual resources which are already theirs. Like Mr. Yates before the oil discovery, they live in ignorance of their vast riches.

Lack Of Faith

Lack of knowledge is not the only reason that Christians are not filled with the Holy Spirit. There are many Christians who may have been exposed to the truth but who, for various reasons, have never been able to comprehend the love of God. They are afraid of Him! They simply do not trust Him.

Trust is another word for faith, and "without faith it is impossible to please God" (Hebrews 11:6). How would you feel if your child were to come to you and say, "Mother, Daddy, I don't love you. I don't trust you any more"? Can you think of anything that would hurt you more deeply? I cannot. And yet, by our attitudes and our actions, if not by our words, most of us say that to God. We live as though God did not exist, even though we give lip service to Him. We refuse to believe His promises that are recorded in His Word.

Many people are afraid to become Christians for fear that God will require the impossible of them — that He will change their plans, require them to give away their wealth, take all the fun from their lives, make them endure tragedies, or something similar.

An outstanding young minister, a seminary honor graduate, once told me, "I have never surrendered my life to Christ because I have been afraid of what He will do to me." Then he told me how, years before, he had had a premonition that if he were to commit his life to Christ, his parents would be killed in a tragic accident. He was afraid to say "Yes" to God for fear his parents would lose their lives — God's test for him to determine the genuineness of his commitment.

You Can Trust God

Now does that sound like a loving Father? Who do you think put that idea into his mind? Certainly not God. It was Satan saying, as he said to Adam and Eve centuries ago, "You can't trust God." But I say you can trust God! He loves you and is worthy of your trust.

Suppose my two sons were to greet me with these words: "Dad, we love you and we have decided that we will do anything you want us to do from now on as long as we live." What do you think would be my attitude?

If I were to respond to their expression of trust in me as many believe God will respond when they surrender their lives to Him, I would take my sons by the shoulders, shake them, glare at them sternly and say, "I have been waiting for this. I am going to make you regret this decision as long as you live. I am going to take all the fun out of your lives — give away your possessions and make you do all of the things you do not like to do."

Of course, I would never respond in that manner. If my sons came to me with such a greeting, I would put my arms around them and say, "I love you, too, and I deeply appreciate this expression of your love for me. It is the greatest gift which you could give me."

God Loves You

Is God any less loving and concerned for His children? No, He has proven over and over again that he is a loving God. He is worthy of our trust. Jesus assures us, "If you then, being evil, know how to give good gifts to your children, how much more shall your Father who is in heaven give what is good to those who ask Him" (Matthew 7:11).

Many students and adults come to me for counsel concerning God's will for their lives. Often they are fearful of what God will ask them to do. Usually I ask them, "Do you believe that God loves you? Do you believe that He has a wonderful plan for your life? Does He have the power to guide and bless your life if you place your trust in Him?"

As a rule, the answers are in the affirmative. I then ask them, "Are you willing to trust Him right now to direct and empower you to live a holy life and to be a fruitful witness for Christ?" By this time most of them are ready to say "Yes" to Him without reservation. They have begun to recognize that their feelings of doubt have been placed there by the enemy of their souls.

Blessing In Return

When you give your life to Christ, you need not worry

about what is going to happen to you. Maybe you are afraid that He will take away your pleasures, cause you to leave your business or profession, take away your wealth, or terminate a friendship or love affair. You may fear that He will send you as a missionary to a remote part of the world where you will lose your life for Him.

He may indeed ask you to do one or more of these things, and again He may not. If He does, you will rejoice in the privilege, for God always blesses those who trust and obey Him. Some of the happiest people I have ever met are serving Christ in remote, primitive parts of the world. Others have given up fame and fortune to follow Him. The Bible reminds us, "The eyes of the Lord run to and fro throughout the whole earth to make Himself strong in behalf of those who love Him, whose hearts are perfect toward Him" (II Chronicles 16:9).

You can trust God. If He leads you to give up anything, he will give you more of His blessing in return than you would ever receive apart from His grace. God alone is worthy of your trust. I invite you to come freely to Christ and say, "Lord, here I am. Take my life and use me for Your glory."

You need not fear what He will do to you. As God reminds us in I John 4:18, "We need have no fear of someone who loves us perfectly; His perfect love for us eliminates all dread of what he might do to us. If we are afraid, it is for fear of what He might do to us, and shows that we are not fully convinced that He really loves us." The Word of God and the experiences of multitudes through the centuries give unqualified assurance that we can trust God with our lives, our all.

How to Be Filled With the Holy Spirit

We are filled with the Holy Spirit by faith. How did you become a Christian? By faith. "For by grace you have been saved through faith; and that not of yourselves, it is the gift of God; not as a result of works, that no one should boast" (Ephesians 2:8, 9). As you therefore have received Christ Jesus the Lord, so walk in Him" (Colossians 2:6).

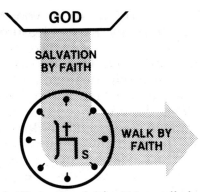

We received Christ by faith. We walk by faith. Everything we receive from God, from the moment of our spiritual birth until we die, is by faith. Do you want to be filled with the Holy Spirit? You can be filled right now, wherever you are, by faith.

You do not have to beg God to fill you with His Holy Spirit. You do not have to barter with Him, by fasting or weeping, or begging or pleading. For a long period of time, I fasted and cried out to God for His fullness. Then one day I discovered from the Scriptures that the "just shall live by faith" (Galatians 3:11). We do not earn God's fullness. We receive it by faith.

Suppose that you want to cash a check for a hundred dollars. Would you go to the bank where you have several thousand dollars on deposit, place the check on the counter, get down on your knees and say, "Oh, please, Mr. Teller, cash my check"? No, that is not the way you cash a check. You simply go in faith, place the check on the counter, and you wait for the money which is already yours. Then you thank the teller and go on your way.

Millions of Christians are begging God, as I once did, for something which is readily available — just waiting to be appropriated by faith. They are seeking some kind of emotional experience, not realizing that such an attitude on their part is an insult to God — a denial of faith, by which we please God.

Heart Preparation

Though you are filled with the Holy Spirit by faith and

faith alone, it is important to recognize that several factors contribute to preparing your heart for the filling of the Holy Spirit.

First, you must desire to live a life that will please the Lord. We have the promise of our Savior, "Blessed are those who hunger and thirst for righteousness for they shall be filled" (Matthew 5:6).

Second, be willing to surrender your life to Christ in accordance with the command of God revealed in Romans 12: "And so, dear brothers, I plead with you to give your bodies to God. Let them be a living sacrifice, holy — the kind He can accept. When you think of what He has done for you, is this too much to ask? Don't copy the behavior and customs of this world, but be a new and different person with a fresh newness in all you do and think. Then you will learn from your own experience how His ways will really satisfy you" (Living Bible).

Confess Each Sin

Third, confess every known sin which the Holy Spirit calls to your remembrance and experience the cleansing and forgiveness which God promises in I John 1:9: "But if we confess our sins to Him, He can be depended on to forgive us and to cleanse us from every wrong. And it is perfectly proper for God to do this for us because Christ died to wash away our sins" (Living Bible).

If you have wronged a brother, have taken that which is not rightfully yours, the Holy Spirit may lead you to make restitution — to right your wrong. If so, obey Him or you will miss His blessing. The blessings of the fullness of God's Spirit come only to those who willingly obey Him.

Jesus promised, "The person who has My commands and keeps them is the one who really loves Me, and whoever really loves Me will be loved by My Father. And I too will love him and will show Myself to him . . . I will make Myself real to him" (John 14:21).

Again, we are not filled with the Holy Spirit because we desire to be filled, nor because we confess our sins or present our bodies a living sacrifice — we are filled by faith. These are only factors which contribute toward preparing us for the filling of the Spirit by faith.

Command And Promise

There are two very important words to remember. The first is *command.* In Ephesians 5:18 God commands us to be filled: "Be not drunk with wine, wherein is excess, but be filled with the Spirit." Not to be filled, controlled and empowered by the Holy Spirit is disobedience. The other word is *promise* — a promise that makes the command possible: "This is the confidence which we have before Him that, if we ask anything according to His will, He hears us. And if we know that He hears us in whatever we ask, we know that we have the requests which we have asked from Him" (I John 5:14, 15).

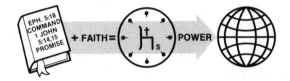

Now, is it God's will for you to be filled and controlled by Him? Of course it is His will — for it is His command! Then right now you can ask God to fill you — not because you deserve to be filled, but on the basis of His promise.

If you are a Christian, the Holy Spirit already dwells within you. Therefore, you do not need to invite Him to come into your life. He did this when you became a Christian and Jesus promised that He will never leave you (Hebrews 13:5). The moment you received Christ, the Holy Spirit not only came to indwell you, but He also imparted to you spiritual life, causing you to be born anew as a child of God. The Holy Spirit also baptized you into the Body of Christ. In I Corinthians 12:13, Paul explains, "For by one Spirit we are all baptized into one body."

There is but one indwelling of the Holy Spirit, one rebirth of the Holy Spirit and one baptism of the Holy Spirit — all of which occur when you receive Christ. Being filled with the Holy Spirit, however, is not a once-and-for-all experience. There are many fillings, as is made clear in Ephesians 5:18. In the Greek language in which this command was originally written, the meaning is clearer than that in most English translations. This command of God means to be constantly and continually filled, controlled and empowered with the Holy Spirit as a way of life.

If you wish to be technical, you do not need to pray to be filled with the Holy Spirit, as there is no place in Scripture where we are commanded to pray for the filling of the Holy Spirit. We are filled by faith. However, since the object of our faith is God and His Word, I suggest that you pray to be filled with the Spirit as an expression of your faith in God's command and in His promise. You are not filled because you pray, but because by faith you trust God to fill you with His Spirit.

What a relief it was to me one day when I read in Romans 8, "The old sinful nature within us is against God. It never did obey God's laws and it never will" (Romans 8:7). I had been trying to make myself good enough to please God, and that is impossible. The Bible says, "The heart is deceitful above all things, and desperately wicked" (Jeremiah 17:9). Therefore, I cannot hope to make myself good enough to earn God's favor. The only way I can please God is through faith. Paul talks about this concept in his letter to the Galatians: "I have been crucified with Christ; and it is no longer I who live, but Christ lives in me; and the life which I now live in the flesh I live by faith in the Son of God, who loved me, and delivered Himself up for me" (Galatians 2:20).

New Master — New Life

The individual who walks by faith in the control of the Spirit has a new Master. The Lord Jesus said, "If anyone wishes to come after Me, let him deny himself and take up his cross, and follow Me" (Matthew 16:24). "Unless a grain of wheat falls into the earth and dies, it remains by itself alone; but if it dies, it bears much fruit" (John 12:24).

Obviously, I cannot control myself and be controlled by the Holy Spirit at the same time. Christ cannot be in control if I am on the throne. So I must abdicate. This involves faith. As an expression of my will, in prayer, I surrender the throne of my life to Him, and by faith I draw upon His resources to live a holy and fruitful life.

The command of Ephesians 5:18 is given to all believers to be filled, directed and empowered by the Holy Spirit, continually, every day of our lives. And the promise of I John 5:14, 15 is made to all believers that, when we pray according to God's will, He hears and answers us. If you pray to be filled with God's Spirit, He will hear and answer you. He will fill you.

Do Not Depend Upon Feelings

Do not think that you have to have an emotional experience or that something dramatic must happen to you. How did you receive Christ? Was it because of some emotional pressure brought to bear upon you? Your emotions may have been involved, but ultimately you became a Christian, not because of your emotional experience, but because of your faith. The Bible says, "For by grace you are saved by faith" (Ephesians 2:8).

The emotional experience was a by-product of an expression of faith or of an act of obedience. The Holy Spirit is not given to us that we might have a great emotional experience, but that we might live holy lives and be fruitful witnesses for Christ. So, whether or not you have an emotional experience is not the issue.

Have you met God's conditions? Do you hunger and thirst after righteousness? (Matthew 5:6) Do you sincerely desire to be controlled and empowered by the Holy Spirit? If so, I invite you to bow your head and pray this prayer of faith right now. Ask God to fill you. Without begging or pleading, just say:

"Dear Father, I need You. I acknowledge that I have been in control of my life and that, as a result, I have sinned against You. I thank You that You have forgiven my sins through Christ's death on the cross for me. I now invite Christ to take control of the throne of my life.

"Fill me with the Holy Spirit as You commanded me to be filled and as You promised in Your Word that You would do if I asked in faith. I pray this in the authority of the name of the Lord Jesus Christ. As an expression of my faith, I now thank You for filling me with Your Holy Spirit and for taking control of my life."

If this prayer expressed the desire of your heart, you can be sure that God has answered it. You can begin this very moment to draw upon the vast, inexhaustible resources of the Holy Spirit to enable you to live a holy life and to share the claims of the Lord Jesus and His love and forgiveness with people everywhere.

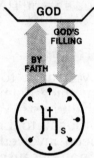

Remember that being filled with the Holy Spirit is a way of life. We are commanded to be constantly controlled by the Holy Spirit. Thank Him for the fullness of His Spirit as you begin each day, and continue to invite Him to control your life moment by moment. This is your heritage as a child of God.

Filled To Share

The primary purpose for which we are filled with the Holy Spirit is to make us witnesses for Christ through the life that we live and the words which we speak. Remember our Lord's final words to His disciples, and through them to us: "You shall receive power when the Holy Spirit has come upon you; and you shall be My witnesses both in Jerusalem, and in all Judea and Samaria, and even to the remotest part of the earth" (Acts 1:8).

The greatest spiritual awakening since Pentecost has, in my opinion, already begun. Millions of Christians are discovering this great source of power which altered the course of history and turned a wicked Roman Empire upside down. That same power, the power of the Holy Spirit is being released through the lives of believing and obedient Christians in our generation to turn our world around and accelerate the fulfillment of the Great Commission in our generation.

Remember, "How to Be Filled With the Spirit" is a transferable concept. I encourage you to master it and to begin to "teach these great truths to trustworthy men who will, in turn, pass them on to others" (II Timothy 2:2, Living Bible).

Review and Thought Questions

1. Why is the average Christian not living in complete obedience to God?

   _____

   _____

   _____

2. Make a list of the priorities in your life right now. What place does *self* have in each?

   _____

   _____

   _____

3. How do these verses describe the riches of Christ?

   Romans 2:4 _____

   _____

   Romans 9:23 _____

   _____

   Romans 11:33 _____

   _____

   Ephesians 1:7 _____

   _____

   Ephesians 3:8 _____

   _____

   _____

Hebrews 11:26 _____

_____

4. Romans 8:16,17 says that we are joint-heirs with Christ. In light of the above answer, what does that relationship mean to you?

_____

_____

_____

a) What promises of God have you claimed?

_____

_____

_____

_____

b) How has claiming them made a specific difference in your life?

_____

_____

_____

5. What do these verses tell you about God's love for you?

Matthew 7:11 _____

_____

John 10:28 _____

_____

_____

II Chronicles 16:9 _____

_____

John 14:21 _____

_____

Hebrews 13:5 _____

_____

6. How is the command of Ephesians 5:18 related to the promise of I John 5:14,15? How can this give you assurance that you are filled with the Holy Spirit?

_____

_____

_____

_____

_____

_____

_____

_____

_____

Discussion questions: 2, 4 (all 3 parts).

CHAPTER STUDY GUIDE

1. As you apply the principles presented in this Concept, being filled with the Holy Spirit will become a way of life for you. A thorough understanding of this Concept will enable you to communicate it more effectively to others.

2. Memorize the following verses and references:
Ephesians 5:18: "And do not get drunk with wine, for that is dissipation, but be filled with the Spirit."
I John 5:14, 15: "And this is the confidence which we have before Him, that if we ask anything according to His will, He hears us. And if we know that He hears us in whatever we ask, we know that we have the request which we have asked of Him."

3. Make this Concept, "How to Be Filled With the Holy Spirit," a way of life by practicing the following:
a. Set aside a special time to be alone with the Lord each day. Be sure that our Lord Jesus Christ is in control of your life and that you are filled with the Holy Spirit as you begin each day. Thank God for what He is going to do in your life and for the way He is going to use you in the lives of others. Ask Him to lead you to those who are in need of Christ's love and forgiveness.
b. Make a practice of breathing spiritually each time you become aware of the need. Simply exhale by confessing your sin and inhale by appropriating the fullness of the Holy Spirit by faith.

AMPLIFIED OUTLINE
Study 1.

Introduction
 A. Learning how to be filled (controlled and empowered with the Holy Spirit is the most important discovery of the Christian life.
  1. You can experience the abundant life Jesus promised.
  2. You can introduce others to Christ.
 B. Even though they had been with the Lord for three years, the disciples were not equipped to carry out

the Lord's Great Commission until they were filled with the Holy Spirit (Acts 1:4, 8).

C. Jesus promised that we would do greater works than He did (John 14:12-14).

1. Obviously we cannot accomplish these greater works ourselves.

2. They will result from the Son of Man, who came to seek and to save the lost, working through us.

3. Our responsibility is to follow Christ; His responsibility is to make us fishers of men (Matthew 4:19).

D. Tragically, multitudes of Christians do not know how to be filled with the Spirit.

1. There is a great contrast between the early church and the present day church.

2. New Testament Christians recognized the new quality of life as Christ living in them.

E. First-century power is available to us today.

1. This news transforms lives.

2. This good news is for you.

I. Who, Why, What?

A. Who is the Holy Spirit?

1. He is God.

2. He is the third person of the Trinity, co-equal with God the Son.

B. Why did the Holy Spirit come?

1. He came to glorify Christ and to lead us into the truth of God's Word (John 16:13, 14).

2. He guides us in our prayer life.

3. He gives us power to witness (Acts 1:8).

4. It is impossible to even know Christ apart from the Spirit (John 3:5).

C. What does it mean to be filled with the Holy Spirit?

1. To be filled with the Holy Spirit is to be filled with Christ and to abide in Him (John 15:1-8).

2. To be filled with the Spirit is to bear twofold spiritual fruit.

      a. Christ, who "came to seek and to save the lost," will, through the power of the Holy Spirit, produce through us the fruit of souls won to the Lord (John 15:16, Matthew 4:19).

      b. As the Holy Spirit controls us, we will mature in Christ and the fruit of the Spirit will become increasingly evident in our lives (Galatians 5:22, 23).

   3. The Word of God will become more meaningful to us.

      a. God's Word is the basis of our spiritual growth (Colossians 3:16).

      b. The Holy Spirit illumines and applies the Word.

      c. A balance between the Word of God and the Spirit of God will result in "the abundant life" which glorifies our Savior.

II. Why is the average Christian not filled with the Holy Spirit?

  A. The average Christian continues to live in defeat and is not filled with the Spirit because of lack of knowledge.

    1. If he knew how much God loved him and the power that was available to him to experience an abundant life, the carnal Christian would no more want to remain carnal than the non-Christian would want to remain a non-Christian.

    2. He does not understand that from the moment of spiritual birth God has made His power available to enable the Christian to go on growing toward maturity in Christ.

    3. The average Christian, not understanding how to be filled with the Spirit by faith, lives a miserable, defeated, roller coaster kind of life (Romans 7:15,25).

    4. The average Christian is not aware of his spiritual heritage.

  B. The average Christian is not filled with the Spirit because of unbelief.

1. Many people are afraid of God; they do not trust Him (Hebrews 3:19, I John 4:18).

2. Many feel that God will require the impossible of them; they doubt the extent of God's love (Matthew 7:11).

3. Many feel that God will take away their pleasures; they do not realize how great is His plan for us (Matthew 6:33).

Study 2.

III. How can you be filled with the Holy Spirit?

A. You are filled with the Spirit by faith.

1. You become a Christian by faith (Ephesians 2:8,9).

2. You also walk in the Spirit by faith (Colossians 2:6).

B. You do not have to beg God for what is already yours (Romans 1:17).

C. Several factors contribute to heart preparation for being filled by faith.

1. You must desire to live a life that will please the Lord (Matthew 5:6).

2. You must be willing to surrender the control of your life to Christ according to the command of God (Romans 12:1,2).

3. You must confess any sin which the Holy Spirit calls to your remembrance and claim His forgiveness (I John 1:9).

D. There are two words to remember in claiming His filling by faith.

1. His command is that we be filled with the Spirit (Ephesians 5:18).

2. His promise is that He always answers when we pray according to His will (I John 5:14,15).

E. It is important to remember:

1. If you are a Christian, the Holy Spirit already indwells you.

2. Being filled with the Holy Spirit, however, is

not a once-and-for-all experience; we are to be constantly filled with the Holy Spirit as a way of life.

3. It is not simply by prayer that we are filled. It is by faith.

F. We can never make ourselves good enough to please God; we must live by faith (Romans 8:7; Jeremiah 17:9; Galatians 2:20).

G. The result of being filled and of walking in the Spirit is that we become dead to self and alive to God (Matthew 6:24; John 12:24).

H. We live by faith. Feelings are valid as a by-product of faith and obedience, but at no time should we depend upon feelings alone.

CHAPTER 4
HOW TO WALK IN THE SPIRIT

Study 1. Spiritual Breathing
Study 2. Be Sure You Are Filled With the Spirit
          Be Prepared For Spiritual Conflict
Study 3. Know Your Rights
          Live By Faith

STUDY 1.

SPIRITUAL BREATHING

"Since I have learned how to walk in the Spirit, the Christian life has become a great adventure for me," said a medical doctor after completing his third Lay Institute for Evangelism. "Now, I want everyone to experience this same adventure with Christ."

Would you like to know how to experience a full, abundant, purposeful and fruitful life for Christ? You can! If you have been living in spiritual defeat — impotent and fruitless, wondering if there is any validity to the Christian life — there is hope for you! What greater promise could Christ have possibly offered to the Christian than the assurance that he can walk daily in the power of the Spirit of Jesus Christ and experience an abundant and fruitful life of purpose and adventure.

FRUITFULNESS
ABUNDANCE

CHRIST-DIRECTED LIFE
† - Christ is in the life
    and on the throne
S - Self is yielding to Christ
• - Interests are directed
    by Christ, resulting in
    harmony with God's plan

Such ability has been promised by no less an authority than Christ Himself, to all who receive Him as Lord and Savior. Here is His promise: 'Truly, truly, I say to you, he who believes in Me, the works that I do shall he do also; and greater works than those shall he do because I go to the Father. And whatever you ask in My name, that will I do, that the Father may be glorified in the Son. If you ask anything in My name, I will do it" (John 14:12-14).

Certain basic spiritual truths, when fully understood and experienced by faith, guarantee revolutionary spiritual benefits. These proven principles can help you to be more consistent in your walk in the Spirit and more effective in your witness for our Savior.

A Supernatural Life

The Christian life, properly understood, is not complex or difficult. As a matter of fact, the Christian life is very simple. It is so simple that we stumble over the very simplicity of it and yet it is so difficult that no one can live it! This paradox occurs because the Christian life is a supernatural life. The only one who can live it is the Lord Jesus Christ.

If I try to live the Christian life in my own fleshly effort, it does become complex, difficult and even impossible to live. But if I invite the Lord Jesus to direct my life; if I know the reality of having been crucified with Christ and raised with Him by faith as a way of life; if I walk in the light as God is in the light — then the Lord Jesus simply lives His abundant life within me in all of His resurrection power.

This fact was dramatically demonstrated in the lives of the early Christians. When the enemies of the Lord saw the way He was fulfilling His promise in the lives of Peter and John and observed their boldness and the remarkable quality of their lives, they were amazed at these obviously uneducated non-professionals and realized what being with Jesus had done for them (Acts 4:13).

I do not wish to suggest that the Christian who walks in the fullness of the Spirit will have no problems. Problems of poor health, loss of loved ones, financial needs and other such experiences are common to all people. However, most of our problems are self-imposed because of our own carnal, selfish actions. The spiritual man is spared from most of these problems. But when the problems do come, the spiritual man can face them with a calm, confident attitude because he is aware of God's resources which are available to him to deal with such problems.

This is not simply a matter of positive thinking, for we are instructed to cast our cares upon the Lord Jesus because He cares for us (I Peter 5:7). The spiritual man knows the trustworthiness of God from experience. The Lord becomes the problem-solver, and the trials and burdens of this world are no longer too great for us when He is carrying the load.

This was at the heart of the apostle Paul's moment-by-moment experience: "I have been crucified with Christ; and I myself no longer live, but Christ lives in me. And the real life I now have within this body is a result of my trusting in the Son of God, who loved me and gave Himself for me" (Galatians 2:20, Living Bible).

Simple And Understandable

The kind of theology which is so profound that it cannot be understood is not only the product of fuzzy thinking, but it is also a direct contradiction of Scripture. Further, certain teaching to which some refer as the "deeper truths" of the Word often lead to a fascination with these "truths" but do not produce holy lives, fruitful witness or a greater love for Christ and commitment to His cause.

The teaching of the Lord was simple and understandable even though some of the truths which He taught were obscure to men whose eyes were spiritually blind. He spoke of the lilies of the field, the sower and his seed, fishing for men, new wineskins, the vine and the branches — simple lessons that were easily understood by His listeners. Jesus communicated with the people; the "multitudes heard Him gladly," they understood Him, and they followed Him.

In a spiritually illiterate world, we must follow the simplicity of our Savior's message and method if we are to communicate His good news to the multitudes. Since God so loved the people of the world, most of whom have little or no knowledge of spiritual truth, and since He gave His only begotten Son to die for our sins that we may have eternal life, it does not seem reasonable to me that one must be a theologian or even a deep student of the Bible (though this is to be desired) before he can experience and share the abundant life of joy and victory that is our heritage in Christ.

SPIRITUAL BREATHING

One of the most important truths of Scripture, the understanding and application of which has enriched my life as has no other truth, is a concept which I like to call "spiritual breathing." This concept has been shared with hundreds of thousands — with revolutionary results — through our literature and various training conferences and seminars.

As you walk in the Spirit by faith, practicing spiritual breathing, you need never again live in spiritual defeat for more than a few minutes at a time. Spiritual breathing, like physical breathing, is a process of exhaling the impure and inhaling the pure, an exercise in faith that enables you to experience God's love and forgiveness as a way of life.

The moment you invited Christ into your life as Savior and Lord, you experienced a spiritual birth. You became a child of God and you were filled with the Holy Spirit. God forgave your sins — past, present and future — making you righteous, holy and acceptable in His sight because of Christ's sacrifice for you on the cross. You were given the power to live a holy life and to be a fruitful witness for God.

Roller Coaster Life

But the average Christian does not understand this concept of spiritual breathing as an exercise of faith and as a result, lives on a spiritual roller coaster. He goes from one emotional experience to another, living most of his life as a carnal Christian, controlling his own life — frustrated and fruitless.

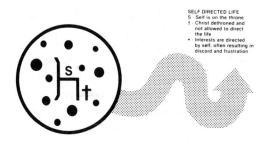

SELF-DIRECTED LIFE
S - Self is on the throne
† - Christ dethroned and
     not allowed to direct
     the life
• - Interests are directed
     by self, often resulting in
     discord and frustration

If this is your experience, spiritual breathing will enable you to get off this emotional roller coaster and to enjoy the Christian life that the Lord Jesus promised to you when He said, "I came that they might have life and might have it abundantly" (John 10:10, Living Bible). As an exercise in faith, it will enable you to continue to experience God's love, forgiveness and the power and control of the Holy Spirit as a way of life.

Exhale — Confess

If you retake the throne, the control center, of your life through sin — a deliberate act of disobedience — breathe spiritually. First, *exhale by confession.* God's Word promises in I John 1:9, "If we confess our sins, He is faithful and just to forgive us our sins, and to cleanse us from all unrighteousness." Confession (*homologeo* in the Greek) suggests agreement with God concerning our sins. Such agreement involves at least three considerations.

First, you must acknowledge that your sin or sins — which should be named to God specifically — are wrong and are therefore grievous to God. Second, you acknowledge that God has already forgiven you through Christ's death on the cross for your sins. Third, you repent, which means that you change your attitude toward your sin. The power of the Holy Spirit will enable you to change your conduct. Instead of doing what your old sinful nature — your fleshly self — wants to do, you can do what God wants you to do.

Inhale — Appropriate By Faith

Next, *inhale, by appropriating the fullness of God's Spirit by faith.* Trust Him now to control and empower you, according to His command to "be filled with the Spirit" (Ephesians 5:18), which actually means to be *constantly and continually* controlled and empowered with the Holy Spirit. According to His promise, He hears us and grants our request because we pray according to His will (I John 5:14, 15). Continue to claim His love, forgiveness and power by faith and continue to have fellowship with Him moment by moment.

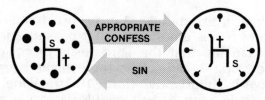

You can get off your spiritual roller coaster, cease to be a carnal Christian and become a Spirit-filled Christian by practicing spiritual breathing. If you are breathing spiritually — exhaling, confessing your sin, and inhaling, appropriating the fullness of the Holy Spirit by faith — you are a Spirit-filled Christian.

Attitude Of Unbelief

What will cause you to become a carnal Christian and fall back into this roller coaster way of life? You become a carnal Christian again when you develop an attitude of unbelief — when you cease to believe the promises of I John 1:9 and I Corinthians 10:13: "No temptation has overtaken you but such as is common to man; and God is faithful, who will not allow you to be tempted beyond what you are able; but with the temptation will provide the way of escape also, that you may be able to endure it."

Paul says in Romans 14:23, "Whatever is not of faith is sin." If you cease to practice spiritual breathing, you will become carnal. You do not become carnal simply by committing one sin or a dozen or a hundred sins provided that you sincerely continue to breathe spiritually. You will become carnal only when you develop an attitude of unbelief and refuse to breathe spiritually.

A man who participated in one of our training conferences a few years ago shared with me his experience when he first realized the practical benefits of spiritual breathing. He had agreed to teach a Sunday school class of young students, and was filled with apprehension because he was not used to teaching students of that age. He planned to arrive at church early in order to make proper preparation for the arrival of his students.

He had asked his family to be ready to leave the house early on that Sunday morning. The family was late getting ready and as he sat in the car in the hot sun, fuming and fussing, waiting for them, he became more and more tense and irritated.

When his family finally got into the car, he exploded with anger, but before he had finished speaking, the Holy Spirit reminded him that his attitude and action did not honor the Lord. Furthermore, he knew that he would be sharing with the children in Sunday school about God's love and forgiveness and patience. By this time he was well aware that he was in no mood for God to use Him.

Changed Attitude

Suddenly he remembered what he had learned about "spiritual breathing." He exhaled by confessing his anger to the Lord, and thanked God that he was already forgiven on the basis of Christ's death for him. Then he apologized to his children, and inhaled by acknowledging afresh the control of the Holy Spirit. He then went on his way rejoicing.

Because he had exhaled — confessed his sin — and inhaled — appropriated the power and acknowledged the control of the Holy Spirit, by faith — his attitude was changed. God was able to use this man to introduce to Christ several young people in his Sunday school class that morning.

Thousands of Christians around the world have shared similar experiences of how this concept of spiritual breathing has brought unusual blessing to their lives and, through them, to the lives of others.

As you exhale and inhale the moment you know that you have sinned, you will recognize greater freedom and power in your life. Simply keep short accounts with God. Do not allow your sins to accumulate.

The Real Evidence

This is not to suggest that we have to sin, but in the words of the apostle John, "My little children, I am telling you this so that you will stay away from sin. But if you sin, there is someone to plead for you before the Father. His name is Jesus Christ, the one who is all that is good and who pleases God completely.

"He is the one who took God's wrath against our sins upon Himself, and brought us into fellowship with God; and He is the forgiveness for our sins, and not only ours but all the world's. And how can we be sure that we belong to Him? By looking within ourselves: are we really trying to do what He wants us to do?

"Someone may say, 'I am a Christian: I am on my way to heaven; I belong to Christ; but if he doesn't do what Christ tells him to, he is a liar. But those who do what Christ tells them to will learn to love God more and more. That is the way to know whether or not you are a Christian. Anyone who says he is a Christian should live as Christ did" (I John 2:1-6, Living Bible).

Critical And Progressive

You will discover that your relationship with the Holy Spirit is both critical and progressive: critical, in that you discover how to appropriate His power by faith; progressive in that you learn how to grow and mature in the Spirit-controlled walk by faith.

A Christian who has walked in the Spirit by faith for many years will generally demonstrate more of the fruit of the Spirit in his life (Galatians 5:22, 23) and be more fruitful in his witness for Christ than one who has just discovered how to walk in the Spirit. You will become aware of such an area of your life — an attitude or an action — that is displeasing to the Lord. Simply breathe spiritually.

Walking in the Spirit through the practice of spiritually breathing is a simple concept. However, there are four important factors which will contribute greatly to an understanding of this great adventure and insure a successful walk in the Spirit. First, be sure that you are filled with the Holy Spirit. Second, be prepared for spiritual conflict. Third, know your rights as a child of God. And fourth, live by faith. Let us look more closely at each of these factors.

Review and Thought Questions

1. What does John 14:12-14 mean to you?

   _____

   _____

   _____

2. What does being crucified with Christ mean? (See Galatians 2:20.)

   _____

   _____

   _____

3. How do the accounts of the following people demonstrate their walk in the Spirit?

   Paul — Acts 18:4-11 (cf. Philippians 4): _____

   _____

   Peter — Acts 3:1-26 (cf. Acts 4:13): _____

   _____

   Stephen — Acts 6:8-15 (cf. 7:51-60): _____

   _____

4. a) What does it mean to you to cast your cares upon the Lord (I Peter 5:7)?

   _____

   _____

   b) How can you do this?

   _____

   _____

   _____

   _____

5. What does the example of the vine and branches in John 15:1-8 mean to you in your Christian life?

_____

_____

_____

6. How would you describe the effects of spiritual fitness as expressed in "spiritual breathing"

Romans 14:23 _____

_____

I John 1:9 _____

_____

I Corinthians 10:13 _____

_____

Ephesians 5:18 _____

_____

I John 5:14, 15 _____

_____

7. What promise does God make to you in I John 2:1-6?

_____

_____

Questions 1, 2, 4 and 5 can be used to stimulate effective group discussions.

STUDY 2.

BE SURE YOU ARE FILLED WITH THE SPIRIT

First, in order to walk in the Spirit, we must be filled with the Spirit. In Ephesians 5:18, we are admonished, "Be not drunk with wine, wherein is excess; but be filled with the Spirit." To be filled with the Holy Spirit is to be controlled and empowered by the Holy Spirit. We cannot have two masters (Matthew 6:24). There is a throne, a control center, in every life — either self or Christ is on that throne. This concept of Christ being on the throne is so simple that even a child can understand it.

My wife and I began to teach our sons this great truth when they were very young. One evening when we were saying our prayers together, I asked our then eight-year-old son, Zac, "Who is on the throne of your life?" He said, "Jesus." I asked our then five-year-old son, Brad, who was on the throne of his life. He answered "Jesus."

The next morning their mother had prepared for breakfast a special dish called "egg in a bonnet." It was a delicious, thick piece of French toast with a hole in the middle, and in that hole was a poached egg. As I was enjoying it, I looked over at our young son. He was not eating the egg nor the toast.

I said, "Brad, eat your breakfast." He replied, "I don't want it." "Of course you do," I said. "You'll enjoy it. Look at me; I am enjoying mine." "Well," he said, "I don't like it and I'm not going to eat it." Being a bit dramatic, he began to release a few tears. I had to make up my mind what I was going to do. I could either say to him, "Now young man, you eat that breakfast or else I will spank you;" or reply, "Forget it. I'll eat it myself."

Who's On The Throne?

However, I thought of a better idea. I asked, "Brad, who is on the throne of your life this morning?" At that, the tears really began to pour. He understood the point I was making. He had learned the concept that Christ must be on the throne; but Christ was not on the throne of his life at that moment. When he regained his composure, he replied, in answer to my question, "The devil and me." I asked him, "Whom do you want on the throne?" He answered, "Jesus."

So I said, "Let's pray," and he prayed, "Dear Jesus, forgive me for being disobedient and help me to like this egg." God heard that prayer, and Brad enjoyed his breakfast. As a matter of fact, he ate it all. You see, he had said that he did not like it before he had even tasted it.

That evening as we were saying our prayers, I asked Zac who had been on the throne of his life that day, and he said "Jesus." Then I asked Brad the same question, and he replied, "Jesus. Oh," he added, "except at breakfast this morning."

It is such a simple truth; in its distilled essence, that is what the Christian life is all about — just keeping Christ on the throne. We do this when we understand how to walk in the control and power of the Holy Spirit, for the Holy Spirit came for the express purpose of glorifying Christ by enabling the beliver to live a holy life and to be a productive witness for the Savior.

Command And Promise

As I said previously, to be sure we are filled with the Holy Spirit (I Corinthians 3:16), we need to remember two important words: *command* — be ye being filled with — constantly and continually controlled and empowered by — the Holy Spirit; and *promise* — if we ask anything according to God's will, He hears us; and if He hears us, He answers us.

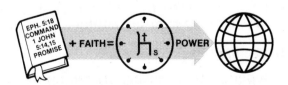

On the authority of God's command we know that we are praying according to His will when we ask Him to fill us — to control and empower us. Therefore, we can expect Him to fill and empower us on the basis of His command and promise, *provided* that we genuinely desire to be filled and trust Him to fill us. Technically, you are filled as an act of faith — not by asking to be filled — in the same way that you became a Christian by faith (according to Ephesians 2: 8, 9) and not merely because you asked Christ to come into your life.

Remember that the Holy Spirit already dwells within you if you are a believer. You do not have to ask Him to come into your life; He is already indwelling you. Your body is a temple of God from the moment you became a Christian. So you simply say to Him, "I surrender my life to You, and by faith I appropriate Your fullness."

The Spirit Reveals Sin

Then continue to breathe spiritually, exhaling whenever the Holy Spirit reveals sin that you need to confess and inhaling as you go on walking in the fullness and control of the Spirit by faith. Some Christians breathe spiritually faster and more often than others.

Exhale only when the Holy Spirit reveals something that needs to be confessed. For some that could be several times each day, while for others it will only be a few times a year.

Avoid being introspective. Do not probe within yourself, looking for sin to confess. Confess only what the Holy Spirit impresses you to confess. Believe God and His Word. Do not seek an emotional experience. If you genuinely hunger and thirst after God and His righteousness, if you have confessed your sin, surrendered the control of your life to Christ and asked God to fill you, believe that you are filled by faith on the basis of His promise. God will prove Himself faithful to His promise.

Fact, Faith, Feeling

Do not depend upon feelings. The promise of God's Word, not our feelings, is our authority. The Christian is to live by faith, trusting in the trustworthiness of God Himself and His Word. This can be illustrated by a train. Let us call the engine *fact* — the fact of God's promises found in His Word. The coal car we will call *faith* — our trust in God and His Word. The caboose we will call *feelings*.

You place coal in the engine and the train runs. However, it would be futile to attempt to pull the train by the caboose. In the same way we, as Christians, should not depend upon feelings or emotions, but in order to live a Spirit-filled life should simply place our faith in the trustworthiness of God and the promises of His Word. Feelings are like the caboose — they will eventually come along in the life of faith, but we should never depend on feelings or look for them. The very act of looking for an emotional experience is a denial of the concept of faith, and whatever is not of faith is sin.

You can know right now that you are filled with the Spirit by trusting in God, His command and promise, and you can go through life with that assurance. In order to walk in the Spirit, then, we must first be filled and then we must continue to breathe spiritually.

BE PREPARED FOR SPRITUAL CONFLICT.

Second, we must be prepared for spiritual conflict if we expect to walk in the control — the fullness and power — of the Holy Spirit. As we have already considered, the Christian life is a supernatural life, and the only one who can live it is Christ. We must be prepared for spiritual conflict, but we should remember that for the Christian the battle is not ours but the Lord's. He promises to fight for us (Exodus 14:14).

The Bible explains that there are three forces — the world, the flesh and the devil — which are constantly waging battle against the believer.

The World

The Bible warns us in I John 2:15-17, "Stop loving this evil world and all that it offers you, for when you love these things you show that you do not really love God; for all these worldly things, these evil desires — the craze for sex, the ambition to buy everything that appeals to you, and the pride that comes from wealth and importance — these are not from God. They are from this evil world itself. And this world is fading away, and these evil, forbidden things are going with it, but whoever keeps doing the will of God will live forever" (Living Bible).

I do not know anyone who loves this world who has ever been used of God in any significant way. There is nothing wrong with money and other material success. However, we are to wear the cloak of materialism loosely. We are to set our affection on Christ and His kingdom, not on the material things of this world. "But take courage; I have overcome the world" (John 16:33).

The Flesh

External forces without and internal forces within us are constantly fighting to win control over us, and we are never free from their pressure. "For the flesh (the old sin nature) sets its desire against the Spirit, and the Spirit against the flesh; for those are in opposition to one another, so that you may not do the things that you please" (Galatians 5:17).

This conflict in our lives will continue so long as we live. There will never be a time when we are free from temptation. All people, no matter how spiritual they are, are tempted and have a tendency toward sin.

There is a difference between temptation and sin. Temptation is the initial impression to do something contrary to God's will. Such impressions come to all men and women, even as they did to the Lord, and are not sin in themselves. Temptation becomes sin when we meditate on the impression and develop a desire which becomes lust and is often followed by the actual act of disobedience.

Yet, this major conflict is largely resolved, when we, by an act of the will, surrender ourselves to the control of the Holy Spirit and face these temptations in His power. "Walk by the Spirit and you will not carry out the desire of the flesh" (Galatians 5:16). For practical daily living we simply recognize our weakness whenever we are tempted and ask the Lord to take care of the problem for us.

The Devil

We are told in I Peter 5:7, 8 to let God have all of our worries and cares, for He is always thinking about us and watching everything that concerns us. We are to be careful — watching out for attacks from Satan, our great enemy, who prowls around like a hungry roaring lion, looking for some victim to tear apart. Satan is a real foe — let there be no mistake about it — and we need to be alert to his cunning and subtle ways, as well as his obvious attempts to defeat and destroy us.

A young minister shared with me one day, "I am afraid of Satan." I said, "You should be afraid of Satan, if you insist on controlling your own life. But if you are willing to let Christ control your life, you have nothing to fear because the Bible says 'Greater is He who is in you that he who is in the world.' " (I John 4:4, Living Bible).

"Satan was defeated 2,000 years ago when Christ in fulfillment of prophecy died on the cross for our sins. Though Satan has great power to influence man, he has only that power which God has granted to him. That is why, in the face of great persecution, the disciples could pray to God in His sovereignty and power, 'They won't stop at anything that You in Your wise power will let them do' " (Acts 4:28, Living Bible).

Stay Out Of The Cage

My minister friend happened to live in a city with one of the largest zoos in the world. I said, "What do you do with lions in your city?" He replied, "We put them in a cage." I said, "Satan is in a cage. Visit the cage in the zoo and watch a lion pacing impatiently back and forth. He cannot hurt you. Even if you go up close to the cage, he still cannot hurt you if you are careful. But stay out of that cage, or you will be in trouble. Get in the cage, and the lion will make mincemeat of you. But you have nothing to fear as long as you stay out of that cage.

"Similarly, you have nothing to fear from Satan as long

as you depend upon Christ and not on your own strength. Remember, Satan has no power except that which God in His wisdom allows him to have."

The apostle Paul warns us, "Put on all of God's armor so that you will be able to stand safe against the strategies and tricks of Satan. For we are not fighting people made of flesh and blood, but against persons without bodies — the evil rulers of the unseen world, those mighty satanic beings and great evil princes of darkness who rule this world; and against huge numbers of wicked spirits in the spirit world" (Ephesians 6:11, 12, Living Bible).

Satan and the forces of darkness are real foes. We must be alert to the way Satan works, but we need not be afraid. We need have no fear of him — if we are willing to trust the Lord — even though he is an expert at inducing Christians to disobey God. But if we continue to be carnal Christians, we had better be ready for some real problems in our individual lives and in our churches.

Review and Thought Questions

1. a) In what areas of your life is "self" on the throne?

   _____

   _____

   b) In what areas of your life is Jesus on the throne?

   _____

   _____

   c) What are you going to do about those areas in which "self" is still in control?

   _____

   _____

2. a) What concrete examples from your life can you give that show the presence of fact, faith and feelings?

   _____

   _____

   _____

   b) What were the results of putting faith in your feelings rather than in the fact of God and His Word?

   _____

   _____

3. What armor used to defend yourself against the world, flesh and devil does Ephesians 6:11-18 describe?

   _____

   _____

   _____

   _____

   _____

   _____

4. What should be your attitude toward desires for worldly things, in light of the teaching and God's promise in Matthew 6:24-33?

_____

_____

_____

5. a) According to Romans 13:14, how can you reduce the opportunities for temptation of the flesh?

_____

_____

b) In what particular area of your life can you apply this method of control?

_____

_____

6. a) What is the prerequisite shown in James 4:7 for successfully resisting the devil?

_____

_____

b) What is God's promise to you?

_____

_____

_____

Discussion questions: 2, 4, 5.

STUDY 3.

KNOW YOUR RIGHTS

If we are going to walk in the Spirit, we need to know our rights as children of God. We need to know our spiritual heritage. We need to know how to draw upon the inexhaustible resources of God's love, power, forgiveness and abundant grace.

One of the most important things we can do to learn who God is, who man is and what our rights are is to spend much time — even at a sacrifice of other needs and demands on our schedules — in reading, studying, memorizing and meditating on the Word of God, and in prayer and witnessing.

Balanced Life

It is impossible to walk vigorously and contagiously in the Spirit without spending time, unhurried time, in fellowship with the Lord in His Word — in prayer and in personal study. We must listen sensitively to Him for His directions for our daily activities as a basis for our daily witness for Christ.

On the other hand, I would hasten to emphasize that, without the regular sharing of your faith in Christ with others, Bible study and prayer can often lead to a spiritually frustrating and impotent life. After many years of working with thousands of Christians, I am convinced that one cannot enjoy the full and abundant life which is our heritage in Christ apart from the proper balance between Bible study, prayer and sharing Christ with others out of the overflow of an obedient, Spirit-filled life. We need to be able not only to experience this great adventure with Christ for ourselves, but also to share this good news with others.

A word of caution is in order at this point. We become spiritual, experience power from God and become fruitful in our witness as a result of faith and faith alone. The Bible clearly teaches that "just shall live by faith." Works are the result of faith.

Result Of Faith

Many Christians are confused on this point. They think

of works (Bible study, prayer and other spiritual disciplines) as the means to — rather than the results of — the life of faith. They spend much time in Bible study and prayer. They may even attempt to witness for Christ and to obey the various commands of God, thinking that by these means they will achieve the abundant Christian life. But they remain defeated, frustrated, impotent and fruitless. Feeling that their problem is that they must not be doing enough, they then spend even more time in prayer and Bible study — all to no avail and leading to even greater frustration and defeat.

Bible study, prayer, witnessing and obedience are the result of the life of faith, not the means to it. As you are filled with the Holy Spirit, the Bible comes alive, prayer becomes vital, your witness becomes effective and obedience becomes a joy. As a result of your obedience in these various areas, your faith grows and you become more mature in your spiritual life. James 2:22 says, concerning the life of Abraham, "You see, he was trusting God so much that he was willing to do whatever God told him to do; his faith was made complete by what he did, by his actions, his good deeds" (Living Bible).

Yes, Bible study, prayer and obedience are important, vitally important, but they should be regarded as the result — the overflow — of the life of faith, not as the means to faith.

Strength In Christ

Paul says,"I want to remind you that your strength must come from the Lord's mighty power within you" (Ephesians 6:10, Living Bible). Jesus Christ, in all of His mighty resurrection power, lives in all of us who have become children of God through faith in Christ (Romans 8; Ephesians 1:9-25; Colossians 1:27-2:10). I do not have any strength in myself.

As a young man in college and later in business, I used to be very self-sufficient — proud of what I could do on my own. I believed that a man could do just about anything he wanted to do on his own if he was willing to pay the price of hard work and sacrifice, and I experienced some degree of success. Then, when I became a Christian,

I was introduced to a whole new philosophy of life — a life of trusting replaced my life of trying.

Now I realize how totally incapable I am of living the Christian life — how weak I am in my own strength and yet how strong I am in Christ. As Paul said,"I can do all things through Him (Christ) who strengthens me" (Philippians 4:13). "God has not given us a spirit of fear; but of power and of love, and of a sound mind" (II Timothy 1:7, King James).

"Greater is He who is in you than he who is in the world" (I John 4:4, Living Bible).

In John 15:4, 5, the Lord stresses the importance of drawing our strength from Him: 'Take care to live in Me, and let me live in you. For a branch cannot produce fruit when severed from the vine. Nor can you be fruitful apart from Me. Yes, I am the vine; you are the branches. Whoever lives in Me and I in him shall produce a large crop of fruit. For apart from Me, you can't do a thing" (Living Bible).

In our own strength we are helpless, impotent, fruitless; we are like branches cut off from the vine if we try to live our own lives, even as Christians. But if we abide in Christ, and He abides in us, it is His life-giving power that is expressed through us and enables us to live and witness for Him.

Fishing For Men

Jesus explained the importance of a fruitful witness in John 15:8 "By this is My Father glorfied, that you bear much fruit, and so prove to be My disciples." In Matthew 4:19 He says, "Follow Me, and I will make you fishers of men." It is our responsibility to follow Him. It is His responsibility to make us fishers of men. What a relief to know that the responsibility of bearing fruit is the Lord's.

All that God expects of us is our availability, our trust and our obedience. We are to live holy lives and tell others about Christ at every opportunity — but their response is dependent upon the working of the Holy Spirit in their lives. Success in witnessing is simply sharing Christ in the power of the Holy Spirit and leaving the results to God.

Work Of The Spirit

I have never led anyone to Christ and I never shall, though I have had the privilege of praying with thousands who have received Christ as a result of my witness. This is the work of the Holy Spirit. Therefore I cannot boast over much fruit or be discouraged over little fruit. The responsibility for fruit belongs to the Holy Spirit, who works in and through me, producing fruit and changing the lives of individuals.

Christ's power is available to all who trust Him. Paul writes, "I pray that you will begin to understand how incredibly great His power is to help those who believe Him. It is that same mighty power that raised Christ from the dead and seated Him in the place of honor at God's right hand in heaven, far, far above any other king or ruler or dictator or leader.

"Yes, His honor is far more glorious than that of anyone else either in this world or in the world to come. And God

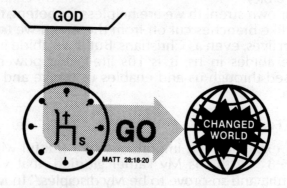

has put all things under His feet and made Him the supreme head of the church — which is His Body, filled with Himself, the Author and Giver of everthing everywhere" (Ephesians 1:19-23, Living Bible).

I Am With You Always

The Lord Jesus commissioned the disciples to go into all the world and preach the gospel, with the promise that He would always be with them. He said,"I have been given all authority in heaven and earth. Therefore go and make disciples in all the nations . . . and then teach these new disciples to obey all the commands I have given you" (Matthew 28:18-20, Living Bible).

He did not say to them, "Go into all the world, and good luck." He said, "And be sure of this — that I am with you always, even to the end of the world" (Matthew 28:18-20). "I will never, never fail you nor forsake you" (Hebrews 13:5, Living Bible).

Our living Savior, the one whom we serve, is the omnipotent God! He is the one who the Bible tells us "is the exact likeness of the unseen God. He existed before God made anything at all, and, in fact, Christ Himself is the creator who made everything in heaven and earth, the things we can see and the things we can't; the spirit world and its kings and kingdoms, its rulers and authorities: all were made by Christ for His own use and glory . . .

"For God wanted all of Himself to be in His Son . . . In Him lie hidden all the mighty untapped treasures of wisdom and knowledge . . . Don't let others spoil your faith and joy with their philosophies, their wrong and shallow answers built on men's thoughts and ideas, instead of on what Christ has said.

"For in Christ there is all of God in a human body; so you have everything when you have Christ, and you are filled with God through your union with Christ. He is the highest ruler with authority over every other power" (Colossians 1:15, 16, 19; 2:3, 8-10, Living Bible).

Every Need Supplied

If we have Christ, we have everything we need, for, as Paul writes to the Colossian church, we are complete in Him. According to your day, so shall strength be given. Do you need love? Our Lord Jesus Christ is the incarnation of love. Do you need joy? He is joy. Do you need peace? Christ is peace. Do you need patience? Christ is patience. Do you need wisdom? Christ is wisdom.

Are you in need of material possessions so that you can better serve Christ? They are available in Him. He owns the cattle on a thousand hills, and I would remind you of His promise to supply the needs of all who trust Him.

Christianity is Christ, and you are complete in Him. He is all you need.

Knowing Christ Better

Therefore, every Christian should give priority to seeking to know Him better. We do this largely through spending much time with Him in reading and meditating on His Word, talking to Him in prayer, obeying His commands and telling others about Him. We cannot really get to know Him well if any one of these three elements is missing from our daily lives.

For example, consider and meditate on this exciting passage from Romans that explains the practical benefits every believer can experience because of Christ's death for us on the cross. Paul writes:

"Adam caused many to be sinners because he disobeyed God, and Christ caused many to be acceptable to God because He obeyed. The Ten Commandments were given so that all could see the extent of their failure to obey God's laws. But the more we see our sinfulness, the more we see God's abounding grace forgiving us.

"Before, sin ruled over all men and brought them to death, but now God's kindness rules instead, giving us right standing with God and resulting in eternal life through Jesus Christ our Lord.

Sin's Power Broken

"Well then, shall we keep on sinning so that God can keep on showing us more and more kindness and forgiveness? Of course not! Should we keep on sinning when we don't have to? For sin's power over us was broken when we became Christians and were baptized to become a part of Jesus Christ: through His death the power of your sinful nature was shattered . . . Your old evil desires were nailed to the cross with Him; that part of you that loves to sin was crushed and fatally wounded, so that your sin-loving body is no longer under sin's control, no longer needs to be a slave to sin.

"So look upon your old sin nature as dead and unresponsive to sin, and instead be alive to God, alert to

Him . . . Do not let any part of your bodies become tools of wickedness to be used for sinning; but give yourselves completely to God — every part of you — for you are back from death and you want to be tools in the hands of God, to be used for His good purposes . . . Don't you realize that you can choose your own master? You can choose sin (with death) or else obedience (with acquittal).

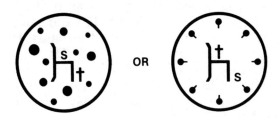

The one to whom you offer yourself — He will take you and be your master and you will be His slave" (Romans 5:19-21; 6:1-3, 6, 11, 13, 16, Living Bible).

Oh, how wonderful to know that these members of our bodies — our eyes, our ears, our lips, our hands, our feet — can be used for the glory of God.

We Do Not Become Puppets

A student asked, "If I give my life to Christ, will I become a puppet?" No. We never become puppets. We have the right to choose — we are free moral agents. God guides and encourages us, but we must act. He does not force us. But the more we understand the love of God, the faithfulness of God and the power of God, the more we will want to trust Him with every detail of our lives. The secret of the successful Christian life is to keep Christ on the throne of our lives. We shall fail in the Christian life only if we as a deliberate act of our wills choose to be disobedient.

One day my wife, Vonette, and I were wading down a shallow stream in Yosemite Park with our two sons. Because the rocks were slippery I was holding my five-year-old, Bradley, by the hand to keep him from slipping on the rocks. Suddenly Brad did slip and his feet went out from under him. We would have had a serious fall and could have been injured had I not held him firmly until he regained his balance. As we continued our walk, Brad looked up into my face with a radiant expression of gratitude and said, "Daddy, I'm sure glad you saved me from falling."

God Holds Us

In the flash of a moment, it was as though God had spoken to me, and I looked up to Him and said, "Father, I am so glad that you have me by the hand. How many times You have kept me from falling!" Oh, this Christian life is wonderful. It is exciting! It is filled with adventure for those who let God control their lives — who walk with Him moment by moment, day by day, allowing Him to "hold their hands."

This personal, intimate walk with Christ, our Savior and our friend, is Christianity — not the struggle, the strain, the labor, the self-disciplining which is usually characteristic of the average, misinformed Christian. If you desire to walk in the Spirit, be sure to know your rights as a child of God, so that you can say with the apostle Paul, "I can do all things through Him (Christ) who strengthens me" (Philippians 4:13).

LIVE BY FAITH

If we are to walk in the Spirit, we must live by faith. Oh, how sad to see wonderful, sincere Christians who have been deceived by a wrong emphasis on emotions. I know of nothing else that has caused so much defeat among Christians. We do not live by feelings. We live by faith. According to Hebrews 11:6, "Without faith it is impossible to please Him." In Galatians 3:11, Paul reminds us, "We live by faith."

Valid emotional feelings are simply the by-product of faith and obedience. There is nothing wrong with feelings. Thank God we have them. Do not be ashamed of feelings, but do not seek them. Never emphasize them. To seek an emotional experience repudiates the command to live by faith and is, in fact, an insult to God. Let emotions find their proper place in your relationship with Christ.

John 14:21 indicates that the most valid way to have an emotional experience is to be obedient to Christ. Jesus said, "He who has my commandments and keeps them, he it is who loves me, and he who loves Me shall be loved by My Father, and I will love him, and will disclose (make real) Myself to him."

Emotional Counterfeits

One of the greatest acts of obedience is to share Christ with others in the power of the Holy Spirit. Since He came to seek and to save the lost and has commissioned us to witness for Him, nothing could please the Savior more. If you want a valid, vital, exciting awareness of Christ in your experience, begin to share Christ with others as a way of life as you walk in the Spirit.

Avoid man-made emotionalism that is generated by resorting to tricks and manipulations of individuals. Many such emotional experiences are a counterfeit of the genuine experience which can be yours through obedience to Christ, our Savior.

We live according to God's promise, trusting in the integrity of God Himself. Faith must have an object, and the object of our faith is God, made known through His Word. God has proven Himself to be worthy of our trust. There are thousands of promises for us contained in God's Word, and no Christian has ever found any one of them to be untrue. When God says something, you can stake your life on it — you can know that He will not fail you.

Thanksgiving Demonstrates Faith

In Romans 8:28 we read one of God's promises to us: "All things work together for good to those who love God, to those who are the called according to His purpose." Do you believe this promise of God? If so, you logically acknowledge the reasonableness of the command of God in I Thessalonians 5:18: "In everything give thanks; for this is God's will for you in Christ Jesus."

Have you learned to say, "Thank You, Lord," when your

heart is broken because of the loss of a loved one? Do you thank God when your body is wracked with pain? When you receive a "Dear John" letter terminating a love relationship? When you have financial reverses? When you fail an exam? When you are unemployed? Do you thank God when you are discriminated against personally, religiously or racially?

You may say that only a fool would give thanks to God under such circumstances. No, not if "all things work together for good to those who love God, to those who are called according to His purpose." If God has commanded us to give thanks, there is a reason for it. This is one of the most exciting lessons I have ever learned — the lesson the saying "Thank You" when things go wrong.

A Better Plan

Before I made this discovery I used to lose my patience when things went contrary to my wishes. Closed doors would often be forced open, if necessary. If they did not open before me, I tried to break them down. I was often tense inside and impatient with others. Then I discovered what a fool I was. Tragically we injure our brothers with our impatience, our criticism, our thoughtlessness. When Christians act this way, the entire Body of Christ suffers.

But God has given us a better plan. We can relax. We can say "Thank You" when the whole world is crumbling around us, because our God is sovereign and omnipotent. He holds the world in His hands, and we can trust Him. He loves us. And He promises to fight for us.

He has commanded us to cast all of our cares upon Him, for He cares for us (I Peter 5:7). He personally visited Earth and took our sins upon Himself, and He is waiting to bless and use us. But He will not bless and use us if we are worried and unbelieving. He will not bless and use us if we complain and criticize and find fault.

Some time ago, a young woman came to Arrowhead Springs for one of our training institutes. After one of my lectures, she came for counsel. Through her tears she shared how her dearest had been killed in an accident. The young woman had been driving the car when he was killed. They were coming home from their engagement party, and an oncoming automobile crossed the center line, forcing her off the road into a telephone pole.

The tragedy was compounded by the guilt she felt because she had been driving the car. Her heart was broken. "What shall I do?" she pleaded.

Have You Thanked God?

Months had passed and she had gone to psychiatrists, psychologists, ministers and many others seeking counsel. She said, "If you can't help me, I fear for my sanity." I asked her if she were a Christian, and she said, "Yes." We read Romans 8:28 and I asked her, "Do you believe that all things work for good?" She said, "Yes, I believe that."

We turned to I Thessalonians 5:18. She read it aloud: "In all things give thanks, for this is the will of God in Christ Jesus concerning you." I said to her, "Have you thanked God for the loss of your loved one?" She was shocked and could hardly believe she heard me correctly. Looking at me in disbelief, she said, "How can I thank God for such a tragic loss?"

"You do not trust God, do you?" I asked. "Yes, I trust God," she insisted. "Then why not show that you do?" I asked. "Will you pray and tell God that you trust Him and give thanks in everything?" As we knelt together, she prayed through her tears, "God, I don't understand, but I know I can trust You; and I do say, 'Thank You.' "

Demonstrating Faith

When she said, "Thank You," she was saying to God, "I will trust You." The Bible says that without faith you cannot please God (Hebrews 11:6) and the best way to demonstrate faith is to say, "Thank You." You may think that you hate God because you have lost a loved one, your inheritance, your money, your business or your health. You may ask, "Why did God do this to me?" But God says, "In everything give thanks." Unbelief is sin and displeases God, according to Hebrews 3:17-4:2 and Romans 14:23.

That young lady came to my office early the next morning literally bubbling with joy. She said, "Last night I slept without medication for the first time since the accident. And this morning when I awakened, my heart was filled with praise and thanksgiving to God. I just cannot understand it, but I know that it has something to do with what you taught me about saying 'Thank You' to God." I could share hundreds of similar stories about Christians whose lives have been transformed by learning the simple lesson of saying "Thank You" in all things.

Some years ago there was a desperate need for more than a half million dollars toward the purchase of Arrowhead Springs, the Campus Crusade for Christ International Headquarters. The future of a great worldwide ministry was at stake. Because of a technicality, our financial world had crumbled, and there appeared to be no hope. The whole ministry was in danger of being destroyed and my own reputation would be shattered.

When word came to me from a friend that the money which we had been promised was no longer available, I fell to my knees and said, "Lord, what am I to do?" I opened my Bible to look for help and assurance. And I was reminded that all things work together for good to those who love God, that without faith, it is impossible to please Him, and that the just shall live by faith. I read the command from God to give thanks in everything.

God Is Faithful

So I got back down on my knees and thanked God for what had happened. I thanked Him through my tears. I thanked Him that in His wisdom and love, He knew better than I what should be done and that out of this chaos and uncertainty would come a miraculous solution to our problem. There on my knees, while I was giving thanks for the disappointment I was feeling, God began to give me the genuine assurance that a miracle was really going to happen. Within ten days God did provide an almost unbelievable solution to our problem — a miracle. He demonstrated again that, when we trust Him, He is faithful and worthy of our trust.

Trust God More

One of the greatest privileges is to trust God. Learn how

to walk by faith. I am still learning and am confident that one day I shall be able to trust God for infinitely greater things than those for which I am now able to trust Him. What a great opportunity is ours to walk with the King of kings every day of our lives, from the time that we awaken in the morning until we go to bed at night.

For many years it has been my practice to begin my day the night before by reading God's Word, meditating upon the attributes and trustworthiness of our wonderful Lord before I go to sleep at night. Then throughout the nightwatches, when my subconscious mind takes over, I am thinking about Christ. When I awaken in the morning, my first thoughts are of Him.

I usually awaken with a psalm of praise on my lips, and with an attitude of thanksgiving: "Oh, Lord, I thank You that I belong to You. I thank You that You live within me, and I thank You that You have forgiven my sins. I thank You that I am a child of God.

"Now, as I begin this day, and as I continue throughout the day, I thank You that You walk around in my body, love with my heart, speak with my lips and think with my mind. I thank You that, You promised to do greater things through me than You did when You were here on the earth. By faith, I acknowledge Your greatness, Your power, Your authority in my life, and I invite You to do anything You wish in and through me."

Then I slip out of bed to my knees, as a formal act of acknowledging His lordship. I try to begin the day right, walking in the fullness of His power. What an adventure awaits those who trust the Lord.

Moment By Moment

In summary, may I remind you that if you desire to walk moment by moment, day by day, in the fullness and power of God's Spirit, you must:

First, be sure that you are filled with the Spirit, by faith — on the basis of God's command to be filled and by claiming His promise that, if we ask according to His will, he will hear and answer.

Second, be prepared for spiritual conflict. The enemy is a real foe to be reckoned with. The world, the flesh and the devil will assail.

Third, know your rights as a child of God. Our strength must come from the Lord. We must abide in Him.

And finally, live by faith, drawing daily upon His strength, His wisdom, His power and His love, giving thanks in all things.

Why should a Christian desire to walk in the fullness and control of the Holy Spirit moment by moment as a way of life? There are several important reasons: to please and honor the Lord, who delights to have fellowship with His children; to enjoy a fuller, richer, more exciting life with our Savior and with others; and to be more fruitful in our witness for our Savior.

Sharing Christ with others as an expression of gratitude and as an act of obedience to the Lord is the natural result of walking in the fullness of the Holy Spirit.

We are commanded to be witnesses for the Lord; therefore, not to be so involved and committed is to disobey Him and would indicate that the Christian is not walking in the control of the Holy Spirit.

Continue To Breathe Spiritually

As you walk in the Spirit and faithfully apply the revolutionary concept of spiritual breathing, you can become a member of the great army of effective Christian disciples whom God is raising up around the world to work, to plan, to pray and to witness for Christ — to help fulfill the Great Commission of our Lord in this generation.

Review and Thought Questions

1. What does prayer mean to you?

   _____

   _____

2. What do these verses say about prayer?

   Hebrews 4:15, 16 _____

   _____

   James 5:16 _____

   _____

   I Samuel 12:23 _____

   _____

   James 1:5 _____

   _____

3. a) How do you achieve the abundant Christian life?

   _____

   _____

   b) Does "abundant" mean that your life will be free
      from struggles and hardships? Explain.

   _____

   _____

4. What do these verses say about witnessing?

   Acts 1:8 _____

   _____

   Matthew 28:18-20 _____

   _____

   John 15:8 _____

   _____

Matthew 4:19 _____

_____

5. How can you break sin's power in your life?

_____

_____

6. What place do feelings have in a life of faith?

_____

_____

7. What do these verses say about thanksgiving?
   I Thessalonians 5:18 _____

_____

Philippians 4:11 _____

_____

Ephesians 5:20 _____

_____

Psalm 95:2 _____

_____

Philippians 4:6 _____

_____

8. a) What does it mean to trust God and walk moment by moment with Him?

_____

_____

   b) What does John 14:21 tell you about how to have an obedient walk with Christ?

_____

_____

Discussion questions: 1, 5, 6, 8.

CHAPTER STUDY GUIDE

1. The application of the principles outlined in this Concept will enable you to live a consistent Spirit-controlled life.

2. Memorize the following verses and references:
Galatians 5:22, 23: "But the fruit of the Spirit is love, joy, peace, patience, kindness, goodness, faithfulness, gentleness, self-control; against such things there is no law."
I Thessalonians 5:18: "In everything give thanks; for this is God's will for you in Christ Jesus."

Your memory work will be easier and more lasting if you review it daily for the entire week rather than try to complete it in just one day.

3. Make this Concept, "How to Walk in the Spirit," a way of life through practicing the following:

a. Begin each day by praying and by reading or studying God's Word, as time allows. Make sure that you are filled with the Holy Spirit as you begin each day. During the day, whenever you find yourself back in control of your life with self on the throne, breathe spiritually: exhale — confess your sin, and inhale — appropriate again the fullness of the Holy Spirit.

b. Conclude your day by thanking God for enabling you to walk in the Spirit during the day, and by reading God's Word and praying.

c. Make a point of giving thanks as an expression of your faith for every difficult situation that comes your way during each day, as well as for the blessing.

AMPLIFIED OUTLINE

Study 1.

Introduction

    A. Every person can experience a full, abundant, purposeful and meaningful life (John 14:12-14).

        1. The supernatural Christian life is not complex or difficult, but there is a paradox to it.

           a. It is so simple that we stumble over its simplicity.

   b. It is so difficult — because it is a supernatural life — that only Christ can live it.

   2. The secret of the Christian life is to walk in the Spirit and thus allow the Lord Jesus to live His abundant life within us in all of His resurrection power (Acts 4:13).

   3. Even the Christian has problems, but he can freely cast all of these problems on the Lord (I Peter 5:7; Galatians 2:20).

B. The teachings of our Lord are simple and understandable.

I. "Spiritual breathing" is the key to our appropriating God's spiritual provision for us moment by moment.

A. When we receive Christ as our personal Savior, we experience a spiritual birth, we become children of God, our sins are forgiven and we are filled with the Spirit.

B. The average Christian is not drawing on his resources in Christ, but is living on a spiritual roller coaster going from emotional experience to another, in control of his own life frustrated and defeated.

C. "Spiritual breathing" will enable us to get off this emotional roller coaster and to enjoy the abundant Christian life Jesus promised (John 10:10).

   1. Exhale by confessing our sins (agreeing with God concerning them) (I John 1:9).

      a. Acknowledge — agree with God — that our sins are wrong.

      b. Acknowledge — agree with God — that He has already forgiven us because of Christ's death on the cross for our sins.

      c. Repent, or change our attitude toward our sin, and experience a change in our conduct through the enabling power of the Holy Spirit.

   2. Inhale by appropriating the fullness of God's Spirit by faith.

      a. His command, and thus His will, is that we can

be filled with the Spirit (Ephesians 5:180.
  b. His promise is that He always grants our requests when we pray according to His will (I John 5:14, 15).
D. A spiritual Christian becomes a carnal Christian again when he ceases to believe I Corinthians 10:13 and I John 1:9 — when he develops an attitude of unbelief (Romans 14:23b).
  1. We should not allow sins to accumulate in our lives (I John 2:1-6).
  2. Our relationship with the Holy Spirit is both critical and progressive.
    a. The power of the Holy Spirit is appropriated by faith.
    b. A spiritual Christian will learn to grow and mature by faith, demonstrating the fruit of the Spirit in his life (Galatians 5:22, 23).

Study 2.

II. Be sure that you are filled with the Holy Spirit.
  A. In Ephesians 5:18 we are commanded to be filled with the Spirit which means to be controlled and empowered by the Holy Spirit.
  B. Either Christ or self is on the throne and in control of our lives, for no man can serve two masters.
  C. Remember two important words in order to be sure that you are filled with the Holy Spirit.
    1. *Command* — be filled with the Spirit (Ephesians 5:18).
    2. *Promise* — if we ask anything according to God's will He hears and answers (I John 5:14,15).
  D. We are filled with the Spirit by faith, just as we received Christ by faith (Ephesians 2:8,9) and not just because we ask Him into our lives.
  E. If you are a Christian, you are already indwelt by the Holy Spirit (I Corinthians 3:16), so you simply

need to ask Him to take control of your life, and then continue to breathe spiritually whenever the Holy Spirit reveals something you need to confess.

F. Do not look for nor depend upon feelings.

III. Be prepared for spiritual conflict.

A. Though we must be prepared for spiritual conflict, we must also remember that the battle is not ours, but the Lord's (Exodus 14:14).

B. Three forces wage war against the unbeliever:

1. The world.

a. The Bible warns us not to love the world (I John 2:15-17).

b. No one who is in love with the world can be used of God in a significant way.

c. We can have confidence of victory in this area for Christ has overcome the world. (John 16:33b).

2. The flesh.

a. The flesh — our old sin nature — is at war with the Spirit (Galatians 5:17).

b. This conflict will continue as long as we live.

c. Temptation (the initial impression to do something contrary to God's will) is not in itself sin. It becomes sin as we meditate on it and desire develops into lust, which is often followed by an actual act of disobedience.

d. The conflict is resolved as we surrender continually to the control of the Spirit (Galatians 5:16).

3. The devil.

a. Satan is a real foe, seeking to destroy us (I Peter 5:7,8).

b. We have the assurance that "greater is He who is in us than he who is in the world" (I John 4:4b).

c. Satan was defeated 2,000 years ago at the cross and God's power is sovereign over him (Acts 4:28).

         d. God's spiritual armor provides our safety against Satan (Ephesians 6:11,12).

Study 3.

IV. Know your rights as a child of God.

    A. It is impossible to know and experience our resources in Christ without spending time with the Lord, who is the source of our strength (Ephesians 6:10).

    B. Good works are a result of a life of faith (James 2:22).

    C. Jesus Christ, in all of His resurrection power, actually lives within the Christian (Romans 8; Ephesians 1:19-23; Colossians 1:27–2:10).

    D. We are weak in our own strength but strong in Christ (Philippians 4:13; II Timothy 1:7; I John 4:4; John 15:4,5).

    E. As we learn of and draw upon our resources in Christ, we will be enabled to be the fruitful witnesses He commands us to be (John 15:8; Matthew 4:19).

       1. It is our responsibility to follow Him.

       2. It is His responsibility to make us effective fishers of men.

    F. The resurrection power of Christ is available to every Christian to help carry out the Great Commission of our Lord (Ephesians 1:19-23; Matthew 28:18-20; Hebrews 13:5).

    G. If we have Christ, we have everything we need, for we are complete in Him (Colossians 1:15,16,19, 2:3,8-10).

    H. In Romans 5 and 6 we have an explanation of how God's resources become available to us when we receive Christ (Romans 5:19-21; 6:1-3,6,11,13,16).

    I. Though God does not force us to obey Him contrary to our wills, the more we understand our resources in Christ, the more we will desire to do God's will. For in Christ we can do all things (Philippians 4:13).

V. Live by faith.

   A. We do not live by feelings; we live by faith (Hebrews 11:6; Galatians 3:11).

      1. Valid feelings are the by-product of faith and obedience (John 14:21).

      2. To seek an emotional experience repudiates God's command to live by faith.

   B. As Christians, the object of our faith is made known through His Word.

      1. We can trust the great promise of God's Word that all things work together for good if we love God (Romans 8:28).

      2. On the basis of this promise, we can logically follow His command in I Thessalonians 5:18 to give thanks in all things.

   C. God has commanded us to cast all of our cares upon Him (I Peter 5:7).

   D. The best way to demonstrate faith is to give thanks in all things.

      1. This pleases God (Hebrews 11:6).

      2. Unbelief displeases God (Hebrews 3:17–4:2; Romans 14:23).

   E. From the time we awaken in the morning until we go to bed at night we should walk with God, trusting Him and thanking Him for every circumstance of our lives.

CHAPTER 5
HOW TO WITNESS IN THE SPIRIT

Study 1. Be Sure You Are a Christian
Study 2. Be Sure There Is No Unconfessed Sin in Your Life
Be Sure You Are Filled With the Holy Spirit
Be Prepared to Share Your Faith in Christ
Pray
Study 3. Go
Talk About Jesus
Expect Results

STUDY 1.

"I have been in Christian work for more than 25 years," he said, "but have never introduced anyone to Christ until this week at Arrowhead Springs. Your message on how to witness in the Spirit and an understanding of how to present the gospel through the use of the Four Spiritual Laws changed my life. Never before have I been so happy. Now, I know something of the abundant life Jesus promised."

This Christian leader was beaming with newfound joy as he shared how that week, for the first time in his life, he had introduced not one person but two people to our Savior. One of his student friends had prayed with six people who expressed their desire to receive Christ while another student at the Institute for Evangelism had introduced eight people to the Savior.

During that week of the student leadership training institute, hundreds of students and the few adults in attendance had, through a prayerful presentation of the "most joyful news ever announced," been used of God to pray personally with more than 900 people who received Christ through their witness.

Tens of thousands of students, laymen and pastors are experiencing how to witness in the Spirit with joyful and revolutionary results.

The Most Important Experience

There is no experience in life more exciting and

spiritually rewarding than the adventure of sharing Christ with others. All over the world, I ask two questions of thousands of Christians — young and old, rich and poor, new Christians and people who have been Christians for more than half a century. I have asked these questions of some of the most wealthy and famous people in the world. The answers are always the same, no matter whom I ask.

The first question is, "What is the most important experience of your life?" "Knowing Christ as my Savior is absolutely the most important experience in my life," is the inevitable answer.

The second question is: "What is the most important thing that you can do to help another person?" Again, the answer is always the same: "Help him to know Christ."

I am sure that, if you are a Christian, you would give the same answers to these two questions. Yet, how sad it is that so few Christians are sharing Christ with others. As a matter of fact, we are told that it takes more than 1,000 lay people and six pastors to introduce one person to Christ in a year!

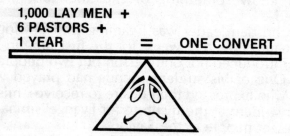

1,000 LAY MEN +
6 PASTORS +
1 YEAR   =   ONE CONVERT

Obviously there is something wrong. If you are typical of the majority of Christians today, you have never introduced anyone to Christ. You would like to do so, however, and you know in your heart that this is what God has called you to do. What is the problem?

It is largely twofold. First, the average Christian does not know how to live a victorious, vital, Spirit-controlled life; and second, the average Christian does not know how to communicate his faith in Christ effectively to others.

I meet many sincere Christians who are students of the

Bible and are faithful in prayer, but they are not joyful and excited about their relationship with the Lord. However, I have never met a Christian who is sharing Christ regularly, as a way of life, in the power and control of the Holy Spirit, who is not radiant and joyful.

For example, one of my dear friends, who is one of the great Christian scholars of our day, confessed to a group of fellow believers in one of our lay institutes for evangelism, "I am not a happy, joyful Christian and I seldom witness for Christ."

Later I shared with him some of the truths which I shall share with you about how to witness in the power of the Spirit. God touched his life. He came back that evening bubbling over with joy after a day of sharing Christ. He could hardly wait to tell us what God had done in his life.

He shared how he had talked to two young college students about Christ, and in the process Christ seemed more real to him than ever before.

Many of you spend hours in prayer and some of you spend hours studying the Bible every day, but you are not joyful. You are not living that abundant life which Jesus promised.

A Scriptural Formula

What is the solution to this tragic and frustrating problem? I want to share with you a scriptural formula that can change your life. I can assure you that if you follow this formula, you will experience an abundant life and will be fruitful for God in a way that you have never before known.

But before I share this formula with you, let me call to your attention the fifth chapter of Luke. There we see the Lord speaking to a great multitude on the shore of the Sea of Galilee. Noticing two empty boats standing at the water's edge, He stepped into one which belonged to Simon Peter and asked him to push it out into the water so that He could sit in the boat and speak to the crowd.

When He had finished speaking, He said to Simon, "Put out into the deep water and let down your nets for a catch." And Simon answered, "Master, we worked hard all night and caught nothing, but at Your bidding I will let down the nets." This time their nets were filled so full of fish that they began to tear (Luke 5).

Launch Out In Faith

Some of you may be skeptical — as was Simon. You may have fished for men for years but have yet to introduce your first person to Jesus Christ. Now, you are told that, if you follow this spiritual formula, you will be fruitful. I can understand your skepticism.

But remember also that Peter had fished all night and had caught nothing, not even a minnow. Yet, when the Lord said, "Put out into the deep water and let down your nets," he was obedient, and he caught so many fish that his boat and a friend's boat almost sank with the weight of the load. Peter and his fellow fishermen, James and John, were so overwhelmed at what Jesus had done for them that they left their nets and followed Him.

You will find that sharing Christ according to these spiritual principles which I shall prescribe will enable you to be regularly and consistently fruitful. When you fill your nets with men whom you have introduced to Jesus Christ, you will begin the most exciting, joyful and rewarding experience that this life has to offer.

Eight Ingredients

There are eight ingredients to this spiritual formula. If these are followed carefully and prayerfully, they will transform your life and witness for Christ. You will become a fruitful Christian and will continue to be one for as long as you live.

First, be sure that you are a Christian.

Second, be sure there is no unconfessed sin in your life.

Third, be sure you are filled with the Holy Spirit.

Fourth, be prepared to share your faith in Christ.

Fifth, pray.

Sixth, go.

Seventh, talk about Jesus Christ.

Eighth, expect God to use you.

Now, let us consider each of these points carefully.

FIRST, BE SURE YOU ARE A CHRISTIAN

There are millions of good, moral, religious people who are active in the church but who are not sure of their relationship with God. As an example, in our student and lay institutes for evangelism, which are attended by many sincere and dedicated church members in the community, usually 10-25% of the conferees indicate that they either received Christ or that they gained the assurance of their salvation during the training.

John Wesley, the founder of Methodism, was not sure of his salvation as a young man, even though he was the son of a minister, the leader of the Holy Club at Oxford and a missionary to American Indians. Upon his return to England he met Jesus Christ at an Aldersgate meeting where he heard the reading of Martin Luther's treatise on faith as a preface to the book of Romans.

He explained what happened in his autobiography. "I felt my heart strangely warmed. I felt I did trust Christ, Christ alone, for my salvation; and an assurance was given me that He had taken away my sins, even mine, and saved me from the law of sin and death."

Before the experience at Aldersgate, Wesley had engaged in a frenzied effort to try to earn God's salvation by his good works. There he received the assurance of God's salvation by faith.

We Receive Christ By Faith

No doubt millions of good, religious church members throughout the world are wrestling with the same problem which John Wesley experienced — trying to earn their salvation by good works. Yet, unlike Wesley, they have never understood God's promise that we receive Christ through faith.

"For it is by His grace you are saved, through trusting Him; it is your own doing. It is God's gift, not a reward for work done" (Ephesians 2:8,9, New English Bible).

Some years ago this truth that we become Christians by faith alone was dramatically demonstrated in an experience that I had with a couple from Zurich, Switzerland. Their son, Hans, had become a Christian while studying for his doctorate in meteorology at the University of California at Los Angeles. His parents had been seeking God many years by studying various religions.

When Hans wrote to share with them his newfound faith in Christ, he mentioned my name as the one who had helped him. They responded immediatly, and requested an appointment with me. They wanted to become Christians, too. At great expense, the father, mother and their daughter flew all the way from Zurich to Los Angeles for the express purpose of becoming Christians.

As we talked together in my office, the father said to me, "I have been looking for God for years, but I have not found Him. I went through a period of atheism which was not satisfactory, and in recent years my wife and I have been studying the various world religions. But we have found no answer.

"Some time ago we began to read the New Testament with considerable benefit. As a matter of fact," he said, "we concluded that Jesus had something to do with knowing God, and we said to our Bible teacher, 'We think Christ has something to do with our quest.' The Bible teacher said, 'I think perhaps you are right.' But we were not given any further help.

End Of The Search

"About that time the letter came from Hans explaining how you had helped him to know Christ. We have concluded that you are the one who can help us.

"Now," he said, "we have flown thousands of miles at great expense to hear what you have to say. We want you to tell us what you told Hans."

Well, you can imagine how I felt. What a privilege it was to talk to this wonderful couple about our Savior, the living Christ. To begin, I drew a circle. In the circle I placed a throne, and then I placed self on the throne. I explained to them that in order to become Christians they must be willing to surrender the throne of their lives to Christ.

"You must receive Him as your Savior," I explained. "The Scripture says, . . . 'But as many as receive Him to them He gave the right to become children of God.' (John 1:12). And Jesus said, 'Behold, I stand at the door and knock; if any one hears My voice and opens the door, I will come in to him' (Revelation 3:20).

"You must invite Jesus Christ into your life if you want to become Christians," I said. The husband replied, "Mr. Bright, I do that every day. As a matter of fact, I invite Jesus Christ into my life many times each day."

Saved By Faith Only

Now I was puzzled. What could I possibly add to what they were already doing? I prayed silently, "Lord, Your Word promises wisdom to those who ask in faith. What do I say now?" There came into my mind the promise, "For by grace you have been saved through faith; and that not of yourselves, it is the gift of God; not as a result of works, that no one should boast" (Ephesians 2:8, 9).

I explained to them that it was not enough to invite Christ into their lives. "God honors faith," I said. "He does not honor your invitation to Him to come in. It is your faith in Him and His promise, that if you open the door He will come in, that He honors. You can ask Jesus into your life a thousand times and He will never come unless you believe on the basis of His promise that He will come. You can depend upon Him to keep His promise to come in if you ask Him in as an expression of faith."

I suggested to them that they invite Christ into their lives one more time and that this time they believe His promises; that if they opened the door, He would come in, (Revelation 3:20), and that to "as many as received Him, to them He (God) gave the right to become children of God" (John 1:12). I told them to place their trust in the promises of God and in His faithfulness.

The father sat back in his chair and laughed. He was filled with wonder, gratitude, relief, praise and thanksgiving. At last he had found the one whom he had sought for many years. Then he turned to his wife and spoke to her in German, because she did not understand English as well as he, and she responded in the same way.

Later that night I had the privilege of praying with their daughter, who also received Christ. The entire family — father, mother, brother, sister — was united in Christ. Eventually, I had the opportunity to visit them in Zurich and saw further the miracle of God's grace in their lives.

Assurance Of Salvation

One of my dearest friends during the seminary days was the son of a famous evangelist. He came from a godly home. We met often for prayer. He memorized thousands of verses of Scripture and lived such a disciplined life for God that he was a constant challenge and inspiration to me.

He existed on a special diet of inexpensive food for days at a time, enabling him to live for 12 to 15 cents a day, so that he could give more money to missions. He had completed his bachelor's degree and was studying for his doctorate in theology when he telephoned me one day to say, "Bill, I have just become a Christian."

I was amazed. "You are one of the best Christians I have ever known," I insisted. "I am sure that you have had an emotional experience of some kind." "No," he said, "I have just become a Christian."

He then explained that all through the years, though he had never shared this before, he had experienced conflict and uncertainty. Though he had invited Christ into his life numerous times, he had never before been sure that He had actually come to be his Savior. Never before did he have the assurance of his salvation.

In Appearance Only

A remarkable young woman came to join our staff. My wife and I were very much impressed with her and were confident that she would have a great ministry for Christ. She came from a wonderful Christian family and had attended a Christian kindergarten, a Christian grade school, a Christian high school and a Christian college. She had been an active leader in church activities and was president of the Christian Women's Association in her area. She had even served as a counselor in several

Billy Graham crusades. This young woman demonstrated all of those qualities that one would expect to find in a dynamic, radiant Christian.

In speaking to the staff during a training session, I stressed the importance of being sensitive to the needs of professing Christians who are not sure of their salvation. We are never to assume that those who are unsure of their salvation are Christians, even if they have invited Christ into their lives many times. I told them that they should not try to convince those who doubt their salvation that they are Christians. Rather, they should assume that they are not yet Christians and should prayerfully counsel them and lead them to the assurance of their salvation.

Knowledge Without Life

At the conclusion of my talk this young woman said to me, "I don't think I am a Christian, and I have always had doubts about my salvation. Through the years, I have gone to different ministers and to other Christian leaders for spiritual counsel. I have told them I was not sure I was a Christian.

"They have inevitably responded, 'Well, you believe that Jesus is the Son of God, don't you? You believe that Christ died on the cross for you sins, don't you?' 'Yes,' I would answer. 'Well, then you are a Christian. Don't worry about it. Let's pray, and you just believe that you are a Christian.' But I have never been sure that God heard my prayer. There has been no evidence that Christ has come in. I am afraid I will die without Christ."

That day I had the privilege of sharing the good news with this woman who had been exposed to Christianity throughout her life. This time the Holy Spirit enabled her to trust God and His Word. By faith she received the Lord Jesus, the gracious gift of God's love. Her heart was filled with joy and praise. She was so excited that she called her mother and father, my wife and others to tell them the good news.

Spiritual Birth

Consider Nicodemus, a ruler of the Jews, a brilliant

scholar, a dedicated religious leader. According to tradition he went to the synagogue for prayer four times each day; three times he prayed at home. However, he observed in the life of Jesus something he had never experienced himself.

Nicodemus said to Jesus, "Rabbi, we know that You have come from God as a teacher; for no one can do these signs that You do unless God is with him." Jesus answered and said to him, "Truly, truly, I say to you, unless one is born again, he cannot see the kingdom of God."

Nicodemus said to Him, "How can a man be born when he is old? He cannot enter a second time into his mother's womb and be born, can he?" Jesus answered, "Truly, truly, I say to you, unless one is born of water and the Spirit, he cannot enter into the kingdom of God. That which is born of the flesh is flesh; and that which is born of the Spirit is spirit" (John 3:2-6).

A Changed Life

Perhaps you have never experienced the joy of salvation. There is no reality of Christ in your life. You have never known the wonder, the joy, the assurance that Christ lives in you, that you are a child of God. You may have believed in Christ intellectually for years. You may be active in the church; you may be very moral, religious and godly in the eyes of your neighbors, and yet you have never experienced this new birth. You have never been changed.

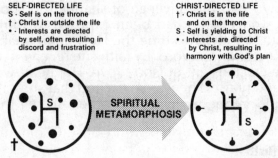

SELF-DIRECTED LIFE
S · Self is on the throne
† · Christ is outside the life
• · Interests are directed by self, often resulting in discord and frustration

CHRIST-DIRECTED LIFE
† · Christ is in the life and on the throne
S · Self is yielding to Christ
• · Interests are directed by Christ, resulting in harmony with God's plan

SPIRITUAL METAMORPHOSIS

Picture in your mind a caterpillar. One day it is just a

hairy worm crawling in the dust. If you give it a course in aviation, it would still be earthbound. If you attached butterfly wings to its body, it would still be unable to fly. But one day the caterpillar weaves about its body a cocoon and some days later, through a metamorphosis, it becomes a butterfly. Where it once crawled in the dust, it now soars in the heavens, a new creature.

In a spiritual sense, that is what must happen to us. A spiritual metamorphosis must take place. This is what happens when Jesus Christ comes to live in our lives.

The Total Person

Becoming a Christian involves commitment of the total person, which can best be illustrated by the marriage relationship. Many years ago, I became aware of a young woman who I thought was the most wonderful girl in the world. As we became better acquainted, we fell in love, but were not married just because we were intellectually involved and loved each other. It was by an act of our wills that we committed ourselves to one another before a minister one day and became husband and wife. In that moment, because of two words, "I do," we became legally married.

As a result, Vonette left her home, I left my home and we started a third home. Now, there was no emotion when I said, "I do." The walls did not shake, nor did lightning flash. As a matter of fact, I felt a little numb. But, we were no less married because I didn't at that moment feel like shouting for joy.

Those two words, which expressed the desire of our hearts, consummated our three-year engagement. My love for my wife has grown through the years, and I have told her thousands of times since that memorable marriage ceremony that I love her. But I have not proposed to her again since we said, "I do."

Commitment Of The Will

So it is in our relationship with Christ. Commitment to Christ involves our entire person — our intellect, our emotions, our will. It is not enough to believe intellectually in Christ as the Son of God; not enough to know that He died on the cross for our sins; not enough to be baptized, to be active in the church and to read our Bibles and pray daily.

One does not become a Christian until, as an act of the will, he receives the gift of God's grace, love and forgiveness — the Lord Jesus Christ. When we receive Him we receive a new nature — we are born into God's family, and we begin to experience eternal life (II Corinthians 5:17).

"God so loved the world that He gave His only begotten Son" (John 3:16). How does one respond when offered a gift he desires? He receives it, of course, and thanks the giver. As you learn more about the Lord and His faithfulness, as well as more about your own needs, you will continue to allow Him to have more and more control of your life.

If you have never yet said to Christ, "I do receive You as my Savior," I encourage you to do so right now. Jesus said, "Behold, I stand at the door and knock; If anyone hears My voice and opens the door, I will come in to him . . ." (Revelation 3:20).

Ask Him to come into your life. Then, on the authority of His promise, thank Him that He has come in as He promised to do. He will not lie to you.

Thank Him

Millions of lives have been changed as a result of receiving Jesus Christ. After you have received Him, never insult Him by asking Him into your life again. The rest of your life, thank Him that He is there. He has promised to be with you always (Matthew 28:20), and He said, "I will never desert you, nor will I ever forsake you" (Hebrews 13:5).

I emphasized this truth at a citywide institute for evangelism, and afterward a woman in her twilight years came to me in tears. She said that she had been a Sunday school teacher for 40 years.

"Seldom has a day passed during those years that I haven't asked Christ into my life," she said. "But I was never sure that he was there. After tonight and for the rest of my life, I am going to say 'Thank You, Lord, that You are in my heart. I am never going to insult You again by asking You to come into my life, because now I am sure that You are already there.' "

Will you do the same? If you have never done so, do it now. Pause for a moment, and if the following prayer expresses the desire of your heart, make it your prayer: "Lord Jesus, I need You. I open the door of my life and receive You as my Savior and Lord. Thank You for forgiving my sins. Take control of the throne of my life. Make me the kind of person You want me to be."

Review and Thought Questions

1. From Ephesians 2:8, 9, what is the basis of salvation?

_____

2. How do you know you are a Christian?

_____

_____

3. What is the difference between asking Christ into your life and believing that He truly has come in?

_____

_____

4. What did Jesus tell Nicodemus about salvation in John 3:2-6?

_____

_____

5. Why is an act of the will so important in becoming a Christian?

_____

_____

6. a) How would you define "faith"?

_____

_____

   b) What place does faith have in your becoming a Christian?

_____

_____

7. What are some of the promises Jesus makes to those who trust Him as Savior?

_____

_____

Matthew 28:20 _____

_____

Hebrews 13:5 _____

_____

Revelation 3:20 _____

_____

John 3:16 _____

_____

_____

_____

_____

Questions 2, 3, 5 and 6 can be used to stimulate effective group discussions.

STUDY 2.

SECOND, BE SURE THERE IS NO UNCONFESSED SIN IN YOUR LIFE

If some sinful attitude or action is hindering your fellowship with God, He cannot live and love through you, and you will not be a joyful Christian or a fruitful witness for Christ. As we read in Hebrews 10, Christ came as God's sacrifice for our sins.

The Old Testament records that the Israelites took their animal sacrifices to the priest who slew the animal and sprinkled its blood on the altar as a covering for their sins. Then, in the fullness of God's time and purpose, as foretold by the Old Testament prophets, Jesus Christ, the Messiah, came to die for us. He came as God's sacrifice to die on the cross for our sins. As a result there is no further need of a sacrifice to be made for our sins (Hebrews 7:27).

We can add nothing to what Christ did for us on the cross. Our tears and our self-imposed disciplines do not add anything to His complete and perfect sacrifice on the cross. The only thing we can do to make Christ's death on the cross meaningful in our lives is to confess our sins and accept His sacrifice as the full and final payment for all of our sins — past, present and future. The Bible says, "If we confess our sins, He is faithful and righteous to forgive us our sins and to cleanse us from all unrighteousness" (I John 1:9).

Agree With God

What do we mean by "confession"? In the original language of the Bible, the word confess, *homologeo*, means to "agree with" or "to say along with." What do we do when we agree with God?

First, we acknowledge that what we have done is wrong. God is holy. No sin can enter His presence. And yet God, who hates sin, loves the sinner. He loves us no matter what we do, but he hates sin. When the Spirit of God says to us, in that still, small voice, "I am grieved with your conduct — your attitude, "we know that what we have done is wrong and we acknowledge — agree with God — that it is wrong.

Second, we acknowledge that the particular sin, as well as all of our sins, was paid for on the cross, and we thank Christ for dying for that sin. Third, we repent. The original meaning of the word "repent" is literally "to have a change of mind." We change our attitude toward our sin, which, of course — through the enabling power of the Holy Spirit — will result in a change of our actions. We will stop doing what has displeased God and will begin doing what pleases Him.

There are those who say, "As a Christian I don't have to confess my sin because Christ has already forgiven me. I can live any way I want to live and do what I want to do and have the best of this world and heaven too."

Such an attitude is totally contrary to Scripture. One who manifests such an attitude probably does not even know Jesus Christ as his Savior. If time and space allowed, I could share with you the tragic results of this thinking on the part of individuals who once were wonderfully used of God, but who no longer walk with the Savior.

The Real Evidence

John, the apostle, deals with this fallacious thinking as follows:

"My little children, I am telling you this so that you will stay away from sin. But if you sin, there is Someone to plead for you before the father. His name is Jesus Christ, the one who is all that is good and who pleases God completely. He is the one who took God's wrath against our sins upon Himself, and brought us into fellowship with God; and He forgave not only our sins, but also the sins of all the world.

"And how can we be sure that we belong to Him? By looking within ourselves: are we really trying to do what He wants us to? Someone may say 'I am a Christian; I am on my way to heaven, I belong to Christ.' But if he doesn't do what Christ tells him to, he is a liar.

"But those who do what Christ tells them to will learn to love God more and more. That is the way to know whether or not you are a Christian. Anyone who says he is a Christian should live as Christ did" (I John 2:1-6, Living Bible).

According to this passage, the professing Christian who does not desire to do God's will has good reason to question whether he is even a child of God. It is true that Christ's death on the cross has paid the penalty for our sins and there is nothing that we can do to add to His sacrifice.

But that which is true from God's point of view, as He looks at us through Christ (Romans 8:1), becomes a reality in our experience only when we confess our sins. The man who refuses to acknowledge his sin — to confess and to turn from doing that which displeases God — is a man who will be weighted down with guilt. He will become so frustrated and spiritually off course that God cannot use him. He will pray and his prayers will not be answered. He may even try to share Christ with others, but no one will respond.

One cannot live a holy life and grieve God's Holy Spirit. Failure to acknowledge sin and judge one's self will result in divine discipline. Because God loves His children, He chastens, corrects and disciplines those who are disobedient. The Scripture says, "If I regard iniquity in my heart, the Lord will not hear me" (Psalm 66:18).

The minute the Spirit of God puts His finger on your sin, confess it. Breathe spiritually. Exhale — confess your sins.

SELF-DIRECTED LIFE
S - Self is on the throne
† - Christ dethroned and not allowed to direct the life
• - Interests are directed by self, often resulting in discord and frustration

APPROPRIATE
CONFESS

SIN

Avoid introspection. Do not look for sin, but as the Holy Spirit makes you aware of something that you have done or are doing, be quick to confess it. Confession of sin is essential for a holy life and a contagious witness for our Lord.

THIRD, BE SURE YOU ARE FILLED WITH THE HOLY SPIRIT

In order to be fruitful in our witness for Christ, we must appropriate by faith the fullness of God's Spirit. We must be sure that we are filled with the Holy Spirit if we expect to live holy lives — to appropriate and exercise the power that is available to us as God's children.

Being filled with the Spirit involves inviting the Holy Spirit to control us — to give us power to live and to make us fruitful witnesses for Him. Two words and two verses are very important. First, remember the word *command*. Ephesians 5:18 tells us, "Be not drunk with wine, wherein is excess; but be filled with the Spirit."

This means that we are to be controlled and empowered by the Holy Spirit as a way of life. It is a command for every believer — not for the evangelist or pastor only, not just for the Sunday school teacher and other Christian leaders, but for everybody who believes in Christ.

Command And Promise

Now relate God's command to His *promise*, found in I John 5:14, 15: "And this is the confidence which we have before Him (in God), that, if we ask anything according to His will, He hears us. And if we know that He hears us in whatever we ask, we know that we have the requests which we have asked from Him."

On the basis of God's command and His promise, if you are willing to surrender the direction of your life to Christ, you can know that He will fill you as you, by faith, appropriate the fullness of God's Holy Spirit.

The Lord Jesus said to the disciples, and through them to us, "I am sending forth the promise of My Father upon you; but you are to stay in the city (Jerusalem) until you are clothed with power from on high" (Luke 24:49).

Then His final words to the disciples before He ascended into Heaven were: "You shall receive power when the Holy Spirit has come upon you; and you shall be My witnesses both in Jerusalem, and in all Judaea and Samaria, and even to the remotest part of the earth" (Acts 1:8).

We say to our staff who are now serving Christ in almost every major country of the world, "Don't go to your assignments unless you know beyond a shadow of a doubt that you are filled with the Spirit."

Only service performed for Christ in the power of the Holy Spirit is pleasing to God. Service performed for Him in the energy of the flesh is time wasted. It dishonors His name and produces spiritual wood, hay and stubble which, on Christ's judgment day, will be burned up (I Corinthians 3:12-15).

Equipped For Service

Being filled with the Holy Spirit equips us for service as witnesses for Christ. Do not make the mistake of thinking that you must experience some great emotion. In fact, emotions can be very dangerous. Pour a gallon of gasoline on the ground, strike a match, and it goes up in flame and smoke — then it is all gone. Dramatic, but wasted.

Many people are so involved in emotions and in seeking experiences that they actually insult God. The Bible says, "The righteous man shall live by faith" (Galatians 3:11), and "Whatever is not from faith is sin" (Romans 14:23b). The very act of seeking an emotional experience repudiates the concept of faith.

There are many times, as I stand in the pulpit or talk to individuals personally, when I do not feel any great surge of spiritual power — no emotion. There are times when, because of much travel, speaking and inadequate rest, my body is weary and my mind is dulled by fatigue; yet, if there is no unconfessed sin in my life, and by faith I claim God's fullness, I know that I am filled with the Spirit even if I do not feel like it. I do not depend upon feelings. I depend upon God's Word — His command and His promise.

By faith you can know that you are filled with the Spirit constantly and continually the rest of your life as you continue to "breathe spiritually" — exhaling as you confess your sins and inhaling as you appropriate God's power by faith. God commands, "Be filled with the Spirit," and He promises that, if we ask anything according to His will, He hears us and answers us.

Surrender Control

If at this moment you know that you are not filled with the Holy Spirit, you can pray right now: "Lord Jesus, I surrender the control of my life to You. I hold nothing back. Take control of my life. I want You to be my Master and my Lord.

By faith I receive the fullness of the Holy Spirit."

If you sincerely prayed this prayer, you can know on the basis of His command and on the authority of His promise that you are filled with the Holy Spirit right now! You can know this by faith — with or without emotions — simply trusting God and His Word. Remember, valid emotions result when you live by faith and when you share your faith in Christ with others in the power of the Holy Spirit. Jesus promised to manifest Himself to all who obey Him (John 14:23).

FOURTH, BE PREPARED TO SHARE YOUR FAITH IN CHRIST

Our student, lay and pastors institutes for evangelism, which have been held all over the world, were designed to train men and women, in a matter of a few hours, how they can live victorious lives and be fruitful in their witness for Christ as a way of life.

I thank God for the way He is using some of the theological seminaries, Bible schools and other such instructional Christian institutions, but you do not need to take long years of training before God can use you. Not everyone has the gift of evangelism, but every believer is called to "do the work of an evangelist" (II Timothy 4:5). All of us have the privilege and responsibility of being witnesses for our wonderful Lord Jesus. Christ's Great Commission in Matthew 28:18-20 is for all Christians.

Through a few hours of intensive training you can learn how to walk in the Spirit and how to communicate your faith in Christ effectively with others through the simple presentation of the Four Spiritual Laws, and other materials.

Some Christians will be more fruitful than others. Do not be distressed if you find that some of your friends are introducing more people to Christ than you are. Simply rest in the knowledge that those who come to Christ through the witness of a Christian are coming as a result of the ministry of the Spirit of God, who alone enables us to bear fruit.

You see, it is our responsibility to abide in Christ — to allow Him to have control of our lives, to walk around in our bodies, to think with our minds, to love with our hearts and to speak with our lips. When we do this, He is the one who

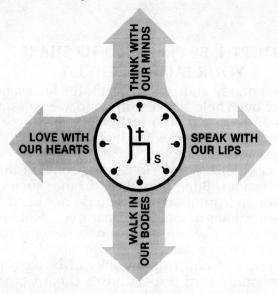

changes the lives of men. We are to abide in Him as the branch abides in the vine and He will produce spiritual fruit through us. It is our responsibility to follow Christ. It is His responsibility to make us fishers of men.

Here on earth He has no lips but ours, no feet but ours and no hands but ours. God has chosen to use men, not angels, to reach the world for Christ and, if we are obedient, He will use us. We can count on it. Remember that success in witnessing is simply sharing Christ in the power of the Holy Spirit and leaving the results to God.

FIFTH, PRAY

The Bible tells us that God is not willing that any should

perish, but that all should come to repentance (II Peter 3:9; I Timothy 2:4). In addition we have the promise that if we ask anything according to God's will, He hears us, and if He hears us, He answers us (I John 5:14, 15). Do you want your loved ones, your friends and neighbors to come to Christ? Then make a prayer list. Begin to claim them for God. God will not contradict Himself. You have the authority and integrity of His Word.

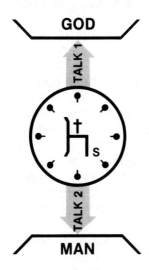

Next, share your faith in Christ with your loved ones and friends in the power of the Holy Spirit, and by faith thank God that He will draw them to Christ (John 6:44). I have prayed for loved ones with whom I used to weep as I pleaded with them to come to Christ. Then the day came when I realized that God was not willing that they should perish — He loved them more than I did — and so I began to thank God in faith that they would become Christians.

God Has Promised

That day has not yet come for some of them. But I no longer weep. I rejoice in the assurance that one day they will come to Christ. God has promised, and He does not lie. I am fully aware that some will not agree with my view of the way God works in answer to prayer. I acknowledge the sovereignty of God and the free will of man.

Well do I know such passages as "He did not do many miracles there because of their unbelief" (Matthew 13:58), "O Jerusalem, Jerusalem, the city that kills the prophets and stones those sent to her! How often I wanted to gather your children together, just as a hen gathers her brood under her wings, and you would not have it!" (Luke 13:34) and "You did not choose Me, but I chose you, and appointed you, that you should go and bear fruit, and that your fruit should remain; that whatever you ask of the Father in My name, He may give to you" (John 15:16).

While the meaning of these passages is not completely clear, as they relate to the subject of our concern and are variously interpreted, there are other passages that seem to me to be completely clear and are more easily understood, such as, "For God so greatly loved and dearly prized the world that He (even) gave up His only-begotten (unique) Son, so that whoever believes in (trusts, clings to, relies on) Him shall not perish — come to destruction, be lost — but have eternal (everlasting) life" (John 3:16, Amplified).

"Come to me all who are weary and heavy laden . . ." (Matthew 11:28), "God demonstrates His own love toward us, in that while we were yet sinners, Christ died for us" (Romans 5:8), "The Lord is not slow about His promise, as some count slowness, but is patient toward you, not wishing for any to perish but for all to come to repentance" (II Peter 3:9), "Who (God) desires all men to be saved and to come to the knowledge of the truth" (I Timothy 2:4).

Pray In The Spirit

I do not suggest that every one who hears the gospel will become a Christian. It is our responsibility to pray for men to come to Christ and to share Christ with them. God alone by His Spirit can produce faith in the hearts of men and change their lives. It is important to remember that only the spiritual man can expect God to answer his prayer for the salvation of loved ones and others.

Consequently, we should not expect a casual, super-ficial prayer of carnal men, "Lord, save everyone," to accomplish much. If you are concerned for the souls of others and expect God to answer your prayers, be sure that you are walking and praying in the Spirit.

Directed Prayer

You may ask, "Can I expect God to draw to Himself everyone for whom I pray while I am walking in the control and power of the Spirit? If so, I will just start walking down the streets or visiting hospital rooms praying for everyone I see." No, this is not what I mean. What I do mean is this: As you walk in the Spirit, the Lord Jesus, who lives within you, who came to seek and to save the lost, and who knows the hearts of all men, will direct you to pray for certain individuals.

According to Philippians 2:13, "For God is at work within you, helping you want to obey Him, and then helping you do what He wants" (Living Bible). Thus, you can know that, as you walk and pray in the Spirit of God and He impresses you to pray for a particular person, that person will come to Christ on the basis of His promise.

And what is His promise? "If we ask anything according to His will, He hears us. And if we know that He hears us in whatever we ask, we know that we have the requests which we have asked from him" (I John 5:14, 15), "(God is) not willing that any should perish, but that all should come to repentance" (II Peter 3:9).

Consider this question: If faith pleases God, which will honor Him most: our pleading and our tears for our loved ones, or our thanksgiving and praise that, according to the promise of His word which we have claimed in believing prayer, they will become Christians?

God's Time Schedule

A word of caution: God's time schedule is not always the same as that of impatient men. Continue to trust and thank Him for the salvation and spiritual growth of those for whom He has impressed you to pray. Do not limit your prayers, however, to praying only for the salvation of men. They continue to need our prayers after they become Christians if they are to become disciples and spiritual multipliers.

Follow the example of our Lord, whose high priestly prayer is recorded in John 17: "I pray not for the world, but for them which Thou hast given me" (John 17:9). Paul and the other writers of the New Testament were frequently requesting prayer for other believers as well as for themselves. Make a prayer list or keep a prayer diary and pray for specific non-Christians and Christians by name, and for specific events. As God answers prayer, record the date and any unusual circumstances involved.

Review and Thought Questions

1. What harm can unconfessed sin do in the life of a Christian?

   _____

   _____

2. What does Hebrews 10:1-18 say about Christ's sacrifice?

   _____

   _____

3. a) How can you make Christ's death and resurrection more meaningful in your life?

   _____

   _____

   b) What does "confession" of sin really mean?

   _____

   _____

   c) What is your general reaction when you sin?

   _____

   _____

4. What promise does I John 2:1-6 give you as a Christian?

   _____

   _____

5. a) What place does discipline (chastening) have in the life of a Christian?

   _____

   _____

b) How have you experienced it?

_____

_____

6. What do these verses say about feelings as related to living the Christian life?

Galatians 3:11 _____

_____

Romans 14:23b _____

_____

John 14:23 _____

_____

7. a) Do you have a prayer list? _____

b) Will you claim God's promise for answers by pledging with Him to pray for others daily?

_____

c) How can you show you really care for others?

_____

d) How would you compare Christ's prayers and prayer life to yours?

_____

_____

_____

_____

_____

Discussion questions: 3, 5, 7c and d.

STUDY 3.

SIXTH, GO

Go tell others about Christ. Do not wait for men to come to you. Go to them with the good news. One of the greatest problems we all face — one of the great barriers in witnessing — is the problem of getting going. There are all kinds of excuses: "I am too busy," or "I am waiting for the Holy Spirit to lead me to someone." We need not wait for the Holy Spirit to "lead us." Our Lord Jesus Christ has already commanded us to go tell the good news to all men.

Remember that the greatest thing that has ever happened to us is knowing Christ, and the greatest thing we can do for another is help him to know Christ. If this is true, we should begin to rethink our priorities. How are you spending your time? Take time every day to share Christ with someone.

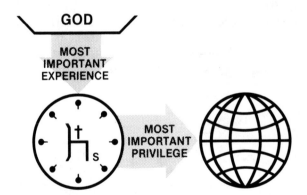

Some of you will be encouraged to know that many on our staff, like myself, are by nature very shy. We do not always find it easy to talk to others about Christ. But since Jesus came to seek and to save the lost and since He lives within us, we simply ask Him to give us the courage to speak forcefully for Him.

Whenever I am alone with a person for a few minutes, I assume I am there by divine appointment to share the good news of God's love and forgiveness. Though I always seek to bring those who are interested to a definite commitment to Christ, I do not feel discouraged when some refuse to receive Him as their Savior and Lord. That is God's responsiblity.

It is my responsibility to tell them the good news in love and with genuine concern. Sharing Christ with others should be a way of life for every Christian. When you awaken each morning, thank the Lord Jesus that He lives within you and ask Him to use your lips to speak of His love and forgiveness at every opportunity throughout the day.

SEVENTH, TALK ABOUT JESUS

Paul said, "Everywhere we go and to all who will listen we preach Christ" (Colossians 1:28, Living Bible). Do not talk about peripheral matters, such as the weather, sports, business, except where necessary for the purpose of becoming acquainted and establishing rapport. Pray and expect God to enable you to introduce His Son into the conversation.

There is a tendency among many Christians merely to encourage others to go to church. This is an important later step, but it does not reach men for Christ. Many

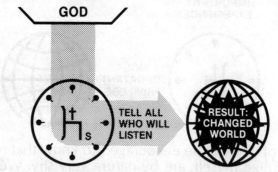

today are antagonistic toward the church, and if we are going to reach them for the Savior, we must talk about the Savior, not about the church. After they receive Christ, most of them will want to become active in the church.

Do not even try to convince people that the Bible is the Word of God. You do not have to prove the Bible — just use it. Use it even with people who say they do not believe it. God has promised to honor His Word (Colossians 1:28, Living Bible).

As you talk to men about the Savior, you will discover that many people are ready to receive Him the very first time you talk to them, as was the experience of the Colossians (Colossians 1:6). Some may need to "ripen" a bit. Be prayerfully sensitive to those with whom you talk.

Ripe Fruit

As a young lad I used to visit my uncle's peach orchard. We would always pick the ripe peaches, but leave the green ones. Two days later, we would return to the same trees and pick more ripe peaches. Every two days we would find yet more ripe ones. So it is in our witness for Christ. We need to be sensitive to people. There are those who are ready to receive Christ, ripe for harvest, and there are those who are not ready. These are like green fruit.

Do Not Argue

Do not argue with those who are not ready. Do not badger them, browbeat them, insult them, nor try to high-pressure them into "making a decision for Christ." Give them something appropriate to read, leave them with a prayer, talk to them later — as the Lord gives opportunity — but continue to look for the ripe ones. They are all around you. Thousands, yes millions, of people whose hearts have already been prepared by the Holy Spirit, are waiting to receive Christ.

On one plane trip, I talked to two people who were "spiritually ripe." One was an 80-year-old woman who received Christ as her Savior. The other, the president of a large corporation, had always believed that Jesus Christ was the Son of God and had died for his sin, but had been too busy with other things to make his commitment to Christ personally.

On the same trip, at Cornell University, where I addressed students and staff, the president of a sizeable business approached me. He was visiting his son who was a new Christian of six months. "I want to thank you for helping my son spiritually," he said. Then I asked if he had ever received Christ. He replied that he had not, but that he wanted to. We bowed in prayer and, to his son's great joy, he committed his life to the Savior.

A maid who came to clean my hotel room received Christ. A taxi driver and a young fishing guide and his father received Christ. Wherever I go, across America and in other countries, in lecture halls on the college campus, or among laymen, there are many who respond eagerly to Christ.

Concentrate On Christ

Today, an ever-increasing number of Christians are constantly being used of God to introduce others to our Savior because they have been trained to talk about Christ in the power of the Holy Spirit. They do not get sidetracked to discuss nonessential matters. That is the reason that the Four Spiritual Laws booklet is so effective — it keeps the conversation centered on the person of Christ, away from distracting issues which direct our attention away from the Lord.

There are many people who express antagonism toward God — they want nothing to do with religion. But when we tell them about Jesus, they are responsive. A taxi driver in Australia said to me, "I gave up all religion in World War II. I want nothing to do with a God who allows people to kill each other."

"Wait a minute," I said. "You are accusing God of something for which man is responsible. It is the evil in man, his sin, that causes him to hate and steal and kill." I explained the difference between religion, which is man's search for God, and Christianity, which is God's revelation of Himself in Christ to man. As I talked to him about the person of Christ, this man's entire attitude changed. Soon he said that he would like to pray with me and receive Christ.

Encourage Response

Do not talk about peripheral things if you expect God to use you. Talk about the Savior — and always encourage those with whom you share to invite Him into their lives. We really haven't "evangelized" until we have given people a chance to respond to the gospel.

Wherever possible, use the Four Spiritual Laws booklet. It makes your presentation of the gospel simple and understandable, and the one with whom you share can use the booklet to share with his loved ones and friends also. Thousands of new Christians are leading others to the Savior in this way.

FINALLY, EXPECT RESULTS

When you talk about Jesus, expect men to respond — not on the basis of positive thinking, but because of your confidence in God, His love, His sovereignty, His power and His promise that He is not willing that any should perish, but that all should come to repentance.

Expect men to respond because our Lord who came to seek and to save the lost has commissioned us to go to

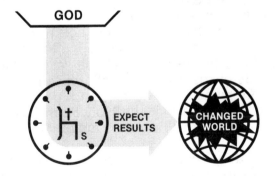

tell everyone the good news and make disciples in all nations. He claimed all authority in heaven and earth and promised to go with His disciples in His resurrection presence.

We are assured of that same presence and power with us today as in that first century. On the basis of such claims and promises of the Lord, it is inconceivable that He would not honor the faithful witness of all who place their trust in Him.

It is interesting to note that while the disciples met with

strong and often bitter opposition, the Christian movement experienced phenomenal growth, as was expressed in Paul's letter to the church in Thessalonica:

"For when we brought you the good news, it was not just meaningless chatter to you, but you listened with great interest. What we told you produced a powerful effect upon you, for the Holy Spirit gave you great and full assurance that what we said was true. And you know how our very lives were further proof to you of the truth of our message" (I Thessalonians 1:5, Living Bible).

Be Positive

There are many Christians who approach others with a negative attitude: "You don't want to become a Christian, do you?" By their negative attitude they unintentionally inhibit others from expressing their need for Christ. Go with the expectancy that God has already prepared the hearts of multitudes who are eager to receive Christ and you will find that he really has.

One of the greatest lies of the centuries is the attitude among Christians that people do not want God. The Christian world has been deceived into thinking that people will not be responsive to the gospel. After more than 30 years of sharing Christ with tens of thousands of students and laymen, individually and in small and large groups, I can tell you that the Holy Spirit has created a hunger for God in the hearts of multitudes around the world.

However, they must be properly approached if we expect them to acknowledge their need and to receive Jesus Christ as their Savior and Lord. They do not want religion. Many of them do not want anything to do with the church at this point. They are not interested in peripheral, spiritual things and religious ritual, but they are interested in Christ. If we confront men and women with the person of Christ in the power of the Holy Spirit, many will respond to His love and forgiveness.

They Respond To Christ

At a pastor's institute in Haiti, more than 1,000

individuals received Christ as 550 pastors and lay preachers prayed with them, one and two at a time, during some four hours of witnessing. At Daytona Beach in Florida, during an Easter vacation, approximately 1,500 staff and students talked with more than 3,500 students who prayed and received Christ.

At Arrowhead Springs, a similar number of trainees talked with approximately 2,000 students who received Christ in one day of witnessing in the Balboa-Newport Beach area. In the racially tense Watts area of South Los Angeles more than 1,000 blacks with whom we talked received Christ on one Saturday afternoon, largely through the witness of whites.

Most of our staff and trainees report that 10%-75% of the people to whom they make a clear presentation of the gospel pray with them to receive Christ. We find that the Spirit of God has prepared the hearts of multitudes of men and women to respond to Christ. As Jesus said, "The fields . . . are white for harvest" (John 4:35).

Jesus said, "And everything you ask in prayer, believing, you shall receive" (Matthew 21:22). Not everyone with whom you share Christ will receive Him as Savior and Lord, but God will use you both to sow and to harvest in His kingdom if you trust Him. "Without faith it is impossible to please Him, for he who comes to God must believe that He is, and that He is a rewarder of those who seek Him" (Hebrews 11:6).

Success In Witnessing

Having stressed the importance of expectancy in seeking to introduce others to Christ, I would remind you again of a statement which we in Campus Crusade for Christ sincerely believe and strongly emphasize, **"Success in witnessing is simply sharing Christ in the power of the Holy Spirit and leaving the results to God."**

If you want your life to be fruitful for the Savior:

First, be sure you are a Christian.

Second, be sure there is not unconfessed sin in your life.

Third, be sure you are filled with the Holy Spirit.

Fourth, be prepared to share your faith in Christ.

Fifth, pray.

Sixth, go.

Seventh, talk about the Lord Jesus Christ.

Eighth, expect results.

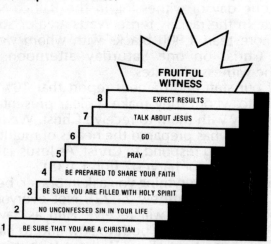

FRUITFUL WITNESS

8 EXPECT RESULTS

7 TALK ABOUT JESUS

6 GO

5 PRAY

4 BE PREPARED TO SHARE YOUR FAITH

3 BE SURE YOU ARE FILLED WITH HOLY SPIRIT

2 NO UNCONFESSED SIN IN YOUR LIFE

1 BE SURE THAT YOU ARE A CHRISTIAN

I can assure you that following this formula will enable you and every other Christian to be fruitful for God as a way of life. This life on earth offers no other adventure that can compare with that of sharing Christ with others.

Review and Thought Questions

1. Examine your current wants and desires. How would you honestly rank your priorities?

   _____

   _____

   _____

2. a) What is your responsibility as a Christian when you are with someone whose spiritual condition you are not sure of?

   _____

   _____

   b) What are some things that may keep you from talking to others about Jesus?

   _____

   _____

3. What does God say about His Word?

   Colossians 1:5, 6 _____

   _____

   _____

   Isaiah 55:11 _____

   _____

   _____

   Ephesians 1:13 _____

   _____

   _____

   _____

   _____

   _____

4. a) What does John 4:35 mean?

_____

_____

   b) What does it mean to you?

_____

_____

5. What is one essential ingredient needed to please Christ (Hebrews 11:6)?

_____

6. Why is it essential to talk about Jesus rather than just talk about the church?

_____

_____

7. What are some important aspects of Christ to present to others?

_____

_____

_____

_____

Discussion questions: 2, 4, 6, 7.

CHAPTER STUDY GUIDE

1. Remember, the most important thing that has happened to you, if you are a Christian, is knowing Christ personally, and the most important thing you can do for another is to share with him how he, too, can know Christ as his Savior and Lord. The application of the scriptural formula in this Concept will enable you to share your faith effectively as a way of life as long as you live.

2. Memorize the following verse, reference and key statement:

Acts 1:8: "But you shall receive power when the Holy Spirit has come upon you; and you shall be My witnesses both in Jerusalem, and in all Judea and Samaria, and even to the remotest part of the earth."

Key statement: Success in witnessing is simply sharing Christ in the power of the Holy Spirit and leaving the results to God.

Remember, your memory work will be easier and more lasting if you review it daily for an entire week rather than try to complete all of it in just one day.

3. Make this Concept, "How to Witness in the Spirit," a way of life through practicing the following:

a. If you are not already familiar with and accustomed to using the Four Spiritual Laws booklet to share your faith in Christ, obtain a copy and practice reading it aloud, just as you would to another person. Simply read the booklet word for word, including the invitation and prayer at the close as well as the material which explains how to know that Christ is in your life.

b. Make a list of those whom you know with whom you should share your faith. Pray for them and then go to them and share the "good news" as contained in the Four Spiritual Laws.

AMPLIFIED OUTLINE

Study 1.

Introduction

    A. The adventure of sharing Christ with others is the

most exciting and spiritually rewarding experience a person can know.

B. There are few Christians who are sharing Christ. We are told that it takes more than 1,000 laymen and six pastors to introduce one person to Christ in a year.

C. There are two basic reasons why the majority of Christians have never introduced anyone to Christ:

1. The average Christian is not living a victorious, vital Spirit-controlled life.

2. The average Christian does not know how to communicate his faith in Christ effectively to others.

D. The truly joyful Christian is one who is sharing his faith. Even though Bible study and prayer are very essential, they are no substitute for witnessing.

E. In Luke 5, we read of Peter catching a great number of fish as he followed the Lord's instruction. This encourages us to believe that we can be effective in fishing for men as we follow the spiritual formula suggested here, which is based on the clear teachings of the Bible.

I.   Be sure you are a Christian.

A. It is not enough to be good, moral, religious, or even to be a member of a church.

1. Many sincere and dedicated church members who have come to training institutes to learn how to share the message of Christ have indicated that during the training they either received Christ or they gained the assurance of their salvation.

2. John Wesley, the founder of Methodism and the son of a minister, had actually served as a missionary before he, himself, became a Christian.

B. We receive Christ through faith (Ephesians 2:8, 9).

C. Like Nicodemus, who, though he was a very religious man, was told that he needed to be born again, every one of us also needs to be born again spiritually (John 3:2-6).

    1. The metamorphosis of a caterpillar illustrates the complete change or spiritual metamorphosis which must take place in our lives.

    2. Commitment to Christ, like marriage, involves the whole person — the intellect, the emotions and the will.

D. Even now you can pray and invite Christ to come into your life if you have not already done so (Revelation 3:20).

E. After you have received Him, do not insult Him by asking Him into your life again. Thank Him daily that He is in your life (Matthew 28:20; Hebrews 13:5).

Study 2.

II.   Be sure there is no unconfessed sin in your life.

A. Sin will prevent you from being a joyful Christian or a faithful witness for Christ.

B. Christ came to be God's perfect sacrifice for our sins — past, present and future (Hebrews 10 and 7:27).

C. When we confess our sins (agree with God concerning them), Christ's death on the cross becomes meaningful in our lives. True confession involves:

    1. Agreeing with God that what we have done is wrong.

    2. Agreeing with God's Word that that particular sin, as well as all our sins, was paid for on the cross.

    3. Repentance — changing our attitude toward that sin — will result, through the enabling power of the Holy Spirit, in changing our actions.

D. Though Christ's death on the cross has paid the penalty for our sins — past, present and future —

and there is nothing we can do to add to His sacrifice, confession of our sins is necessary and Scriptural (I John 2:1-6).

1. There is no condemnation to us if we belong to Christ (Romans 8:1).

2. However, refusing to acknowledge sin hinders our fellowship with God (Psalms 66:18).

III. Be sure you are filled with the Holy Spirit.

A. We are filled with the Holy Spirit by faith. Claim God's command and promise (Ephesians 5:18; I John 5:14, 15).

B. The fullness (control) of the Holy Spirit is absolutely essential for an effective witness for Christ (Acts 1:8).

C. Only service performed for Christ in the power of the Holy Spirit is pleasing to God (I Corinthians 3:12-15).

D. Being filled with the Holy Spirit is a matter of faith — not feelings. "The just shall live by faith" (Galatians 3:11; Romans 1:17). "That which is not of faith is sin" (Romans 14:23).

E. Valid emotions result when we live by faith and obey God (John 14:23).

IV. Be prepared to share your faith in Christ.

A. You can learn, through a few hours of intensive training, how to effectively communicate to others your faith in Christ through the simple presentation of the Four Spiritual Laws and other materials.

B. It is our responsibility to follow Christ. It is His responsibility to make us fishers of men.

V. Pray.

A. God is not willing that any should perish (II Peter 3:9; I Timothy 2:4).

B. If we ask anything according to God's will, He hears and answers our prayers (I John 5:14, 15).

C. Make a prayer list.

D. As you pray, ask the Holy Spirit to draw men to Christ (John 6:44).

1. Though God is sovereign, He has given man the privilege of exercising his free will (Matthew 13:58; Luke 13:34).

2. Still the Bible clearly teaches how great is the love of God and how aggressively He seeks the lost (John 3:16; Romans 5:8; II Peter 3:9; I Timothy 2:3, 4).

E. We must be walking in the Spirit to be sure that God is directing us to pray for that which is according to His will and that which He will answer (Philippians 2:13; I John 5:14, 15).

F. Pray not only for the salvation of men, but also for Christians and their spiritual growth and service (see the example of the Lord in John 17).

Study 3.

VI. Go.

A. Do not wait for men to come to you.

B. Jesus Christ has already commanded us to tell the good news to all men.

C. Arrange your priorities so that you can take time every day to share Christ with someone.

D. Do not be discouraged if some refuse to receive Christ. Success in witnessing is simply sharing Christ in the power of the Holy Spirit and leaving the results to God.

VII. Talk about Jesus.

A. Follow the example of the apostle Paul (Colossians 1:28).

B. Do not be sidetracked with peripheral matters such as talking about the church, defending the Bible (Isaiah 55:11).

C. As you talk about the Savior, you will find that there are many who are ready to receive Him.

D. Avoid arguments and share Christ in love.

VIII. Expect results.

A. One of the greatest lies of the century is that men do not want God.

B. Men are hungry for God.
   1. The Holy Spirit has created this hunger in the hearts of multitudes.
   2. They need only to be properly approached.
C. Trust in God's promises (John 4:35; Hebrews 11:6; Matthew 21:22).

CHAPTER 6
HOW TO INTRODUCE OTHERS TO CHRIST

Study 1. Why Witness?
Study 2. How To Witness
Study 3. Conflict — Assurance

STUDY 1.

"You must bring a lot of happiness into this world," said the young businessman with tears of joy and gratitude sparkling in his eyes. He had just prayed with me and received Christ as his Savior. He and his wife had been looking for God for some time, he said, and now he was eager to take the Four Spiritual Laws booklet home with him so that he could in turn introduce his wife to Christ.

The words of this joyful young Christian have come to my mind again and again: "You must bring a lot of happiness into this world."

For about 30 years I have had the exciting privilege of "bringing a lot of happiness into this world" by sharing the Lord Jesus Christ with thousands of students and laymen around the world.

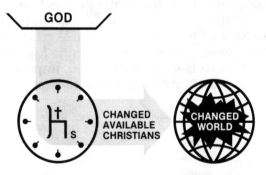

The apostle Paul related this experience to the Colossians, "Everywhere we go we talk about Christ to all who will listen" (Colossians 1:28, Living Bible).

Great Commission

We, the Christians of the 20th century, have the privilege of participating with the living Lord in the fulfillment of His Great Commission in our generation. In our judgment, the only way to change the world is to change individuals. Jesus Christ is the only One who can change people from within. Changed people in sufficient numbers will produce changed campuses, changed communities, changed cities, states and nations — yes, in a very real sense, a changed world. Thus, you can help to change the world by introducing others to Jesus Christ.

One of the greatest misconceptions of the centuries, in my opinion, is the idea so prevalent among Christians that men do not want God. Wherever I go — in this country or in other countries — I find ample proof that just the opposite is true. The Holy Spirit has created a hunger for God in the hearts of multitudes.

Why So Little Fruit?

For many years in many lands I have asked tens of thousands of Christians, "What is the greatest thing that has ever happened to you? The answer has always been, "Knowing Jesus Christ as my Savior."

The second question that naturally follows is, "What, then, is the greatest thing that a Christian can do for another person?" The answer has always been, "Help him to know Christ." Yet, tragically, many Christians have never introduced anyone else to the Lord Jesus.

Basically, there are two good reasons for this. First, the average Christian is living a defeated, impotent, fruitless, carnal life. He is not walking in the fullness and control of

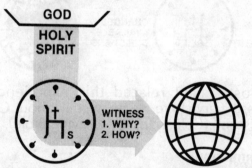

the Holy Spirit. Second, the average Christian has never been trained to communicate his faith in Christ effectively. He has never learned how to begin a conversation about Christ, how to explain the gospel simply and clearly, and how to lead a person to make a decision to receive Christ by faith.

The first problem is thoroughly covered in the concepts explained in previous chapters: Chapter 2 — "How to Experience God's Love and Forgiveness"; Chapter 3 — "How to Be Filled With the Spirit"; Chapter 4 — "How to Walk in the Spirit" and Chapter 5 — "How to Witness in the Spirit."

The second problem I shall discuss in this concept: "How to Introduce Others to Christ."

First, we shall consider *why* we should witness, which relates to motives; and second, *how* we should witness, which relates to methods.

WHY WITNESS?

Let me explain briefly seven good reasons we should witness.

Constrained By Love

First, we should witness because the love of Christ constrains us (II Corinthians 5:15). These are the words of the apostle Paul. Having experienced the love and forgiveness of God in his own life, he wanted everyone to experience this same love. If you really love Christ, you will also want to introduce Him to others.

Christ Commanded

Second, we should witness because Christ has commanded us to do so. He said, "Follow me, and I will make you fishers of men" (Matthew 4:19). "You did not choose Me, but I chose you, and appointed you, that you should go and bear fruit . . ." (John 15:16).

Men Are Lost

Third, we should witness because people without Christ are lost. Jesus said, "I am the way, and the truth,

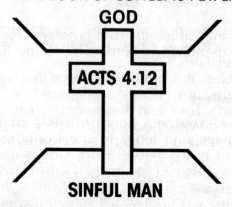

and the life; no man comes to the Father, but through Me" (John 14:6). God's Word declares emphatically, "There is salvation in no one else! Under heaven there is no other name for men to call upon to save them" (Acts 4:12, Living Bible).

Benefits Received

Fourth, we should witness because of the benefits to those who receive Christ. When we introduce others to Christ, they become God's children (John 1:12); their bodies become temples of God (II Corinthians 6:16); all their sins are forgiven — past, present and future (Colossians 1:14). They begin to experience the peace of God (John 14:27); they receive God's direction and purpose for their lives (Psalms 37:23) and they experience the power of God to change their lives (II Corinthians 5:17).

Spiritual Growth

Fifth, we should witness because of the benefits to those who witness. Witnessing encourages spiritual growth. Witnessing leads us to pray and to study God's Word and forces us to depend upon Christ. As we witness in the power of the Holy Spirit, we sow love and joy and peace.

According to the biblical principles of sowing and reaping, we always harvest what we sow and even more (Galatians 6:7). For example, if we sow love, we always harvest love — but always more than we sow. Jesus said, "My nourishment comes from doing the will of God"

(John 4:34, Living Bible). In this passage, reference is made to His experience of witnessing to the Samaritan woman.

Tremendous Privilege

Sixth, we should witness because it is a tremendous privilege. In his second letter to the Corinthians, Paul wrote, "We are Christ's ambassadors. God is using us to speak to you; we beg you, as though Christ Himself were pleading with you, receive the love He offers you — be reconciled to God" (II Corinthians 5:20, Living Bible).

Most people consider it a high honor to serve as an ambassador for the head of their country, the president or king, but as believers in Christ we are ambassadors for the King of kings and Lord of lords!

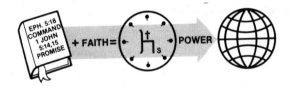

Power To Witness

Seventh, we should witness because the Holy Spirit empowers us to witness. Jesus Christ said, "You shall receive power when the Holy Spirit has come upon you; and you shall be My witnesses . . ." (Acts 1:8). To fail to witness for Christ is to deny the Holy Spirit His right to empower and to use us to introduce others to our Savior.

It is appropriate to remind ourselves again and again that training, materials, methods, techniques and strategies are of no value apart from the enabling and empowering of the Holy Spirit.

Review and Thought Questions

1. How could you begin a conversation about Christ?

   By waiting for an opportunity
   to witness

2. Explain briefly why we should witness.

   basically the Word tells
   us to do that the world can
   be won for Christ.

3. What does the "Great Commission" mean to you? (See Matthew 28:18-20).

   helping to fulfil the mission God
   gave to Jesus when he was here
   on earth.

4. Why do some Christians exhibit so little fruit?

   He is living a defeated Christian life
   & he has not been trained

5. From these verses, how would you define fruit in a Christian's life?

   Galatians 5:22, 23 _Character traits of a_
   Christian

   John 15:16 _Others that we bring to Christ_

   Matthew 7:15-20 _By their actions_

Matthew 13:18-23 *There will be growth*

6. What benefits result from having a personal relationship with Christ?

John 1:12 *He gave us power to become*
Children of God

I Corinthians 6:19 *Our body is the temple*
of the H.S.

Colossians 1:14 *We have forgivness*
of Sins

John 14:27 *We have peace*

II Corinthians 5:17 *He is a new Creator*

7. What does God set aside for all who accept His Son?

I Peter 1:3, 4 *An Inheritance in*
heaven

Ephesians 1:13, 14 *Sealed with the H.S.*

Questions 1, 3 and 5 can be used to stimulate effective group discussions.

STUDY 2.

HOW TO WITNESS

Now, I should like to discuss how we should witness.

As I have already indicated, many devout Christians fail miserably in their efforts to introduce another to Christ simply because they do not know how to go about it.

The Know-How

We cannot over-emphasize the need for training in communicating God's plan of salvation effectively. The story is told of the farmer who had to go to the doctor to have a few stitches made in a cut on his arm. When the doctor charged him $50, he protested vehemently. "But, Doc, "he said, "it didn't take you more than 15 minutes to sew that cut." "I know," agreed the doctor. "I charged you $5 for making the stitches, and $45 for the know-how."

The "know-how" makes the difference between effective and ineffective witnessing. Basically, we witness in two ways: by the way we live, and by the words we speak — by our lives and with our lips. We are specifically commanded to speak the good news with our lips, and that is the aspect of witnessing that we shall discuss here.

Before you can introduce others to Christ, however, there are certain things that you need to know: You must be sure that you are a Christian yourself. (This is discussed in Chapter 1). Then, as a Christian, you must know the empowering ministry of the Holy Spirit (as I have already mentioned, this is covered in Chapters 2, 3, 4 and 5).

You must understand what a nonbeliever needs to know about God, Jesus Christ, and the gospel before he can make an intelligent decision for Christ.

For many years, in our various student, lay and pastors institutes of evangelism, we asked those who participated in the training to help us list everything they felt a person should know before he could make an intelligent decision for Christ.

Distilled Essence

Usually 25 to 50 different suggestions were made, all of

which were written on the chalkboard. We would encourage every person to participate so that every single fact or bit of information that anyone had to contribute was recorded. That list usually included the following:

God loves us.
Man is sinful.
Man is lost.
God loved us so much that He gave His Son.
Christ died for our sins.
Christ arose from the dead.
He wants to come into every life.
We must repent.
We must be born again.
We must receive Jesus Christ.
To as many as receive Him (Jesus), to them God gives the right to become His children.

After all suggestions were exhausted, we asked each participant to read through the Four Spiritual Laws booklet with us and help us eliminate every point listed on the chalkboard that relates to Law One. These points were then removed from the board. We continued through Law Two, Three and Four, following the same procedure. At this point, the chalkboard was always clean, for the distilled essence of the gospel is contained in the Four Spiritual Laws booklet.

Simple Presentation

The content of the Four Spiritual Laws began to crystallize in my thinking during the summer staff training in 1956.

One of our speakers for staff training that year was a Christian layman who was an outstanding sales consultant. He emphasized that to be a successful salesman a man must develop a clear, simple, understandable presentation that he can use over and over again. But then he warned us that when a man becomes weary of hearing himself make the same presentation and develops "presentation fatigue," he often changes the presentation and inevitably loses his effectiveness.

He then compared the witnessing Christian to the secular salesman. To be effective in our communication for Christ, he stressed that we needed to develop a simple, understandable, logical presentation of the gospel which, basically, we could share with everyone. The better and more often we communicated this simple presentation, the more fruitful we would be for Christ.

He illustrated his remarks by telling of several well-known Christians who had their own special presentations. Then he zeroed in on me, saying, "Bill Bright thinks that he has a special message for each of the different groups of student and laymen with whom he works. But, though I have never heard him speak, I would be willing to wager that he has only one message for everyone. Basically, he tells them all the same thing."

The Same Message

To say that I objected to such a suggestion is to put it mildly. The longer he spoke, the more distressed I became. I resented the suggestion that I or anyone else who truly desired to serve the Lord was not led of the Spirit to speak with originality to various individuals according to their particular needs. Furthermore, I resented his using me as an example before the rest of the staff.

But, when it was all over and I was licking my wounds, the most serious of which was a lacerated ego, I began to reflect on exactly what I did share with various people. That afternoon I wrote down my basic presentation and, to my amazement, I discovered that my friend had been right. Without realizing it I had been sharing basically the same thing with everyone. What I wrote that afternoon and later polished is now known as "God's Plan for Your Life," a positive, 20-minute presentation of the claims of Christ, who He is, why He came, and how man can know Him personally.

I asked each staff member to memorize it, and we all began to use it in our personal witnessing. The next year, as we concentrated on sharing the simple presentation of the gospel in total dependence on the Holy Spirit's power, our ministry was multiplied a hundredfold.

"How To"

"God's Plan" was our first written "how to" material — that is, material which explains simply and specifically how an individual can arrive at a desired goal, and also how he in turn can help others to arrive at the same goal. The "how to" approach is, to the best of my knowledge, one of the most needed and most powerful approaches to the Christian life and witness I know anything about.

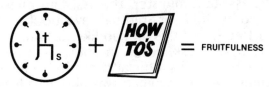

We have found, for example, that the average Christian does not need to be convinced that he should be filled with (controlled and empowered by) the Holy Spirit; he needs, rather, to be shown how to be filled with the Spirit by faith. Similarly, the average non-Christian does not need to be convinced that he should become a Christian. In most cases he simply needs to be shown how to become a Christian.

Condensed Version

Though "God's Plan" was extremely effective, we felt the need for a shorter version. So I prepared a condensed outline, complete with Scripture verses and diagrams; and each member of the staff memorized it. For several years we wrote it out word for word as we shared Christ with others. Then, as more and more people became involved in our training program, it became apparent that we needed to make the presentation available in printed form.

As a result, the Four Spiritual Laws booklet was born. We do not claim that this particular presentation is the only way to introduce others to Christ, or even the best way.

However, we do know that literally tens of thousands of men and women have received Christ through the direct, simple presentation of the gospel contained in this booklet. Millions of copies have been distributed in all of the major languages of the world.

He Disliked Tracts

I think, for example, of a church whose senior pastor had come to Arrowhead Springs for training and was very excited about the presentation of the Four Spiritual Laws. He went back to share his enthusiasm with his church and with his assistant minister. The assistant minister was not impressed by the Four Spiritual Laws booklet. He had a dislike for tracts, and this looked like just another tract. He tossed it on his desk, not even bothering to read it.

A few days later a city official came by to inspect the church facilities. As the woman was about to leave after her inspection, it suddenly occurred to the assistant minister that he had not talked to her about Christ. He looked around quickly, and the only thing he saw was the Four Spiritual Laws booklet which he had tossed aside in disgust some days previously. He gave it to her saying, "Read this," meaning that she should read it when she got home.

Led Herself To Christ

She misunderstood, however, and began to read it aloud in his presence. She read every word, and by the time she got to Law Four, tears were streaming down her cheeks. She came to the prayer and prayed aloud, leading herself to Christ. By this time the assistant minister was so impressed that he came to Arrowhead Springs to find out for himself how he could be a more effective witness for Christ through the training and the use of the Four Spiritual Laws.

Readily Responded

Another heartwarming experience demonstrates the effectiveness of the booklet. There was a man who was greatly admired in his hometown, though he was not a Christian. In fact, he was known as the town skeptic and had been witnessed to repeatedly.

He had befriended the parents of a Christian friend who

felt especially concerned for his salvation. After obtaining a Four Spiritual Laws booklet, his friend decided to call on the skeptic and read it to him. As he finished reading, he asked, "Does this make sense?" The "skeptic" replied that it did. "Is there anything that would keep you from receiving Christ?" "No," was the reply. The two men then knelt together and prayed, and the "skeptic" invited Christ into his life.

When they arose, the friend was rejoicing with the man, who then stunned him with this question, "Is this what you and all the other Christians have been trying to tell me for years?" "Yes," was the reply. "Well," continued his new brother in Christ, "why didn't you tell me? Any man would be a fool not to receive Christ if he really understood what is involved."

The gospel as contained in the booklet had cut right through the barrier of skepticism and indifference so that the skeptic got the message.

Make A List

If you may be inclined to think that the Four Spiritual Laws presentation is too simple, I suggest that you make a list of all the important truths of the gospel that you think should be presented when you witness. Then compare your list with the booklet. You will discover, as I have already demonstrated, that it contains all of the basic truths of the gospel.

Now, with all of these things in mind, let me give you some simple suggestions that will help you to introduce others to Christ.

First, you should begin every day with prayer, asking the Holy Spirit to empower and lead you to those whose hearts He has prepared. (Study Chapter 9, "How to Pray.")

Second, it is extremely important to relate to people in a loving, natural, personal way. Avoid being mechanical. Everyone responds to love. (Study Chapter 8, "How to Love by Faith.") As you walk in love, the Spirit of God will confirm to those with whom you are sharing Christ that you are genuine and authentic, that you are not simply trying to win an argument or promote a cause, and that you have taken time to talk to them because you truly love them with God's love.

Some Green Fruit

Not everyone will be prepared to receive Christ or even be positive in his response. Some may even be antagonistic, but God wants you to sow the seed or to be an instrument of harvest. In either case, relax and let Him do what He wants to do through you.

Remember, just as all fruit in the orchard is not ripe at the same time, so some individuals will be ripe for harvest and others will still be green — not yet ready to respond to the gospel. Consider every appointment a great privilege and opportunity, not a legalistic responsibility. Think of God's great love, of what knowing Him has meant to you and what it will mean to others when they receive Christ. Make sharing your faith in Christ a way of life.

Many Benefits

There are many benefits which result from using a presentation such as the Four Spiritual Laws. Let me list some of them:

It enables you to open your conversation easily.

It begins with a positive statement.

It presents the gospel and the claims of Christ clearly and simply.

It gives you confidence in your witnessing because you know what you are going to say and how you are going to say it.

It enables you to be prepared at all times and to stick to the subject without getting off on tangents.

It allows you to be brief and to the point.

It offers suggestions for growth, including the importance of the church.

And, of special importance, it is a "transferable technique" whereby those whom you introduce to Christ can be encouraged to lead still others to Christ.

Many Christians are effective in their own personal ministries, but are unable to communicate their technique to their spiritual children so that they can communicate it to *their* spiritual children, generation after generation. Yet this is the very thing that Paul exhorted Timothy, his young son in the faith, to do.

"For you must teach others those things you and many others have heard me speak about. Teach these great truths to trustworthy men who will, in turn, pass them on to others" (II Timothy 2:2, Living Bible).

The Four Spiritual Laws is such a simple, transferable technique that it enables those who receive Christ to go immediately to friends and loved ones and tell them what they have done, and it enables them to show those friends and loved ones how they, too, can make a commitment to Christ.

Be Concise

A minister came to share his frustration with me over his lack of effectiveness and fruitfulness in witnessing for Christ. "What do you say when you seek to introduce a person to Christ?" I inquired. He explained his presentation, which was very long and complicated. I sensed that the large number of Bible verses he used confused most people and prevented them from making an intelligent decision.

I challenged him to use the Four Spiritual Laws presentation daily for the next 30 days and report to me at the end of that time. When I saw him two weeks later, he was overflowing with joy and excitement. He said, "By simply reading the booklet to others, I have seen more people come to Christ in the last two weeks than I had previously seen in many months. It is hard to believe."

Practical Truths

Countless letters report from people who have benefited from receiving training in how to be controlled and empowered by the Holy Spirit and how to use this simple presentation. One man expressed what many say, "These truths are so practical that I have applied them in my daily life and am now experiencing victory when defeat used to be the common result. Before receiving training and reading your materials, walking in the Spirit was not a way of life for me and consequently I was not interested in communicating my faith."

Another shared, "I was afraid at first, but the Lord has changed my attitude, and now I want to go out witnessing. I thank God with all my heart for this change."

A woman who had served with her husband as a missionary in Africa for many years gave this report, "You should have seen the transformation in my husband when he returned from a Lay Institute for Evangelism. He wanted to share the Four Spiritual Laws booklet with everyone — students, fellow teachers, policemen, garage attendants . . . He even shared in the pool with water up to his neck! And the best part of all is that he keeps on doing it."

Just Get Started

But even a Spirit-controlled person with a tested and trusted tool in his hands can expect barriers of resistance in sharing Christ with others. One of the most difficult barriers to overcome in witnessing is just getting started. No matter who you are or where you are, opportunities are always available. Assume that whenever you are alone with another person for more than just a few moments it is a divine appointment and an answer to your prayer.

I witness regularly to porters, elevator operators, hotel maids, taxicab drivers, filling station attendants and people in numerous other types of work. On a plane, it is often easy to engage the stewardess or a seatmate in conversation by having in hand either a Bible, a Four Spiritual Laws booklet or some other piece of literature.

Following a group meeting, whether a church service, a Bible study, large evangelistic meeting or some similar gathering, you may wish to introduce yourself to different individuals. Then after a warm greeting, proceed with the following questions in a way that is natural for you: "What did you think of the meeting?" "Did it make sense to you?" "Have you made the wonderful discovery of knowing Christ personally?" "You would like to, wouldn't you?"

Have You Heard

Then ask if he has ever heard of the Four Spiritual Laws and proceed to read them to him. If he has already heard of the Four Laws, ask his opinion, review the booklet with him and give him the opportunity to receive Christ if he has not already done so.

The same approach can be used in distributing and in asking people to read other Christian literature and materials. After they have read the literature or listened to the lecture, you may wish to ask the same previous four questions, substituting "article" or "lecture" for "meeting."

There are many effective ways to establish contact. After a cordial, friendly greeting, you can say:

"Have you ever heard of the Four Spiritual Laws? This little booklet is one of the most widely read books in the world. Millions of copies have been distributed in every major language."

"The content of this booklet has changed my life."

"I would like to share this little booklet that has really meant a lot to me. Almost everyone I have shared it with has said that it was meaningful to them. Have you ever heard of the Four Spiritual Laws?

"The contents of this booklet has been used to change the lives of thousands. It contains truths that I believe will be of great interest to you. I would like to have you read it and give me your impression."

"A friend of mine recently gave me this little booklet which really makes sense to me. I would like to share it with you. Have you ever heard of the Four Spiritual Laws?"

This direct approach can best be employed when you have only a few moments with an individual. If you have a more unhurried opportunity, you may find it helpful to take a few minutes to establish rapport by sharing a few things of personal interest about yourself and asking the other person about himself, his business, profession or family.

Then you can proceed to explain that you are a Christian and have discovered a booklet that has been a great help to you and that you would like to share with him. Then ask, "Have you ever heard of the Four Spiritual

Laws?" As you prayerfully depend upon the Holy Spirit, He will give you wisdom in making the transition. However, no presentation will be effective unless God has already prepared the other individual's heart.

Some Not Prepared

Although multitudes of people have been prepared by the Holy Spirit to receive Christ, you will inevitably meet individuals whose hearts are not prepared. You can give these people special literature to read and encourage them to read the New Testament, particularly the Gospel of John. Pray for them and, whenever possible, arrange to meet them in a later appointment.

Be Friendly

In making the presentation, show love. Be casual, friendly, warm and speak with confidence. Some of you may recall the comic radio salesman, "Elmer Blurt," who always followed his timid knock on the door with, "I guess there's probably nobody home, I hope, I hope, I hope!"

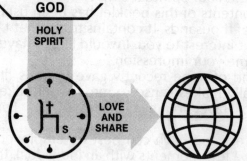

You do not need to try to impress people with your brilliance, but neither should you use a half-hearted hesitant approach that suggests, "I don't suppose you would like to become a Christian, would you?"

Read The Booklet

When you share the Four Spiritual Laws, do not elaborate with personal illustrations, which often confuse the one to whom you are speaking. Simply read through the booklet. Generally, it is wise for the one who is doing the witnessing to read aloud from the booklet, holding it at an angle so that the one with whom it is being shared can read along with him.

It is also helpful to use a pencil or something similar to point to the lines and words being read, to insure better concentration. There will be times when the Holy Spirit will lead you to stop and explain something that may be unclear. Normally, however, it is more effective to read through the booklet before stopping to explain or answer questions.

If the person to whom you are witnessing raises questions, you should say, "Let's remember that question and come back to it in a moment, after we have finished reading the booklet." Of course, be sure to answer the question later.

Some time ago I was speaking to a group of pastors in Dallas. A university chaplain asked if I would go with him to a nearby university campus to demonstrate how to use the Four Spiritual Laws booklet with students. He gathered about a dozen students, most of whom were Christians. I gave them each a copy of the Four Spiritual Laws booklet and asked them to follow along silently as I read the booklet aloud.

Although I have shared Christ with thousands of people in individual counseling sessions through the years, I am a rather reserved person and do not always find it easy to witness. As I sat there reading the booklet aloud to the students, I began to receive all kinds of negative impressions from the enemy who was trying to discourage me and put doubts into my mind such as, "These students will laugh at you. They are too intelligent to be responsive to such a simple presentation. You need a more intellectual approach. Don't go too far; don't be a fanatic. People will be turned off. They will think you are crazy."

But knowing that I am free from Satan's power as I obey and simply trust the Lord, I could say, "Greater is He who is in me (Christ) than he who is in the world (Satan)" (I John 4:4). So I kept on reading, knowing from experience

222 HANDBOOK OF CONCEPTS FOR LIVING

that God would honor this presentation as He has on thousands of other occasions, for He has promised to honor His word.

When I came to the prayer, it suddenly seemed that a chorus of voices was saying to me, "You are not going to read this prayer and make a fool of yourself before these sharp students, are you? But I read the prayer, and then I said, "If this prayer expresses the desire of your heart, pray it with me silently. Make it your own prayer."

God Worked In Their Hearts

Then I read the prayer aloud a second time. When I finished the prayer I looked up and saw tears running down the cheeks of one of the young women. She came up to say that she had prayed the prayer and knew that the Lord Jesus had come to live in her heart. Later a young man came to receive Christ.

Before I left, the chaplain introduced me to another young woman who had just received Christ. As far as I know, all the rest except one were Christians. The remaining one had been reared as an atheist, but was very sobered by what he had heard and was also on the verge of receiving Christ.

Through the simple reading of the gospel, as contained in the Four Spiritual Laws booklet, the Spirit of God worked in the hearts of these young men and women in a marvelous way, as He usually does when any Spirit-controlled person shares this presentation.

Again, let me say that as you read the booklet, there will be times when the Holy Spirit will lead you to stop reading and explain something which may be unclear to the one with whom you are sharing. Normally, however, it is much more effective to read through the booklet and give opportunity for the individual to receive Christ without unnecessary comment. Personal illustrations should be used only when necessary to answer a question or clarify a point.

Review and Thought Questions

1. In what specific ways did you witness by the way you lived today? (Remember, a witness can be either positive or negative.)

   By the way we live and by the way we speak

2. Why did Jesus Christ come to earth?

   Luke 19:10 _____

   _____

   John 10:9, 10 _____

   _____

3. How would you present Christ to a non-believer? Write out the references of the verses you would use and why.

   _____

   _____

   _____

4. What does it mean to really love someone (in a non-romantic involvement)?

   _____

   _____

   _____

5. What role does the Holy Spirit play in evangelism?

   John 6:63 _____

   _____

   _____

Romans 8:16 _____

_____

Romans 8:26 _____

_____

II Corinthians 3:17 _____

_____

I Peter 3:18 _____

_____

6. What role does Satan play in keeping people from accepting Jesus?

II Corinthians 5:4 _____

_____

Ephesians 2:2, 3 _____

_____

I Timothy 4:1 _____

_____

7. Explain I Timothy 3:16. Why could it also be called the whole gospel in a nutshell?

_____

_____

_____

_____

_____

_____

_____

Discussion questions: 1, 3, 4, 7.

STUDY 3.

CONFLICT — ASSURANCE

Generally, you will find that most people agree with the first three spiritual laws and are not likely to ask many, if any, questions. Thus, you can proceed to Law Four.

The material contained on pages 8 and 9 in the booklet will help you to determine whether or not a person is ready to receive Christ. You will observe two circles, one representing the self-controlled life, the other the Christ-controlled life. Ask the question contained in the booklet,

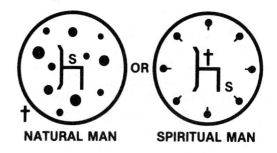

NATURAL MAN   **SPIRITUAL MAN**

"Which circle represents your life?" Then ask, "Which circle would you like to have represent your life?" In most cases the one with whom you are sharing will answer the first question, "The circle on the left," and the second question, "The circle on the right."

A Necessary Preparation

Repentance is a necessary preparation for receiving Christ, as illustrated by these two diagrams. Repentance means to change your attitude, which results in a change of action. However, it should be clearly understood that one does not become a Christian because he repents, but because he receives Christ by faith as explained in John 1:12 and Ephesians 2:8, 9.

Further, we need to explain that a genuine acceptance of Christ as Savior results in a new birth and in His becoming our Lord. For as John explains: "My little children, I am telling you this so that you will stay away from sin. But if you sin, there is someone to plead for you before the Father. His name is Jesus Christ, the one who is all that is good and who pleases God completely. He is the one who took God's wrath against our sins upon Himself, and brought us into fellowship with God; and He is the forgiveness of our sins, and not only ours but all the world's.

"And how can we be sure that we belong to Him? By looking within ourselves: are we really trying to do what He wants us to? Someone may say, 'I am a Christian; I am on my way to heaven; I belong to Christ.' But if he doesn't do what Christ tells him to, he is a liar. But those who do what Christ tells them to will learn to love God more and more. That is the way to know whether or not you are a Christian." (I John 2:1-5, Living Bible).

There are many people who profess to be Christians, who go through the "ritual" of Christianity, but do not give any evidence that they are Christians. By our obedience to the Lord Jesus Christ through the enabling of the Holy Spirit, we demonstrate that we belong to Him.

Opportunity To Pray

The next crucial point in sharing Christ is to help those who want to receive Him as their Savior to know exactly what to do. As you continue to read from the booklet, explain how one can receive Christ through prayers.

Read the prayer aloud and then ask, "Does this prayer express the desire of your heart?" If the answer is "Yes," say, "You can pray this prayer right now if you really mean it, and Christ will come into your life as He promised." Then pause for prayer, with the suggestion that if the individual will pray aloud, you can pray with him.

If there is a long silence, you may suggest that the individual pray after you. Be sensitive. Do not offend by "forcing" the prayer. He may wish to pray his own prayer rather than the suggested prayer. Should the individual wish to pray silently, suggest that he say "Amen" when finished. At this point, you pray.

No Response?

If he does not want to make a commitment at this

point, exercise caution to avoid offending the one with whom you are sharing Christ. Do not try to badger, argue or high pressure him into making a "decision" for Christ. Christ said, "No one can come to Me, unless the Father who sent Me draws him" (John 6:44).

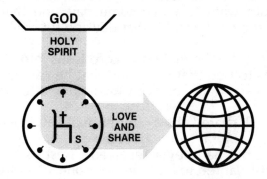

The important thing is not what you do, but what the Holy Spirit does through you (I Corinthians 3:6). You and I do not have the ability to bring anyone to Christ. Remember, *SUCCESS IN WITNESSING IS SIMPLY SHARING CHRIST IN THE POWER OF THE HOLY SPIRIT AND LEAVING THE RESULTS TO GOD.*

If He Is Not Ready

However, there are several additional things you can do to help the individual who does not receive Christ after you have read and discussed the booklet together up to the prayer. First, always maintain a positive and loving attitude. You may wish to say, "Quite likely you will want to receive Jesus Christ as your Savior one day. Let me show you what will happen when you do invite Christ to come into your life."

Then proceed to explain the assurance of salvation by reading the rest of the booklet. If the response is positive, give the person another opportunity to receive Christ by inviting him to pray with you. You will find that many will be ready to pray by the time you have read the entire booklet.

Pray Later

Some will want to pray then, while others may wish to pray at a later time after they better understand what is involved in receiving Christ. Be sure to leave the individual with the understanding that this is a decision he will no doubt want to make some day, and that he should reread the booklet later that day and receive Christ on his own.

Suggest that he invite the Lord Jesus into his life before he goes to bed that night and that he call you as soon as he does so. Many receive Christ alone after the interview is over.

Once, I shared the Four Spiritual Laws booklet with a famous general who agreed with the content of the booklet but had never received Christ as his Savior and Lord. He wanted to but had not done so. I offered to pray with him, but he said he would prefer to pray the prayer after I left. I promised to pray for him and said goodbye.

The next morning I called him to inquire, "Did you pray that prayer?" "I certainly did," he responded warmly and enthusiastically, "just as I promised I would."

There are two other things you might find helpful. You could share your personal testimony and, as the Holy Spirit leads you, give another opportunity for the individual with whom you are sharing to receive Christ in prayer. Or it may be helpful to simply review the booklet, explaining it clearly one law at a time and asking after each law, "Does this make sense?"

Assurance

Another important consideration in sharing Christ with others is the necessity of leading the new Christian to full assurance of faith in Christ. All of the material in the booklet following the prayer is specifically designed to aid you in helping the new Christian to be sure of his salvation.

After an individual has prayed, ask the following questions, contained on page 6 of the Four Spiritual Laws booklet. Did you receive Christ into your life? According to His promise, contained in Revelation 3:20, where is He right now in relation to you?

If the reply is, "Well, He is in the world," or "He is in heaven," ask the question again, emphasizing ". . . but where is He in relation to you?" Explain that, according to Revelation 3:20, Christ said He would come into our lives. Ask, "Would He mislead you? On what authority do you know that God has answered your prayer?"

Then explain that our authority is the trustworthiness of God Himself and His Word. Together read I John 5:11-13. Emphasize that we can know we have eternal life on the basis of these promises from God's divinely inspired Word.

One time I shared the gospel, as explained in the Four Laws, with a man who received Christ but had no assurance of his salvation. After reading this particular passage to him, I asked, "What would happen if you died today?" He replied, "I'm afraid that I would go to hell."

But as I reread the I John passage several times, I saw light come to his eyes and radiance to his face. The Holy Spirit had broken through the resistance that he had built up for 50 years, and this man finally saw God's truth and received Christ into his life by faith.

Don't Depend On Feelings

Always explain the importance of faith. Review and explain the meaning of Ephesians 2:8, 9. Warn against the danger of depending upon feelings. One of Satan's great lies is that you must have some kind of emotional experience when you receive Christ. But the Word of God says we are to live *by faith*.

Explain the train diagram on page 12 of the booklet. The Christian life is not lived according to feelings but according to faith in God and His Word. Study this truth carefully and always make it clear to the person with whom you are sharing Christ.

Also read and explain briefly and clearly the five things that have happened to the new Christian, as listed on page 13 of the booklet.

When the individual is assured, on the basis of God's Word, that Christ is in his life, suggest that each of you pray aloud, thanking God for what He has done. The very act of thanking God demonstrates faith and often contributes to the assurance of salvation.

Continue with suggestions for Christian growth and the importance of becoming active in a local church, as explained on pages 14 and 15.

Follow Up

Proper follow-up of the new Christian cannot be overemphasized. You should secure the name and address of each individual with whom you pray. This can be done tactfully and without offense if you give the person your name and address first.

Then arange to meet with the new Christian for spiritual counsel and follow-up not more than 48 hours later, the very next day if possible. In any event, send the name and address to the Follow-up Department, Campus Crusade for Christ, Arrowhead Springs, San Bernardino, CA 92414. We want to help every new convert to become mature in Christ.

Staff there will send the new believer a series of Bible study letters and other materials that emphasize assurance of salvation; the importance of reading the Bible; prayer; the ministry of the Holy Spirit; the importance of baptism and of actively serving Christ through the local church; the importance of sharing Christ with others; and a number of other truths that every new Christian should know.

God Used The Letters

Many received the assurance of their salvation just by reading and studying the materials that we sent them. One young woman dropped by to thank me for sending her the series of follow-up letters.

"After receiving Christ," she said, "I was plagued with

serious doubts. I even became resentful about you and your letters to me. Then, miracle of miracles, God used your letters to answer my questions and to help me surrender my will to Christ. Now I have made application for Campus Crusade for Christ staff and have just been accepted. I am so happy, and I want to thank you again for writing those follow-up letters. I wouldn't be here today had it not been for them."

In addition to taking advantage of the follow-up letters, you have a responsibility to follow up the individual *personally,* wherever possible. If you can't meet personally, send a personal letter of encouragement to the new Christian.

Along with individual follow-up you can help encourage new Christians to grow and to begin to win and build others through small discipleship groups, home Bible studies, Sunday school, and church.

Training Available

Campus Crusade for Christ wants to serve you and the entire Body of Christ not only by helping to train you to share your faith more effectively but also by helping to train and build up those whom you introduce to Christ. In addition to the Four Spiritual Laws booklet, other materials are available to assist you in your Christian growth and witness for Christ.

Witnessing as a way of life requires training as a way of life. If the business world depends upon a continuous training program to promote greater sales of a secular product, how much more important it is that Christians participate in a continuous training program through the local church.

We want to help you. Training in the most effective use of these practical tools is available through student, lay, pastor, executive and military conferences held across America and in most major countries of the world.

For specific information regarding training and available materials, write to:

Campus Crusade for Christ International
Arrowhead Springs
San Bernardino, CA 92414

I challenge you to perform an experiment for the next 30 days. Each day, ask God to lead you to someone whose heart has been prepared for your witness. Go prayerfully and in the power of the Holy Spirit. In the spirit of the apostle Paul, "talk about Christ to everyone who will listen."

Present the gospel as contained in the Four Spiritual Laws and expect God to use you. At the end of 30 days, I am sure that you will be convinced, as multitudes of others have been convinced, that there is no greater adventure in life than introducing others to our matchless Savior.

Remember, "You can bring a lot of happiness into this world" by sharing Christ with others.

If this prayer expresses the desire of your heart, make it your own: "Lord Jesus, I thank You for Your love for me. I thank You that through Your death and resurrection my sins have been forgiven and I am able to live a victorious and fruitful life for You each day. As an expression of my love for You and for all men, and in obedience to Your command, I want to give daily priority to introducing others to You. Thank You for Your promise to make me fruitful if I follow You. Amen."

Review and Thought Questions

1. How would you explain the difference between a Spirit-controlled life and a self-controlled life?

   _____

   _____

   _____

2. What is repentance?

   asking forgiveness

   Change of mind

   _____

3. How does one become a Christian?

   John 1:12 *After you receive Christ*

   He gives power to become Children

   Ephesians 2:8, 9 *By grace through faith*

   John 5:24 *Hear the word & believes will*

   have everlasting life

4. What does I John 2:1-5 tell you about how you can know you are a Christian?

   If we keep his Commandments

   we know him

   _____

5. Why should anyone want to be a Christian?

   _____

   _____

   _____

6. a) What promises do you find in I John 5:11-13?

_____

_____

b) Why are they important?

_____

_____

7. Name just one person you will talk to personally about Jesus Christ in the next month.

_____

_____

_____

_____

Discussion questions: 1, 5, 6a and b.

CHAPTER STUDY GUIDE

1. The application of the principles outlined in this Concept will enable you to have an effective ministry in introducing others to Christ.

2. Memorize the following verses and references:

I Corinthians 2:1, 2: "And when I came to you brethren, I did not come with superiority of speech or of wisdom, proclaiming to you the testimony of God. For I determined to know nothing among you except Jesus Christ and Him crucified."

I Peter 3:15: "But sanctify Christ as Lord in your hearts, always being ready to make a defense to every one who asks you to give an account for the hope that is in you, yet with gentleness and reverence."

3. Make this Concept, "How to Introduce Others to Christ," a way of life by doing the following:

   a. Be prepared to share your faith with others. Get a copy of the Four Spiritual Laws booklet. Read it over several times aloud as if you were sharing it with someone else. After you have done this, ask a Christian friend to let you share the booklet with him. Have him play the part of an interested non-Christian.

   As you read, hold the booklet at an angle so that he can follow along. use a pencil or a similar object to point to what is being read to insure better concentration on his part. Give the person an opportunity to respond at appropriate places. Go through the prayer as if the person were receiving Christ.

   Go through the portions of the booklet on assurance and growth. At the conclusion, practice making a follow-up appointment to get back together with the person sometime within the next 48 hours. Follow the suggestions in this Concept on how to share the Four Spiritual Laws.

   b. Prayerfully make an appointment with a friend who you feel will be open and interested in the claims of Christ. Tell him you would like to share with him something that has been meaningful to you. Then go in the power of the Holy Spirit. As you meet with him and share the Four Spiritual Laws, give him an opportunity to respond and to pray to receive Christ. Be prayerfully sensitive to his response.

Go through the assurance and follow-up sections of the booklet. If he receives Christ, make an appointment with him to meet for follow-up sometime within 48 hours. You may want to give him the Concept booklet, "How to Be Sure You Are a Christian," to read before you meet with him again. When you do meet together, work the Bible study in the back of "How to Be Sure You Are a Christian."

c. Prayerfully make a list of other people with whom you feel God would have you share Christ. Pray for the people on your list daily. Make appointments with these people one by one. Take those who receive Christ with you as you share Christ with others. Keep adding to the list as God lays particular people on your heart, and seek to talk to one, two or three of these people a week, depending on your schedule.

d. Begin sharing Christ with people you do not know personally. Be prayerfully sensitive to God's leading, and be sensitive to the persons with whom you share. Follow the suggestions on pages 30-33.

e. Make sharing Christ with others a way of life. Learn to share naturally both with friends and strangers. Develop a spiritual sensitivity to those with whom you share. Go with others you know are effective in sharing their faith; you can learn from them. Also take along other people who can learn from you as you share Christ.

f. Put your plan for sharing in writing. Follow through on your plans. Then keep accurate records of your sharing experiences.

AMPLIFIED OUTLINE
Study 1.

I. Despite the joy and fulfillment witnessing can bring,

many Christians have never introduced a single person to Christ. There are basically two reasons for this:

A. The average Christian is living a defeated, frustrated, carnal life. He is not, by faith, allowing the Holy Spirit to fill and control him according to God's command and promise (Ephesians 5:18; I John 5:14, 15).

B. Also, the average Christian has never been trained to communicate his faith effectively.

II. Why should we witness?

A. Because "the love of Christ constrains us" (II Corinthians 5:14).

B. Because the Lord Jesus has given the command to witness (Matthew 28:19; Matthew 4:19; John 15:16).

C. Because men are lost without Christ (John 14:6; Acts 4:12).

D. Because of the benefits that come to those who receive Christ.

    1. They become sons of God (John 1:12).

    2. Their bodies become temples of God (II Corinthians 6:16).

    3. All their sins are forgiven — past, present and future (Colossians 1:14).

    4. They begin to experience the peace of God (John 14:27).

    5. They receive God's direction for their lives (Psalms 37:33).

    6. They experience the power of God to change their lives (II Corinthians 5:17).

E. Because witnessing for Christ helps us to grow spiritually (Galatians 6:7).

F. Because it is a tremendous privilege to witness for Christ (II Corinthians 5:20).

G. Because we are empowered by the Holy Spirit to witness (Acts 1:8).

Study 2.

III. How to witness.

   A. Recognize that we witness by the way we live and by the words we speak, but recognize that living a good life is no substitute for actively sharing our faith in Christ with others.

   B. Begin each day by asking the Holy Spirit to lead you to ones whose hearts He has prepared to receive Christ.

   C. Make sharing your faith in Christ a way of life.

   D. Use the Four Spiritual Laws booklet for added benefits for your witnessing.

      1. It enables you to open your conversation easily.

      2. It begins with a positive statement.

      3. It presents the gospel and the claims of Christ clearly and simply.

      4. It gives you confidence in your witnessing because you know what you are going to say and how you are going to say it.

      5. It enables you to be prepared at all times and to stick to the subject without getting off on tangents.

      6. It makes it possible for you to be brief and to the point.

      7. It includes an invitation to receive Christ.

      8. It offers suggestions for growth, including the importance of the church.

      9. It presents a "transferable technique" whereby those whom you lead to Christ can be encouraged to lead others to Christ (II Timothy 2:2).

   E. Use the Four Spiritual Laws booklet in various ways.

      1. Share it with individuals whom you meet even briefly.

      2. Share it with others following a group meeting, etc.

      3. Share it with friends, acquaintances.

F. Relate the contents of the Four Spiritual Laws booklet in a loving, natural, personal way.

Study 3.

G. Whenever possible, be sure to give each person an opportunity to receive Christ after you have shared the gospel as contained in the Four Spiritual Laws booklet. This should be done in prayer as an expression of faith.
   1. Don't try to "high pressure" people into making a "decision" for Christ.
   2. Remember that success in witnessing is simply sharing Christ in the power of the Holy Spirit and leaving the results to God.
H. Seek to follow up those whom you have the privilege of introducing to Christ.
   1. Whenever possible, arrange to meet with the new Christian no more than 24 to 48 hours later.
   2. If it is not possible to follow up personally, write personal follow-up letters.
   3. You can send his name and address to Campus Crusade for Christ to receive further Bible study material for Christian growth.
   4. Introduce the new Christian to other materials for evangelism and growth.
   5. Encourage the new Christian to participate in one of the training institutes offered by Campus Crusade for Christ.

CHAPTER 7
HOW TO HELP FULFILL
THE GREAT COMMISSION

Study 1. Who? What?
Study 2. Why? When? Where?
Study 3. How?

STUDY 1.
WHO? WHAT?

Today we live in a world of rapid and radical change. Men's hearts are filled with fear and dread, frustration and despair. Man cannot seem to cope with his pressing problems — economic instability, pollution, energy shortages, the rising tide of crime and violence, high divorce rates, the drug-and-sex-oriented youth culture and widespread political, social and moral decay.

World leaders themselves are pessimistic, fearing that some madman will push the button and incinerate mankind. The late Sir Winston Churchill said, "Our generation may well live to see the end of what we call civilization."

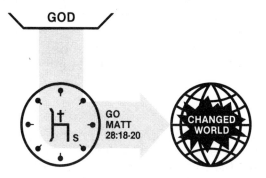

Oh, what an hour for Christians to become involved in what could well become the greatest spiritual harvest since Pentecost! This dark and desperate hour is an hour of destiny for Christians, the hour for which we were born, the hour in which we must "shine like beacon lights" and set in motion a sweeping spiritual revolution that will turn the tide and reveal to mankind in the glorious gospel of Christ the ultimate answers to the problems of the world.

The Great Commission

In one of my first classes in journalism, I learned that the lead paragraph in a good news story usually answers six basic questions: Who? What? Why? When? Where? How?

If I had the privilege of writing a news story about the greatest events of all the centuries, one of the most important would be a small meeting on a mountain in Galilee where our risen Lord gave His disciples a global strategy that is known as the Great Commission. Had this meeting not been held and had our Lord's command not been given, it is quite likely that no one who reads these pages would now be experiencing the love, forgiveness, joy and purpose of God's matchless grace available to all who believe in Christ.

Jesus said to them, "All authority has been given to Me in heaven and on earth. Go therefore, and make disciples of all the nations, baptizing them in the name of the Father and the Son and the Holy Spirit, teaching them to observe all that I command you; and lo, I am with you always, even to the end of the age" (Matthew 28:18-20).

Christ's Great Commission is the greatest *plan* ever given to men, by the greatest *person* who ever lived, concerning the greatest *power* ever revealed and with the greatest *promise* ever recorded. To understand more fully the Great Commission, as well as its implications in our lives, we need to answer the six basic questions.

WHO?

First, who gave the Great Commission and to whom was it given? Who would have the audacity to say, "I have been given all authority in heaven and earth"? Only Jesus Christ. He is the unique Son of God. His miraculous birth, substitutionary death and bodily resurrection are the most important events in human history.

God became man! The apostle Paul wrote: "And He is the image of the invisible God, the first-born of all creation. For in Him all things were created, both in the heavens and on earth . . . For in Him all the fullness of Deity dwells in bodily form, and in them you have been made complete, and He is the head over all rule and authority" (Colossians 1:15, 16).

Jesus Christ died on the cross and was raised from the dead to save men from sin and to give eternal life to all

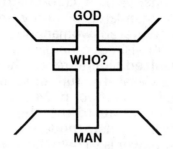

who receive Him. The result was a spiritual revolution that changed the first-century world and altered the course of history.

Need we be reminded that our 20th-century world needs changing? Jesus of Nazareth, the greatest person who ever lived, has caused the most changes for good in the entire history of mankind through changing the lives of men.

Historian Phillip Schaff said, "Jesus of Nazareth, without money and arms, conquered more millions than Alexander, Caesar, Mohammed and Napoleon. Without science and learning, He shed more light on things human and divine than all the philosophers and scholars combined. Without the eloquence of schools, He spoke words of life such as were never spoken before nor since, and produced effects which lie beyond the reach of orator or poet.

"Without writing a single line, He has set more pens in motion and furnished themes for more sermons, orations, discussions, works of art, learned volumes and sweet songs of praise than the whole army of great men of ancient and modern time. Born in a manger, crucified as a malefactor, He controls the destinies of the civilized world and rules a spiritual empire that encircles the globe."

Men Transformed

Christ changes men and nations. Wherever His message goes, men are transformed. It was said of our Savior by the great missionary statesman, Dr. Samual Zwemer, "The gospel not only converts individuals, but changes society. On every mission field from the days of William Carey, the missionaries have carried a real social gospel. They established standards of purity and hygiene, promoted industry, elevated womanhood, restrained anti-social customs, abolished cannibalism, human sacrifice and cruelty, organized famine relief, checked tribal wars, and changed the social structure of society" (*Evangelism Today: Message, Not Method*, p. 24).

The apostle Paul wrote to the church in Ephesus, "I pray that you will begin to understand how incredibly great His (God's) power is to help those who believe Him. It is that same mighty power that raised Christ from the dead and seated Him in the place of honor at God's right hand in heaven, far, far above any other king or ruler or dictator or leader.

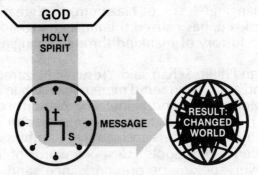

"Yes, His honor is far more glorious than that of anyone else either in this world or in the world to come. And God has put all things under His feet and made Him the supreme Head of the Church — which is His body, filled with Himself, the Author and Giver of everything everywhere" (Ephesians 1:19-23, Living Bible).

Christ's ability to change men is based solely on the fact of who He was and is. He claimed and proved that He is indeed the Son of God.

To Whom Was The Great Commission Given?

Christ's Great Commission involves not merely the 11

disciples to whom He originally gave it, but everyone who believes in Him. Therefore, it is every Christian's responsibility to be vitally and continuously involved in helping to fulfill the Great Commission.

Shortly after Jesus gave the Great Commission, God the Holy Spirit, on the day of Pentecost, transformed and empowered the lives of the disciples. Before Pentecost, one had denied our Lord and all had deserted Him. However, from that day on, they went out boldly, at the cost of their lives, to proclaim the message of God's love and forgiveness in Christ.

Somehow we have the idea that the early Christians were different from us — that they possessed a quality of life which we cannot attain. But the people to whom Jesus gave this Great Commission were common, ordinary working people, plagued with the same weaknesses that we have. The only difference between most of them and the majority of us is that two outstanding things happened to them.

First, they came to have complete confidence in a resurrected Lord triumphant over death — one who lived within them and was coming again to reign on earth. Second, they were filled with the Holy Spirit. Today, if enough Christians were completely committed to our resurrected and returning Lord and were controlled and empowered by His Spirit, we would turn our world upside down and experience a 20th-century spiritual revolution like that of the first century.

WHAT?

Now, let us consider the question, "What is the Great Commission?" For many years I have signed my letters, "Yours for fulfilling the Great Commission in this generation." Considering the magnitude of the task, with a world population of more than four billion people in 210 countries and protectorates, many people ridicule this possibility. I have been reminded repeatedly that "the Great Commission has not been fulfilled since the first century, if then, and is not likely to be fulfilled in our generation either."

But to those who ridicule any serious, systematic attempt to fulfill the Great Commission, I would merely cite a modern-day man-made program that demonstrates the plausibility and possibility of reaching the entire population of the world with the gospel and discipling tens of millions in all of the nations.

The United States Space Commission designed and executed a plan to put man on the moon within nine years from the drawing board stage. It is estimated that mass media made it possible for more than one-fourth of the world's population to see the first two men land on the moon. Is God four times more powerful than the directors of that mass media project?

Part of the pessimism we see is the result of spiritual ignorance concerning what is actually involved. Let me explain exactly what the Bible teaches concerning the Great Commission.

A Chance To Hear

First of all, the command of our Lord involves winning men to Himself, baptizing them, teaching them what He taught, building them as disciples and sending them forth as His ambassadors in such numbers that every person in each country of the world would hear "the most joyful news ever announced — that in Jesus Christ we have salvation!"

This does not mean that every person will hear the gospel in our generation. There are those who may never hear the gospel. But it does mean that we should seek to make a prayerful, intelligent presentation of the gospel to every living person and leave the results to God.

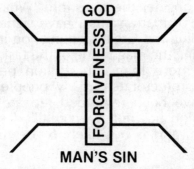

Also, it does not mean that the majority who hear the gospel will become Christians, but it does mean that they will at least have a chance to hear and believe. For some, one presentation of the gospel is all that is necessary, as Paul reported concerning the Colossian Christians: "The same Good News that came to you is going out all over the world and changing lives everywhere, just as it changed yours that very first day you heard it and understood about God's great kindness to sinners" (Colossians 1:6, Living Bible).

And to the Thessalonians, Paul wrote, "For when we brought you the Good News, it was not just meaningless chatter to you; no, you listened with great interest. What we told you produced a powerful effect upon you, for the Holy Spirit gave you great and full assurance that what we said was true. And you know how our very lives were further proof to you of the truth of our message" (I Thessalonians 1:5, Living Bible).

Christ commanded: "Make disciples in all nations." How many disciples, He didn't say; but He unquestionably meant enough to saturate the entire community, city, state or province and nation with the good news, and to train other disciples.

Preach and Teach

Christ did not commission us to *Christianize* all nations; he called us to *evangelize* and *disciple* them. Our responsibility is to preach and teach Christ's dynamic gospel; it is the Holy Spirit's responsibility to make our witness effective. With the responsibility, however, Christ also gave us everything necessary for success.

When you go forth to represent the Lord Jesus Christ as His disciple, you can be assured that you are representing the one person who possesses all power, wisdom and authority. You have everything when you have Him. No power can resist you as you go in faith as His ambassador. We have the promise, ". . . Greater is He who is in you than he who is in the world" (I John 4:4). Also, there is the assuring word that even "the gates of hell shall not prevail against it (the Church)" (Matthew 16:18).

Almost 200 years ago, when William Carey (called "the father of modern missions") began his pioneer ministry, only 25% of the nations of the earth had heard the gospel. Today every nation in the world is receiving the gospel either through trained disciples, radio, television or the printed word.

But, even though there is a witness for Christ in every nation, the Great Commission is not fulfilled, and it will remain unfulfilled until there are sufficient disciples in every nation to saturate totally that nation with the gospel. We must become as interested in making disciples as we are in getting decisions, more interested in spiritual multiplication than we are in spiritual addition.

Review and Thought Questions

1. Many have argued that the Great Commission was only for the apostles to whom it was originally given and is not for us today. Name two things in Matthew 28:20 that prove the Great Commission is intended for Christians today. _____

_____

_____

2. a) How does Ephesians 1:19-23 express God's power?

_____

_____

   b) What additional fact does Jeremiah 32:17 bring out?

_____

_____

3. a) Why is it important that Jesus is who He said He is, the Son of God?

_____

_____

_____

   b) How would you describe His character?

_____

_____

_____

4. What does it mean to be Christ's ambassador?

_____

_____

_____

5. Why is it critical that we take the news of Jesus Christ to every land?

_____

_____

_____

6. List some reasons that the New Testament church has such a great impact (I Thessalonians 1:5-10)

_____

_____

_____

_____

_____

_____

_____

_____

Questions 3 and 4 can be used to stimulate effective group discussions.

STUDY 2.

WHY? WHEN? WHERE?

Why should we, as Christians, devote ourselves completely to helping to fulfill the Great Commission? There are at least three good reasons. First, Christ has commanded us to do so. Second, men are lost without Christ. And third, men everywhere are hungry for God. Let us consider each of these reasons.

Christ Commanded

First, we must go because Christ has commanded us to go. The athletic coach presents a list of rules and standards to the athletes and says, "These are the things you must do if you expect to be a part of the team." The men subscribe to these rules, or they don't make the squad.

The employer says to the employee, "Here are the rules," and the employee follows these rules, or he loses his job.

In time of battle the commanding officer orders the soldier, "Do this," and he does it, or he is threatened with court-martial and may jeopardize his life and the lives of others. Similarly, our Lord has issued an order — "Go and make disciples —" and no true believer can take our Lord's command lightly.

Through His People

But most Christians have never taken this command of our Lord seriously. We have been playing at church while our world is aflame. We are like men and women who straighten pictures on the walls of a burning building. We are dealing with peripheral issues when it is the hearts of men and women that need to be changed.

The problems in the world that are threatening to engulf humanity can be solved only in Christ. And Jesus Christ has chosen to get His message out through His people, whom He has clearly commanded to go and tell the good news everywhere.

If we take our Lord seriously, we must direct ourselves fully — time, talent and treasure — to the fulfillment of the Great Commission, not out of a sense of legalistic duty, but out of a sense of gratitude and loving debt for what Christ has done for us. If we want to obey Him, He has said, "Go," and that is sufficient reason for going.

Men Are Lost

Second, we must obey our Lord's command because men are lost without Christ. Jesus said, "I am the way, and the truth, and the life; no one comes to the Father, but through Me" (John 14:6).

That may sound narrow, but that is what the Lord Jesus said, and Jesus Christ is God! For many years I have asked

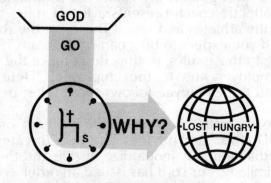

people all over the world if they have found God. Apart from those who have met Christ in a personal, vital encounter, the answer, in general, is, "I am looking for God; I hope to find Him, but I haven't found Him yet!"

No man will ever find God until he receives Christ. "There is salvation in no one else! Under all heaven there is no other name for men to call upon to save them" (Acts 4:12, Living Bible). Do you really believe that men without Christ are lost?

A young man, counseling with the famous evangelist Dwight L. Moody, asked: "Mr. Moody, do you think my parents really believe that I am lost? My father is the Sunday school superintendent of our church, but he has never talked to me about Christ. Do you really think they believe that I am lost?"

Has it occurred to you that some of your family and friends, your neighbors and associates who do not know

Christ are spiritually lost according to the clear teaching of Christ Himself?

As the apostle John records, "And who is the greatest liar? The one who says that Jesus is not Christ. Such a person is anti-Christ for he does not believe in God the Father and in His Son. For a person who doesn't believe in Christ, God's Son, can't have the Father either. If you do you will always be in close fellowship with both God the Father and His Son" (I John 2:22-24, Living Bible).

Prepared To Die

An experience that helps to demonstrate that religion does not satisfy and that men are lost without Christ took place when I was speaking to a large group of students from several campuses in southern California. On this occasion, a young Muslim, together with many others, remained after the meeting to receive Christ. After all the others had gone, he approached me saying, "I would like to talk with you in privacy."

We went aside into a little room where we were alone. He said, "I have come from a very devout Muslim family in my country. My father is a man of great influence and wealth; I am here studying cinema, getting my master's degree. I have been looking for God for years, but I have never been able to find Him. Six months ago, when I came to the States, a doctor friend gave me a New Testament, and I have been reading it.

"As I have read it, I have become aware that Jesus is the God whom I am seeking. Tonight, as you spoke, it was as though He knocked at the door of my heart. I would like to ask Him in, but if I do, I must be prepared for many problems.

"I shall have to write to my father and tell him what I have done, and he will disown me. If he disowns me, he will cut off my allowance. If I have no income, I will lose my coveted degree; I will also lose my student visa and will have to go back to my country. In my country there are still devout Muslims who kill other Muslims when they become Christians. If I receive Christ tonight, I must be prepared to die."

Obviously, I did not press him; this was a matter far too serious for human intervention. I could only pray and ask God to complete His work in his heart. You see, God does not call upon you and me to "force" decisions for Christ. We are human instruments through whom the Holy Spirit does his work.

"I Am Ready"

About 30 minutes later, this young Muslim interrupted the silence by saying, "I am ready." Having counted the cost, he was saying in essence, "I am ready to die, if need be, so that I might know that my sins are forgiven, so that I might know that I have eternal life."

Even though this young man had been exposed to religion all of his life, he now understood that men are lost without Christ. We both wept as we knelt together in prayer. What an experience to realize that here was one for whom Christ was so important that he was willing to give his life, if need be, in order to know Him as his Savior.

Some time later, after this man had endured much hardship and persecution at the hands of some of his fellow students from his former religion, I asked him, "Are you sorry that you committed your life to Christ?" He assured me that he was not sorry. His father did disown him; he lost his financial support from his family. He was forced to leave the university and was unable to complete his work for his long-sought degree in cinema.

Though I tried to keep in touch, I regret to say that I lost contact with him. It is my understanding that he returned home to his country and possibly to his death. However, if he did die, he did not die in vain. My own commitment to Christ, as well as that of many others, was made all the stronger by his faith. The Word of God is emphatically clear: "And there is salvation in no one else; for there is no other name under heaven that has been given among men, by which we must be saved" (Acts 4:12).

Men Are Hungry

Third, we must obey our Lord's command to go

because men everywhere are hungry for God. Man's hunger for God has been demonstrated in thousands of ways since the beginning of the ministry of Campus Crusade for Christ. As part of our training program at Arrowhead Springs and elsewhere around the world, we spend several hours each week in actual person-to-person evangelism in the local communities, at the beaches and in public gatherings.

Frequently, hundreds pray and receive Christ in a single afternoon. More than 3,000 blacks in the Watts area of Los Angeles received Christ in a single afternoon through the personal contact of some 1,600 predominantly white staff and students. More than 2,000 received Christ in one day of sharing on the beaches of southern California.

When 10,000 Koreans at a Leadership Training Institute went out to share Christ, more than 16,000 people indicated that they wanted to receive Christ.

Mexico, India

During one three-day Easter holiday, at least 17,000 people heard that they could have a personal relationship with Jesus Christ from 155 nationals in Mexico and 25 Latin American Campus Crusade staff, and 1,245 indicated they had prayed and received Christ.

Campus Crusade staff in India prayed that 5,000 students would receive Christ in a single year, and God answered with more than 5,000 new believers.

During a period of approximately six months four Campus Crusade athletic teams, two singing groups, and Andre Kole, a well-known illusionist, presented the claims of Christ to 351,000 students in 629 appearances. More than 50,000 indicated they had prayed and received Christ as their Savior. Many thousands of additional students and laymen have made commitments to Christ through the ministry of other staff members and thousands whom they have trained.

The average Christian has been conditioned to think negatively about the non-Christian's response to the gospel. This attitude prevails when one seeks to reach students, intellectuals and top executives. Yet, properly approached, many of these leaders respond to the claims of Christ.

Student Leaders

Some time ago, I was afforded a remarkable opportunity to see this demonstrated in a dramatic way as I spoke at a very important student convention, attended by the top leaders of 133 colleges and universities. The student representatives from each campus included the student body president, editor of the newspaper and a few other key students.

A few weeks before the convention, the Vice President of the United States, who was the scheduled speaker, found it necessary to be released from his speaking engagement because of a very important and urgent assignment for the President.

I received a call from the student body president of Stanford University, who was also the program chairman. Would I substitute for the Vice President? Of course, I was honored to do so. But what was I to say, on such short notice, to this select group of student leaders?

I decided to speak to them about the greatest leader the world has ever known. My message was about the person of Jesus Christ — who He is and why He came to this earth. I spoke for 45 minutes. When I finished, there was a standing ovation — not for the speaker, I am convinced, but for Christ, about whom I had spoken. Scores of these students stood in line for almost an hour to express their appreciation, and many of them expressed an interest in knowing Christ personally. Several prayed and received Christ as a result.

One day I began to share Christ with a porter in a hotel where I was staying. He was very discouraged. "Porters aren't very important," he said. "Everyone looks down on porters." I put my arm around his shoulders and said, "I want you to know that God loves you and I love you. In His sight you are just as important as the most famous person in the world."

The Holy Spirit had prepared his heart for the "good news," and soon he received Christ as his Savior as we bowed in prayer. All over the world men are hungry for

God because the Spirit of God has created this great hunger in their hearts and souls.

WHEN

When will the Great Commission be fulfilled? The Great Commission is our Lord's idea, and only He in His omniscience knows when and how it will be fulfilled. However, since He gave us the command, and has promised to equip us to do His will, we must assume that He means for us to fulfill the Great Commission in each generation.

When the apostle Paul wrote to the church in Thessalonica, he said, "For the Word of the Lord has sounded forth from you, not only in Macedonia and Achaia, but also in every place your faith toward God has gone forth, so that we have no need to say anything" (I Thessalonians 1:8).

Paul seems to be saying that wherever he went throughout Macedonia and Achaia, he found that the gospel and the testimony of the Thessalonians had preceded him. In other words, widespread evangelization had occurred to such an extent that Paul himself apparently could find no one who had not already heard the gospel message in this area.

Luke wrote of Paul's preaching in Ephesus: "And this took place for two years, so that all who lived in Asia (a province in Asia Minor) heard the word of the Lord, both Jews and Greeks" (Acts 19:10). This verse does not necessarily mean that *every single person* in Asia Minor had been personally confronted with the gospel through Paul's witness. However, it does seem to indicate that the area was evangelized in an overall sense.

Therefore, in light of God's inspired Word, we may set forth a definition of the initial fulfillment of the Great Commission. It is the preaching of the gospel to such an extent that the percentage of those *who are known* to have heard it will be sufficiently great as to suggest that the rest of the nation has also heard the message, in one way or another.

However, the widespread proclamation of the gospel is only the beginning; we must not stop there. We must go on with the objective of giving as many people as possible an opportunity to receive Christ in a person-to-person encounter with the gospel, and then seek to include them in the local church where they will be taught and encouraged to mature in their Christian lives.

WHERE

Where must we go to fulfill the Great Commission? We must go to the whole world. However, Jesus Himself gave us a strategy to follow. Just before He ascended into heaven, He told the disciples, "But you shall receive power when the Holy Spirit has come upon you; and you shall be My witnesses both in Jerusalem, and in all Judea and Samaria, and even to the remotest part of the earth" (Acts 1:8).

Begin to share Christ as a way of life in your Jerusalem — your home, your neighborhood, your campus or class-

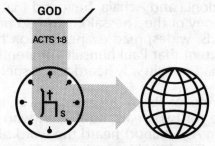

room, your office, or your factory. Seek ways to present Christ in your community, your state, your nation, which is your Judea, and to help spread His good news to the entire world through your prayers, your financial investments and your personal involvement.

Review and Thought Questions

1. Why should we care about telling others of Christ?

_____

_____

_____

2. a) What does John 14:6 say?

_____

_____

   b) Why is this important?

_____

_____

_____

3. a) What sacrifice was the rich young ruler unwilling to make in Luke 18:18-23?

_____

_____

   b) What do you think were some of the consequences of his decision?

_____

_____

4. a) Why is it that some people respond eagerly when presented with the claims of Christ and others don't?

_____

_____

   b) How would you respond to someone in the latter category?

_____

_____

5. a) What does the word "witness" mean to you?

_____

_____

   b) How is it used in the Bible?

   Proverbs 14:5 _____

_____

   Isaiah 55:1-7 _____

_____

   Acts 20:17-23 _____

_____

6. How would you describe Jerusalem, Judea and Samaria
   in relation to your world today (cf. Acts 1:8)?

_____

_____

_____

7. What is involved in the fulfillment of the Great Commission? Explain the role of both evangelism and
   discipleship in its fulfillment.

_____

_____

_____

_____

_____

_____

_____

_____

Discussion questions: 4, 5a, 6, 7.

STUDY 3.

HOW?

For most people, the big question is *how* is the Great Commission to be fulfilled and *how* can I help?

Perhaps you are thinking, "I am convinced that men are lost without Christ and that multitudes are ready to receive Him. I want to obey our Lord Jesus Christ by helping to fulfill the Great Commission, but what does God want me to do? How do I begin?"

This great task can be accomplished only as millions of Christians develop a personal strategy that ties in directly to the global strategy of our Lord. Let me illustrate by giving you our overall strategy in Campus Crusade for Christ.

More than 30 years ago, God gave to this ministry a vision and a strategy — a strategy that has been implemented through the years — for helping to fulfill our Lord's command.

In the United States, there are more than 3,000 campuses representing over 13 million students. In addition, there are some 25,000 high schools with more than 22 million students. These students represent a major source of manpower to help reverse the decadent tide in our nation and help change the world. They need to be reached for Christ *now*.

It is the goal of Campus Crusade for Christ International, working together with other Christian organizations and local churches dedicated to these same goals, to help train key Christian leaders — to work full time or as volunteers on each of these high school and college campuses — organizing meetings and making personal contacts — taking the gospel to as many students as possible and discipling those who respond. Already, on hundreds of campuses, tens of thousands of students are hearing the gospel and responding.

Our ministry to lay people is a direct outgrowth of the Campus Ministry. As God continued to do a mighty work in the the lives of thousands on many college campuses, laymen began to ask, "How do you account for the miraculous results of the ministry of Campus Crusade among students? Can't you give us the same kind of training you give your staff and students?"

Thus, in 1959 I began to speak at many day-long Lay Institutes for Evangelism in various cities throughout the nation. Shortly after that, the Lay Ministry (now called Here's Life, America) was born, and it has since produced some remarkable results.

The day-long institutes soon became week-long and spread city- and state-wide, encompassing hundreds of churches and thousands of lay people. In Seattle, Wash., alone, hundreds of churches sent a total of 4,200 delegates to receive training in how they could experience and share the abundant life in Christ.

Arm Of The Church

Since its inception, Campus Crusade has served as an arm of the local church, helping to encourage, motivate and train Christians to reach out to others with the timeless message of God's love and forgiveness.

In 1972, EXPLO '72 drew 80,000 students and lay people to Dallas, Texas, for training in evangelism and discipleship. Two years later, at EXPLO '74 in Seoul, Korea, similar training was given to 323,000 delegates from 78 countries. According to officials, as many as 1.5 million people attended one evening rally.

In 1976, we sought to motivate Christians to believe God for further miracles during Here's Life America — a movement to help reach the United States and Canada with the gospel. As a result, some 325,000 Christians from 15,000 churches of many denominations worked side by side to help saturate their communities for Christ. Now as part of Here's Life, World many thousands of trained Christians overseas are helping to reach their cities, towns and tribes with the claims of Christ. As we work with churches, Christian organizations and mission groups throughout the world, our goal is to help introduce one billion people to Christ by the end of 1988. Through the ministry of local churches and some 2,500 planned training centers, these Christians will be encouraged to grow spiritually and to share their faith with others.

Other Ministries

To help implement the total saturation of our world with the gospel, numerous other ministries have naturally evolved within Campus Crusade for Christ. For example, the Military Ministry helps to reach millions of service men and women stationed on military installations around the world. The "P.S." (prison) Ministries carries the message of Christ to prisoners, parolees, probationers and their families. Specialized outreaches through music groups, athletic teams, multimedia presentations and a world-famous illusionist point audiences to the person of Christ. The International Ministries helps to win and disciple thousands of the 260,000 international students now studying in the U.S. The Mass Media Ministry, through the means of literature, audiovisuals, films, tapes, radio and television, is helping to proclaim the gospel to additional millions around the world.

To The Whole World

Both in the United States and in most of the major countries of the world, our basic strategy is the same. Through a multiplication movement of *winning* people to

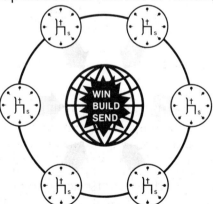

Christ, *building* them in the faith and *sending* them to the world with the good news of God's love and forgiveness, tens of thousands have been introduced to our Lord Jesus Christ.

Winning Individuals

Every conceivable program of winning men and women to Christ is used — personal evangelism; large evangelistic meetings; evangelistic home Bible studies; telephone surveys; literature, films, cassette tapes, radio, television; direct mail; evangelistic coffees, teas, breakfasts, luncheons and banquets; wide-scale literature distribution.

Buiilding In Faith

Our strategy for building men and women in the Christian faith includes getting them involved in the fellowship and instruction offered through the local church, home Bible studies and small discipleship groups. Christians are taught how to walk in the love of Christ and in the power of the Holy Spirit. They learn about God's unconditional love; His total forgiveness and acceptance made possible for us in Christ because of His death on the cross for our sin; and His resurrection power available to us. They also learn how to study His word.

Christian growth is accelerated rapidly as individuals are taught how to share Christ with others and are encouraged to share their faith in Him regularly as a way of life.

Sending Individuals

Sending men and women to the world is the inevitable result of a proper emphasis on winning and building. The individual who rightly understands the love and forgiveness of God and who has been properly instructed to communicate his faith in Christ will not be satisfied to remain a carnal, impotent, fruitless, mediocre Christian. Like the disciples whose nets were miraculously filled with fish, such an individual will "forsake all and follow Christ."

Priority of Prayer

Any successful strategy to help evangelize the world must emphasize the importance of prayer. Millions of faithful prayer disciples are urgently needed to pray daily. We are asking God to raise up millions of Christians to become a part of the Great Commission Prayer Crusade, prayer soldiers who will faithfully intercede daily for a mighty spiritual awakening throughout the entire world.

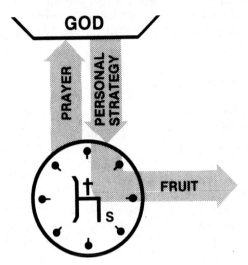

A Personal Strategy

The fulfillment of the Great Commission can be accomplished only as millions of Christians develop a personal strategy that ties in directly to Christ's global strategy. One Christian with a personal strategy, focusing all of his efforts, can magnify and multiply his fruitfulness beyond measure. "But," you may ask, "what is a personal strategy?"

A personal strategy is a deliberate plan of action by an individual to accomplish a specific goal. Since the goal of every sincere believer should be to help fulfill the Great Commission, his personal plan should include evangelizing and discipling — adding and multiplying.

When you personally introduce another to Christ, that is *spiritual addition*. But when you deliberately disciple the new Christian and help him to win, disciple and send others who will do the same to still others, that is *spiritual multiplication!*

Multiplication was the method Jesus Himself used as He concentrated much of His time on teaching the 12 disciples. And the apostle Paul specifically commended this principle to Timothy, his son in the faith: "And the things which you have heard from me in the presence of many witnesses, these entrust to faithful men, who will be able to teach others also" (II Timothy 2:2).

Consider this situation: Suppose you led five people to Christ and began to work with them, teaching them to feed themselves from the Word of God and to share their faith with others. Suppose that within one year those five began to train five others. Now there are 25. In another year, as each of those 25 introduces five others to Christ and begins to build them, the number grows to 125. At that rate, the entire population of our world, theoretically, could be reached in just 14 years!

Of course, things don't always happen in neat one-year segments. But developing a personal strategy enables us to move forward in obedience to our Lord's command and to concentrate our energies on our primary calling of helping to fulfill the Great Commission. Paul emphasizes this:

"No soldier in active service entangles himself in the affairs of everyday life, so that he may please the one who enlisted him as a soldier" (II Timothy 2:4).

Unless we develop a personal strategy, the fulfillment of the Great Commission will remain an unrealized dream.

It all boils down to this easy equation: *GOAL* minus *PLAN* minus *ACTION* equals *DREAM*.

GOAL plus *PLAN* plus *ACTION* equals *REALITY!*

But you may wonder *how* to develop a personal strategy. Let me make some simple, Scriptural suggestions.

Commitment

First, be sure that you are committed to Christ and are filled with the Holy Spirit. Millions of people who are active in the church are not sure they are Christians. I state this on the basis of years of interacting personally with thousands of professing Christians.

There are also thousands of guilt-ridden, carnal

Christians who have become so frustrated and off-course that God cannot use them. In each case, there is a lack of faith or trust in God. Basically, the average Christian does not believe God will do what He promises to do.

You are encouraged in Romans 12:1, 2 ". . . to present your bodies in a living and holy sacrifice, acceptable to God, which is our spiritual service of worship. And do not be conformed to this world, but be transformed by the renewing of your mind, that you may prove what the will of God is, that which is good and acceptable and perfect."

We can trust the loving will of God. I have seen thousands of defeated, impotent, fruitless Christian students, laymen and pastors whose lives have been transformed as a result of presenting themselves to God as a once-and-for-all act of worship.

Contract With God

My wife and I were very materialistic and ambitious before we became Christians. However, the more we studied the Bible and became aware of the love and grace of God, the more we wanted to serve Him. One day we knelt in our home near Hollywood and signed a contract with the Lord, as a formal act of relinquishing the title deeds of our lives to Him.

We each made a list of all the things that we had desired before we received Christ and began to follow Him. We had very luxurious appetites!

"Lord," we prayed, "we want to surrender all of our own plans and desires to You. By Your enabling grace and power we are turning our backs upon the things that have encumbered us in order that we might serve You better. You have commanded us to seek first the kingdom of God. Now we want to seek You and Your way above everything else. We want to serve You and do whatever You want us to do, and go wherever You want us to go, whatever the cost."

Today, Vonette and I own very little of this world's goods — only a few personal items. We don't own our home, which we rent, or even a car, though a friend provides a car for our use. We do not even have a savings account. We literally live from day to day. But, oh what an adventure it is to live for Christ — to serve the King of kings and Lord of lords without the hindrances and encumbrances of the past.

This may not be what God will call you to do. But whatever your situation, you can trust a loving God when you surrender every life ambition to Him. There is no other experience in life that compares with seeking first the kingdom of God, keeping Christ in control of our lives, doing what He calls us to do and being an instrument through whom He changes lives. This is real living — life at its highest and best.

You may be interested to know that a short time after we committed our lives irrevocably to Christ, He gave me the vision for launching the worldwide ministry of Campus Crusade for Christ.

Pray In Faith

Second, pray in faith that God will guide you in developing your personal strategy. Ask God for an effective strategy to reach your immediate area of influence for Christ. You do not have to design your own strategy — simply discover the plan that God has already designed!

Jesus was a perfect example. While on earth He discussed every major decision and turning point in His life with His heavenly Father. And as you pray, expect God to provide both the strategy and the wisdom to implement it. Expectant faith pleases God.

Strategy Outline

Third, outline the strategy God reveals in answer to your prayers. Make lists of specific people with whom you can share Christ. Consider specific groups with which you are involved and develop a strategy to reach each one. Begin with your family. Remember that in your home, more than in any other place, your life will be your testimony. Trust God continually to fill you with His Spirit, so that your actions — the fruit of the Spirit — will bear witness to what Jesus has done in your life.

Plan how you can reach the people with whom you

work. Seek those you know are Christians, and ask them to join you in evangelizing your office. In your church, make yourself available to your pastor. Offer to teach Sunday school and especially to be a part of the visitation/evangelism team. Encourage other members of your church to develop their own strategies.

Invite your neighbors for an evangelistic coffee, tea or dessert, or start a neighborhood evangelistic Bible study. Tell your friends what Christ has done in your life and that He can do the same in theirs.

Way Of Life

Pray for the people to whom you want to talk. Then go to them. Tell them of God's love and forgiveness, available through Jesus Christ. Give them the opportunity to receive Him. Share your faith as a way of life — seek to talk about Christ with everyone you meet. As people trust Him as Lord and Savior, help them to grow in their faith and involve them in the cycle of multiplication.

Invite them to join you in an effort to saturate your entire community with the message of Christ.

Utilize the mass media — radio, television, newspapers and magazines — to reach every person possible with the good news. Prayerfully investigate opportunities to influence people within the communications media for Christ and to encourage Christians to enter public office. Allow Christ to expand your faith as He reveals His strategy to you, remembering that He has a perfect plan which must be followed in order for you to help fulfill the Great Commission in your community.

Training And Materials

Fourth, learn everything you can about how to accomplish your personal strategy in helping to fulfill the Great Commission. Thousands of students, laymen and pastors are taking advantage of the training and materials available through Campus Crusade for Christ to learn how to win men to Christ, build them in the faith and send them to the world with the good news of God's love and forgiveness.

Write to Campus Crusade for Christ, Arrowhead Springs, San Bernardino, CA 92414 to request more specific information on available training. I also encourage you to investigate the training in evangelism and discipleship offered by your church and other Christian organizations.

May I encourage you to write out your own personal strategy today. List people with whom God has impressed you to share Christ. This is spiritual addition. For spiritual multiplication, list people you would like to train to experience and share the abundant life in Christ. Then begin immediately to work out your strategy.

Aggressive Evangelism

Finally — and this is an absolute must— *give your attention to aggressive evangelism.* Take the initiative to help fulfill the Great Commission where you live. Claim your relatives, friends, neighbors and business associates for Christ in prayer. Then present His claims to them. As you implement this personal strategy, think beyond your local goals to the world-wide goal of fulfilling the Great Commission. This will prevent your becoming side-tracked on a time-consuming tangent.

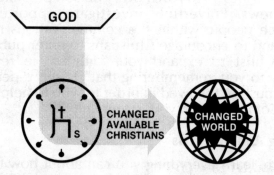

Under the Holy Spirit's guidance, you can proceed with complete confidence to plan your work and work your plan. Every Christian, whether a student, homemaker, businessman, pastor or missionary, needs a personal strategy to help reach his community or area of influence.

In this changing and chaotic period of history, sincere,

thinking Christians dare not be satisfied with the status quo, or business as usual. Whoever you are, wherever you are, if you are available, God will use you to help change this world!

Communist Growth

In 1903 Lenin started communism with 17 people. In 1917 he took over Russia with only 40,000 followers. Today communists control more than one-third of the world's population and have greatly influenced and infiltrated most of the rest of the world. Why are they taking the world? Because of their dedication. For example, a young communist who broke his engagement wrote this letter to his fiancee explaining his decision:

"We communists have a high casualty rate. We are the ones who get shot and hung and ridiculed and fired from our jobs and in every other way made as uncomfortable as possible . . . We live in poverty. We turn back to the party every penny we make above what is absolutely necessary to keep us alive. We have been described as fanatics; we are fanatics.

"Our lives are dominated by one great overshadowing factor: the struggle for world communism . . . it is my life, my business, my religion, my hobby, my sweetheart, my wife and my mistress, my bread and my meat. I work at it in the daytime and dream of it at night . . . Therefore, I cannot carry on a friendship, a love affair or even a conversation without relating it to this force which both guides and drives my life . . . I've already been in jail because of my convictions, and if necessary, I'm ready to go before the firing squad!"

Dedication Of Disciples

Such was the dedication of the disciples and other first-century Christians. Such has been the dedication of every servant of God who has made any significant impact for Christ and His kingdom. We must not merely match that commitment — we must exceed it. God is looking for disciplined soliders of the cross, completely committed Christians through whom He can accomplish mighty exploits for His kingdom.

Dr. James Stewart, one of the most famous New Testament scholars of our time, said, "If we could but show the world that being committed to Christ is no tame, humdrum, sheltered monotony, but the most exciting, thrilling adventure the human spirit can ever know, those who have been standing outside the church and looking askance at Christ will come crowding in to pay allegiance; and we might well expect the greatest revival since Pentecost."

I believe that. I believe that millions of Christians are awakening to the fact that we must be about our Father's business. As I observe God's working in the lives of men and movements around the world, I am convinced that the greatest spiritual awakening since Pentecost has already begun.

Like the apostle Paul, many are telling others about Christ. Many are following his example when he said, "Everywhere we go we talk about Christ to all who will listen, warning them and teaching them as well as we know how. We want to be able to present each one to God, perfect because of what Christ has done for each of them" (Colossians 1:28, Living Bible).

Real Significance

Some time ago, I was visiting Rome. One evening as I sat in the Roman Forum, I saw and heard portrayed, through the medium of light and sound, the drama of ancient Rome. For almost a thousand years, Rome ruled the world. Into that Forum had come the conquering generals to be honored for their conquests and to receive their laurels.

Into the Forum had come the heads of various countries that made up that great Empire. Here the senators met to legislate the laws that governed Rome. In that Forum, Julius Caesar had been assassinated. Here was a place that vibrated with history and drama. I was enthralled as I sat there.

Earlier that afternoon, I had visited a dungeon cell across the street from the Forum, where it is believed that the apostle Paul had spent the last few months of his life. Had I been living in those days, and had I visited Paul in the dungeon cell, it is not likely that I would have been as impressed with this "bond slave of Christ" as I would have been with many of the leaders of Rome.

Paul probably was neither a commanding figure nor an eloquent speaker, according to his own admission; but here was a man with a brilliant mind, a flaming heart and an anointed pen — a man who had linked his life with the risen Christ. He was a man chosen and anointed of God. He shared Christ's vision and burden for the world, and he was committed to the fulfillment of the Great Commission in obedience to Christ's command.

What God did in that dungeon cell had far more significance than the activities within the Roman Forum. God took that life that was yielded to Him and used it to help change the course of history. Today we are Christians, worshipping Jesus Christ, largely because of what God did through the apostle Paul.

Call To Discipleship

Just as God used Paul and millions of others like him through the centuries, so He is looking for men and women in our time through whom He can accomplish mighty exploits for His kingdom.

Jesus said, "Go ... and make disciples in all the nations." In order to make disciples, we must be disciples ourselves. Like begets like. We produce after our kind. The man who is committed to Christ and understands how to walk in the fullness of the Spirit will influence and help produce the same kind of Christians.

Jesus said, "If anyone wishes to come after Me, let him deny himself, and take up his cross daily and follow Me" (Luke 9:23). Jesus also said, "Anyone who wants to be My follower must love Me far more than he does his own father, mother, wife, children, brothers, sisters — yes, more than his own life — otherwise he cannot be My disciple" (Luke 14:26, Living Bible).

For some, such a call to discipleship may sound too hard. Perhaps this thought was in Peter's mind when he told the Lord, "We have left everything and followed

You." Jesus said, "Truly I say to you, there is no one who has left house or brothers or sisters or mother or father or children or farms for My sake and for the gospel's sake, but that he shall receive a hundred times as much now in the present age, houses and brothers and sisters and mothers and children and farms, along with persecutions; and in the world to come, eternal life" (Mark 10:28-30).

The fulfillment of this promise in the lives of all who seek first Christ and His kingdom has been attested to times without number — not always in material things, of course, but in rewards far more meaningful and enriching.

Christ First

I shall never forget the concern of my wife, Vonette, when I explained to her at the time of my proposal that I loved Jesus Christ more than I loved her and that He would always have first place in my life and in our home.

Though she did not understand such a "fanatical" attitude on my part at that time, she later surrendered her life to Christ and now says with me, "Christ is first in my life."

It is because of our individual commitments to and love for Him that we love each other and consider each other all the more. Truly Christ has enriched our individual lives and our ministry far beyond anything we could ever have dared to dream. We say with the famous missionary statesman, C. T. Studd, "If Christ be God and died for me, there is nothing too great that I can do for Him."

Significant Movement

You and I have the privilege of being part of the most significant movement of all the centuries, the movement to help fulfill the Great Commission of our Lord in this generation. I invite you to join with millions of other Christians who are putting aside their personal ambitions, their selfish desires, their own pleasures, and are saying with the apostle Paul, "I am a slave of Jesus Christ" (Romans 1:1).

I will give my attention, my time, my talents, my treasure to Him for the fulfillment of the Great Commission. From the time I awaken in the morning until I go to bed at night, I want to be a part of His great strategy for the world.

Will you surrender your life totally and unreservedly to Christ and make yourself available to help fulfill the Great Commission in this generation? It may mean sacrifice. For some it may mean death — martyrdom — but can you think of a greater leader to follow than the Lord Jesus Christ? Is there a greater cause than His to which you can give yourself? Do you, as an expression of your love and gratitude to Chirst for you and as an act of obedience to His command, want to help fulfill the Great Commission in this generation?

The Commitment

If it is your desire to commit yourself to help fulfill His command, make the following prayer your prayer: "Dear Father in heaven, I stand at attention. I make myself available to You to do with as You wish. I want to be a man (woman) of God through whom You can bring Your message of love and forgiveness in Christ to all people everywhere.

"I invite You to cleanse me, to empower me, to lead me, to inspire me, to teach me, to cause me to do that which will bring the greatest honor and glory to Your name. Enable me by Your Holy Spirit to contribute my maximum to the fulfillment of the Great Commission in my time. I ask this in the wonderful name of the Lord Jesus, Amen."

If you have prayed that prayer, you have indicated your commitment to Jesus Christ. Through the investment of your time, your talent and your treasure, you can help fulfill the Great Commission of our Lord in this generation. Remember, through the power of the indwelling Christ, you can help to change the world.

Review and Thought Questions

1. How would you explain the "abundant life in Christ?

_____

_____

_____

2. What place does prayer have in the fulfillment of the Great Commission?

_____

_____

_____

3. a) What personal strategy of evangelism did Paul exhibit in Acts 13 and 14?

_____

_____

   b) What additional strategy did he employ in Acts 18:1-11?

_____

_____

   c) What personal strategy do you (or will you) use?

_____

_____

4. What are the essential ingredients of a personal strategy?

_____

_____

_____

_____

5. How does II Peter 1:3-8 amplify (or explain) the multiplication principle?

_____

_____

_____

6. List five people you would like to train (disciple) to share the gospel, or one person you can ask to disciple you.

_____

_____

_____

7. What commitment will you make regarding your answer to Question #6?

_____

_____

_____

8. How would you define "aggressive evangelism"?

_____

_____

_____

9. How would you describe Peter's commitment to the Lord in Mark 14:29-52? _____

_____

and in Acts 4:5-31? _____

_____

What changed him?

_____

_____

Would you describe yourself as "on fire" for the Lord? Why or why not?

_____

_____

_____

10. What personal commitment(s) have you made to God?

_____

_____

_____

11. How will you begin to fulfill these commitments?

_____

_____

_____

_____

_____

_____

Discussion questions: 1, 8, 9 (last part), 10, 11.

CHAPTER STUDY GUIDE

1. The application of the principles outlined in this Concept will enable you to have a vital part in helping to fulfill the Great Commission in this generation.

2. Memorize the Great Commission as given in Matthew's Gospel:

Matthew 28:18-20: "And Jesus came up and spoke to them, saying, 'All authority has been given to Me in heaven and on earth. Go therefore and make disciples of all the nations, baptizing them in the name of the Father and the Son and the Holy Spirit, teaching them to observe all that I commanded you; and lo, I am with you always, even to the end of the age.' "

3. Make this Concept, "How to Help Fulfill the Great Commission," a way of life by practicing the following:

a. The Great Commission can never be fulfilled apart from the ministry of the Holy Spirit, apart from planning, or apart from hard work. Choose a particular day, and set aside several hours for prayer and planning. Find a quiet place to be alone with the Lord. Spend a prolonged time in prayer with God. Ask Him to lead and direct you concerning the investment of yourself — your time, talent and treasure — in helping to fulfill the Great Commission.

Then, with a pencil and paper, begin to make tentative plans for what you feel God would have you do. Your plans may relate to your neighborhood, to your place of work, to your local church and community, to your state or nation, or to the entire world. Let the Lord lead you. This planning will just be a start. You will revise your plans many times, but you need to get started.

b. Begin to put your plans into operation. This may involve talking to certain people about Christ. It may involve recruiting other people to help you accomplish your particular goals and plans. As you implement your plans, you will find that some of your ideas will work and some won't. Don't be afraid to try and to fail. You will learn from your mistakes.

Learn to eliminate the things that don't work and to continue to use the things that do work. Remember that the more people you can train and involve in the fulfillment of the Great Commission, the more you have multiplied your own efforts. Multiplication is the key. .

c. Plan to obtain further personal training that you should have in order to be better equipped to fulfill your plans. Training enables you to learn from the experiences of others. Training should be a lifetime process.

AMPLIFIED OUTLINE

Study 1.

The Great Commission of the Lord is the greatest *plan* ever given to men, by the greatest *person* who ever lived, concerning the greatest *power* ever revealed and with the greatest *promise* ever recorded.

I. Who gave the Great Commission and to whom was it given?
  A. Only Christ could say, "I have been given all authority in heaven and earth."
    1. He is the unique Son of God.
    2. He died on the cross and was raised from the dead to save men from sin and to give eternal life to all who receive Him.
    3. He has caused more changes for good than anyone else in the entire history of mankind.
    4. He changes men and nations.
    5. "In Christ there is all of God in a human body; so you have everything when you have Christ, and you are filled with God through your union with Christ. He is the highest ruler with authority over every other power" (Colossians 2:9, 10).
  B. The Great Commission was given to the disciples and to every Christian.

1. Through the power of the Holy Spirit the disciples went out boldly, at the cost of their lives, to proclaim the message of God's love and forgiveness through Christ, resulting in a changed world.

2. We, too, need to have confidence in our resurrected Lord, to be filled with the Holy Spirit and to be available to help turn our world upside down for Christ.

II. What is the Great Commission?

A. It involves making disciples in all nations (Matthew 28:19) so that they in turn can saturate their nations with the good news and can train other disciples.

B. It is a command to seek to make a prayerful, intelligent presentation of the gospel to every living person.

1. Some will not hear, or if they hear, will not comprehend.

2. Also, though not all who hear will become Christians, many will respond, some after only one presentation (Colossians 1:6).

Study 2.

III. Why should we devote ourselves completely to helping to fulfill the Great Commission?

A. Because Christ has commanded us to go and make disciples (Matthew 28:19).

B. Because men are lost without Christ (John 14:6).

C. Because the Holy Spirit has created a hunger for God in the hearts of people everywhere, as evidenced by the many who respond when the gospel is shared in the power of the Holy Spirit.

IV. When will the Great Commission be fulfilled?

A. Since God has given the command and has equipped us to do His will, we must assume He wants it fulfilled in our generation and in every generation.

B. The initial fulfillment of the Great Commission is the preaching of the gospel to such an extent that the percentage of those who are known to have heard it will be sufficiently great as to suggest that the rest of the nation has already heard the message, in one way or another.

V. Where must we go to help fulfill the Great Commission?

A. We must go to the whole world.

B. We must follow Christ's strategy and begin in our own Jerusalem (Acts 1:8).

Study 3.

VI. How is the Great Commission to be fulfilled?

A. More than 30 years ago, God gave to Campus Crusade a vision for helping to fulfill the Great Commission, which includes a strategy:

1. To help reach the more than 3,000 college campuses with more than 13 million students.

2. To help reach the 22 million students in 25,000 high schools.

3. To work with laymen, pastors and churches in both metropolitan and rural areas of each of the 50 states.

4. To work with military personnel in the United States and abroad.

5. To use special evangelistic teams and to help win and disciple internationals now studying in the United States.

6. To use literature, films, tapes, radio and television to win and disciple additional millions.

7. To extend a similar strategy to each of the 210 nations and protectorates in the world and thereby:

a. Win men and women to Christ.

b. Build them in the faith.

c. Send them to help win and disciple others.

8. To emphasize the importance of prayer.

B. You can have a personal strategy to use your time, talent and treasure to help fulfill the Great Commission.

   1. A personal strategy is a deliberate plan of action by an individual to help fulfill the Great Commission.

   2. When you personally introduce another to Christ, that is spiritual addition.

   3. When you deliberately disciple the new Christian and help him to win, disciple and send others, who will win and disciple still others, that is spiritual multiplication.

C. Use these spiritual suggestions for developing your personal strategy.

   1. Be sure you are committed to Christ and are filled with the Holy Spirit (Romans 12:1, 2).

   2. Pray, in faith, that God will guide you in developing your personal strategy.

   3. Outline the strategy God reveals in answer to your prayers.

   4. Learn everything you can about how to accomplish your personal strategy.

   5. Give your attention to aggressive evangelism.

   6. Embark on a continuous course of training in Christian growth and witnessing as a way of life.

CHAPTER 8

HOW TO LOVE BY FAITH

Study 1. God Loves Us
Study 2. Command To Love
    Our Inability To Love
Study 3. We Love With God's Love
    We Love By Faith

STUDY 1.

The beautiful ballroom of the Marriott Motel in Chicago was crowded to capacity with more than 1,300 college students and Campus Crusade staff. They seemed to hang onto every word as I explained one of the most exciting spiritual discoveries I have ever made: how to love by faith.

For years I had spoken on the subject of love. I had a beautiful four-point outline:

First, God loves us unconditionally.

Second, we are commanded to love others — God, our neighbors, our enemies.

Third, we are incapable of loving others in our own strength.

Fourth, we can love others with God's love.

But, as in the case of most sermons on love, something was missing. Then some years ago in an early hour of the morning, I was awakened from a deep sleep. I knew that God had something to say to me. I felt impressed to get up, open my Bible and kneel to read and pray.

What I discovered during the next two hours has since enriched my life and the lives of tens of thousands of others. I learned *how* to love. With this discovery, God gave me the command to share this wonderful truth with Christians around the world. In that life-changing time of fellowship with the Lord I was given a fifth point for my sermon on love: *We love by faith.*

Greatest Thing In The World

Love is the greatest thing in the world — the greatest

privilege and power known to man. Its emphasis in life and word changed the course of history as the first-century Christians demonstrated a quality of life never before witnessed on this earth. The Greeks, Romans and Jews hated one another. The very idea of love and self-sacrifice was foreign to their thinking. When they observed that Christians from many nations, with different languages and cultures, actually loved one another and sacrificed to help each other they responded in amazement, "Behold how these people love one another!"

I challenged the students at the Marriott to become a part of a 20th-century revolution of love. I suggested that they make a list of all the individuals they did not like and begin to love them by faith.

Early the next morning, a young woman with sparkling eyes and face aglow said to me, "My life was changed last night. For many years I have hated my parents. I haven't seen them since I was 17, and now I am 22. I left home as a result of a quarrel five years ago and haven't written or talked to them since, though they have tried repeatedly to encourage me to return home. I determined that I would never see them again. I hated them.

"Before becoming a Christian a few months ago, I had become a drug addict, a dope pusher and a prostitute. Last night you told me how to love my parents and I could hardly wait to get out of that meeting to call them. Can you believe it? I now really love them with God's love and can hardly wait to see them."

Everybody wants to be loved. Most psychologists agree that man's greatest need is to love and be loved. There is no barrier that cannot be dissolved with the mighty force of love — God's love. "Love never fails!" (I Corinthians 3:8).

Eros, Phileo, Agape

There are three Greek words translated into the one English word "love." *Eros* is a word which suggests sensual desire; it does not appear in the New Testament. *Phileo* is used for friendship, or love for one's friends or relatives, and conveys a sense of loving someone because he is worthy of our love. *Agape* is God's love — the purest, deepest kind of love — expressed not through mere emotions but as an act of one's will.

It is God's supernatural love for us revealed supremely through our Lord's death on the cross for our sins. It is the supernatural love He wants to produce in us, and through us to others by His Holy Spirit. *Agape* love is given because of the character of the person loving, rather than because of the worthiness of the object of that love. Sometimes it is referred to as love "in spite of" rather than "because of."

A New Commandment

The Lord Jesus gave to His disciples — and through them to us and to all believers — a new commandment: "Love each other just as much as I love you" (John 13:34, Living Bible). What kind of love? It was and is the very

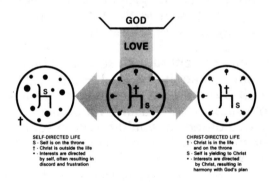

same love which God the Father expresses for His only begotten Son, the Lord Jesus.

It is the very same love which the Son demonstrated on the cross by dying for our sins. It is this same divine, supernatural, unconditional, everlasting, unchangeable love which God has now made available to us with the command that we are to love one another.

This promised love was given to the disciples on the day of Pentecost with the outpouring of the Holy Spirit. As a result, they were not only able to love each other as Christ's disciples, but they could also love their enemies, the very ones who crucified our Lord.

This same divine love — *agape* is available to us. It is

not merely an emotional experience, but it is a divine, supernatural power originating with the Father and coming from Him to the Son, to the disciples, to us and to the world.

Importance Of Love

God underscores the importance of this kind of love through the inspired pen of the apostle Paul, as recorded in I Corinthians 13. In this beautiful and remarkable passage of Scripture, we are reminded that, apart from love, anything that we might do for God or man is of no value.

Consider these words, "If I had the gift of being able to speak in other languages without learning them, and could speak in every language there is in all of heaven and earth, but didn't love others, I would only be making noise. If I had the gift of prophecy and knew all about what is going to happen in the future, knew everything about everything, but didn't love others, what good would it do?"

"Even if I had the gift of faith so that I could speak to a mountain and make it move, I would still be worth nothing at all without love. If I gave everything I have to poor people, and if I burned alive for preaching the gospel but didn't love others, it would be of no value whatever" (I Corinthians 13:13, Living Bible). In other words, no matter what we do for God and for others, it is of no value unless we are motivated by God's love — for God and for others.

But what is this *agape*? How does this kind of supernatural love express itself?

Love Is . . .

In this chapter, Paul continues by describing *agape*: "Love is very patient and kind, never jealous or envious, never boastful or proud, never haughty or selfish or rude. Love does not demand its own way. It is not irritable or touchy. It does not hold grudges and will hardly even notice when others do it wrong. It is never glad about injustice but rejoices whenever truth wins out."

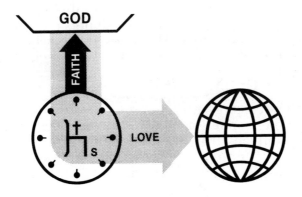

If you love someone you will be loyal to him no matter what the cost. You will always believe in him, always expect the best of him, and always stand your ground in defending him. All the special gifts and powers from God will someday come to an end, but love goes on forever . . . There are three things that remain — faith, hope and love — that keep on forever; and the greatest of these is love" (I Corinthians 13:4-13).

In the next chapter, the apostle Paul, inspired by the Holy Spirit admonishes us, "Let love be your greatest aim" (I Corinthians 14:1, Living Bible).

Every person needs to know five things about love.

GOD LOVES US

First, God loves us. He loves us with *agape* love — the love described in I Corinthians 13. He loves us so much that He sent His Son to die on the cross for us, that we might have everlasting life (John 3:16). His love is not based on performance. Christ loves us so much that, while we were yet sinners, He died for us (Romans 5:8). His love for us is unconditional and undeserved.

God loves us in spite of our disobedience, our weakness, our sin and our selfishness. He loves us enough to provide a way to abundant, eternal life. The cross clearly demonstrates the highest expression of unconditional love. From the cross Christ cried out, "Father, forgive them for they know not what they are doing" (Luke 23:24). If God loved those who are sinners that much, can you imagine how much He loves those who are His children through faith in Christ and who seek to please Him?

Love Awaits

The parable of the prodigal son, as recorded in Luke 15, illustrates God's love for His children. A man had two sons. The younger one asked his father for his share of the estate, packed his belongings and took a trip to a distant land, where he wasted all of his money on parties and prostitutes.

About the time that his money was gone, a great famine swept over the land and he began to starve. He finally came to his senses and realized that his father's hired men at least had food to eat. He said, "I will go to my father and say, 'Father, I have sinned against you and against heaven and am no longer worthy of being called your son. Please take me on as a hired man.' "

He decided to return to his home. While he was still a long distance away, his father saw him coming and was filled with loving pity. He ran to his son, embraced him and kissed him. I believe that the reason the father saw his son coming while he was still a long distance away was that he was praying for his son's return and spent much time each day watching that lonely road on which his son would return.

Even as the son was making his confession, the father interrupted to instruct the servants to kill the fatted calf and prepare for a celebration — his lost son had repented, he had changed his mind and had returned to become a part of the family again.

God demonstrated His love for us before we were Christians, but this story makes it obvious that God continues to love His child who has strayed far from Him. He eagerly awaits his return to the Christian family and fellowship. Even when we are disobedient, He continues to love us, waiting for us to respond to His love and forgiveness. As Paul reminds us in Romans 5:9, 10:

"And since by His blood He did all this for us as sinners, how much more will He do for us now that He has declared us not guilty? Now He will save us from all of God's wrath to come. And since, when we were His enemies, we were brought back to God by the death of His Son, what blessings He must have for us now that we are His friends, and He is living within us!" (Living Bible).

More Than Enough

The story is told of a modern-day prodigal son who had quarreled with his parents and had left home in anger. After leading a life of partying and sin, he finally boarded a train and headed for home. As the train neared his farm, he related to the man seated next to him that he had written a letter to his parents, asking their forgiveness and begging that they take him back. If they wanted him back, they were to tie a white rag to the old elm tree in the back yard.

"I can't look," he said to his seat partner. "You look for me. I'm afraid." As they rounded the bend, his neighbor peered out the window and exclaimed, "Look! There's not only one rag — there are hundreds! Every branch is covered!" If human parents love this way, do you think God loves any less?

The love that God has for us is more than enough! No Christian, even though he has sinned, ever need fear that God has ceased to love him. In John 17:21, 23, Jesus prays to the Father, "My prayer for all of them (the disciples and believers of all ages) is that they will be of one heart and mind, just as You and I are, Father . . . I in them and You in Me. All being perfected into one — so that the world will know You sent Me and will understand that You love them as much as You love Me" (Living Bible).

Love Disciplines

This is a staggering, overwhelming truth that is almost impossible to comprehend. We need have no fear of someone who loves us perfectly (I John 4:16-19). We need never be reluctant to trust God with our entire lives, for He truly loves us. And the almost unbelievable part of it is that He loves us even when we are disobedient.

Even on the human level, loving parents recognize the reasonableness of such love. I find that I love my sons as much when they are disobedient as I do when they are good, though for their sakes, because I do love them, I sometimes find it necessary to correct them. So it is in our relationship with God. When we are disobedient He chastens or corrects us because He loves us.

Chastening should not be confused with wrath or punishment. The Bible says that "those whom the Lord loves He disciplines (chastens), and He scourges every son whom He receives. It is for discipline that you endure; God deals with you as with sons; for what son is there whom his father does not discipline?

"But if you are without discipline, of which all have become partakers, then you are illegitimate children and not sons. Furthermore, we had earthly fathers to discipline us, and we respected them; shall we not much rather be subject to the Father of spirits, and live?

"For they disciplined us for a short time as seemed best to them, but He disciplines us for our good, that we may share His holiness. All discipline for the moment seems not to be joyful, but sorrowful; yet to those who have been trained by it, afterwards it yields the peaceful fruit of righteousness" (Hebrews 12:6-11).

God is merely "child-training" us. He is not paying us back for the sins that we have committed.

Furthermore, God never chastens us as punishment for sins. Christ's death on the cross has once and for all satisfied the wrath and justice of God for the believer's sin. God chastens and disciplines us to help us grow and mature spiritually.

Such chastening is likely to be a grievous experience, but it can be avoided by confessing our sins. According to I Corinthians 11:32, "But when we are judged, we are disciplined by the Lord in order that we may not be condemned along with the world."

God's Love Is Constant

The early Christians endured persecution, hardships and unbelievable suffering. Yet Paul wrote to them, "Who then can ever keep Christ's love from us? When we have trouble or calamity, when we are hunted down or destroyed, is it because He doesn't love us anymore? And if we are hungry, or penniless, or in danger, or threatened with death, has God deserted us?"

No, for the Scriptures tell us that for His sake we must be ready to face death at every moment of the day — we are like sheep awaiting slaughter, but despite all this, overwhelming victory is ours through Christ who loved us enough to die for us.

For I am convinced that nothing can ever separate us from His love. Death can't, and life can't. The angels won't, and all the powers of hell itself cannot keep God's love away. Our fears for today, our worries about tomorrow, or where we are — high above the sky, or in the deepest ocean — nothing will ever be able to separate us from the love of God demonstrated by our Lord Jesus Christ when He died for us" (Romans 8:35-39, Living Bible). Such love is beyond our ability to grasp with our minds, but it is not beyond our ability to experience with our hearts.

Aware of something of the magnitude and significance of God's love, the angel reassured the frightened shepherds on the night of our Lord's birth with these words, "Don't be afraid! I bring you the most joyful news ever announced, and it is for everyone! The Savior — yes, the Messiah, the Lord — has been born tonight in Bethlehem" (Luke 2:10, 11, Living Bible).

Review and Thought Questions

1. a) What is unconditional love?

   _____

   _____

   b) How do you show love to others?

   _____

   _____

2. How would you obey the command of John 13:34?

   _____

   _____

   _____

3. List the qualities of love given in I Corinthians 13. State
   briefly what each means to you.

   _____

   _____

   _____

   _____

4. What things do you need to know about God's love?

   _____

   _____

   _____

5. What place do you feel discipline has in love? Why?

   _____

   _____

   _____

   _____

6. What does Romans 8:35-39 tell us about God's love?

_____

_____

_____

7. How could you express love in the following situations?

at home _____

_____

at school _____

_____

at work _____

_____

at church _____

_____

at a sporting event _____

_____

8. How would you explain the difference between *eros, phileo* and *agape love?*

_____

_____

_____

_____

_____

_____

_____

_____

Questions 1, 3, 5 and 7 can be used to stimulate effective group discussions.

STUDY 2.

COMMAND TO LOVE

Second, we are commanded to love.

A certain lawyer asked Jesus, "Sir, which is the most important command in the law of Moses?" Jesus replied, " 'You shall love the Lord your God with all your heart, soul and mind.' This is the first and greatest commandment. The

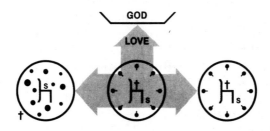

second most important is similar: 'Love your neighbor as much as you love yourself.' All the other commandments and all the demands of the prophets stem from these two laws and are fulfilled if you obey them. Keep only these and you will find that you are obeying all the others" (Matthew 22:36-40, Living Bible).

Why Love God

The question may come to your mind, *why does God want our love?* Isn't this selfish? God in His sovereignty and love has so created man that he finds his greatest joy and fulfillment when he loves God with all his heart and soul and mind and loves his neighbor as himself.

There was a time early in my Christian life when I was troubled over the command to love God so completely. How could I ever measure up to such a high standard? Two very important considerations have helped me to desire to love and please Him completely.

First, the Holy Spirit has filled my heart with God's love, as promised in Romans 5:5. "For we know how dearly God loves us, and we feel this warm love everywhere within us because God has given us the Holy Spirit to fill our hearts with His love" (Living Bible).

Second, by meditating on the wonderful things God has done and is doing for me, I find my love for Him growing. I love Him because He first loved me (I John 4:19).

How could God love me so much that he was willing to die for me (Romans 5:8)? Why should God choose me to be His child, as is stated in John 15:16? By what merit do I deserve to be His ambassador to tell this good news of His love and forgiveness to the world? On what basis do I deserve the privilege of His constant presence and His indwelling Spirit, and of His promise to supply all of my needs according to His riches in glory?

Why should I have the privilege — denied to most of the people of the world who do not know our Savior — of awaking each morning with a song in my heart and praise to Him on my lips for the love, joy and peace that He so generously gives to all who place their trust in His dear Son, the Lord Jesus?

Loving God First

I was a new Christian when I proposed to Vonette, who is now my wife. She had been an active church member, though I discovered later that she was not a Christian at that time. Imagine her distress when, in my new zeal for Christ, I explained to her that I loved God more than I loved her and that He would always be first in my life.

I failed to explain, nor did I even realize at the time, that it was exactly because of my love for God that I was able to love her so much. Later, before we were married, she too experienced God's love and forgiveness and became His child.

Through the years He has become first in her life also, and because He is now first in each of our lives, we enjoy a love relationship that we otherwise could not know. Though my responsibilities in His service take me to many parts of the world and I have often been away from her, our sons and our home, we both find our joy and fulfillment in Him. The times when we have been privileged to be together as a family have been all the richer because of our mutual love for Him and His love for us.

The person who has not yet learned to love God and to seek Him above all else and all others is to be pitied, for he is denying himself the blessings that await all who love God with all their heart, soul and mind.

Love Demonstrated

This deep insight into the love and trustworthiness of God was revealed to John, the beloved apostle, as recorded in his first epistle: "God showed how much He loved us by sending His only Son into this wicked world to bring to us eternal life through His death. In this act we see what real love is: it is not our love for God, but His love for us when He sent His Son to satisfy God's anger against our sins.

"Dear friends, since God loved us as much as that, we surely ought to love each other too. For though we have never yet seen God, when we love each other, God lives in us and His love within us grows ever stronger. And He has put His own Holy Spirit into our hearts as a proof to us that we are living with Him and He with us.

"And furthermore, we have seen with our own eyes and now tell all the world that God sent His Son to be their Savior. Anyone who believes and says that Jesus is the Son of God has God living in him, and he is living with God. We know how much God loves us because we have felt His love and because we believe Him when He tells us that He loves us dearly.

"God is love, and anyone who lives in love is living with God and God is living in him. And as we live with Christ, our love grows more perfect and complete; so we will not be ashamed and embarrassed at the day of judgment, but can face Him with confidence and joy, because He loves us and we love Him too.

"We need have no fear of someone who loves us perfectly; His perfect love for us eliminates all dread of what He might do to us. If we are afraid, it is for fear of what He might do to us, and shows that we are not fully convinced that He really loves us. So you see, our love for Him comes as a result of His loving us first" (I John 4:11-19, Living Bible).

First Love Lost

Those Christians who find comfort and security in their church dogmas and creeds, in their commitment to certain Christian standards of ethics and conduct, or in their involvement with social issues, would do well to meditate on the first five verses of Revelation 2.

This portion of Scripture records God's message to the church at Ephesus. He commends the church for nine good qualities then goes on to say, "Yet, there is one thing wrong; you don't love Me as at first! Think about those times of your first love (how different now!) and turn back to me again and work as you did before; or else I will come and remove your candlestick from its place among the churches" (Revelation 2:4, 5, Living Bible).

A similar message from God is given to the church at Laodicea: "I know what you have done, and that you are neither hot nor cold! I could wish that you were either cold or hot! But since you are lukewarm and neither hot nor cold, I intend to spit you out of My mouth! All those whom I love I correct and discipline. Therefore, shake off your complacency and repent" (Revelation 3:15, 16, 19, Phillips).

Loving Our Neighbors

It is natural for us to fulfill the command to love our neighbors as ourselves if we truly love God with all our heart, soul and mind. If we are properly related to God on the vertical, we shall be properly related to our fellow man on the horizontal.

For example, billiard balls rolling freely on a table naturally bounce away from each other because of the nature of their construction. But if we tie strings to several balls and lift them perpendicular to the table, the balls will cluster together as a result. When individual Christians are vitally yoked to Christ and related to God, and are walking in the Spirit, loving Him with all their heart, soul and mind, they will fulfill God's command to love others as themselves.

The apostle Paul explains this by saying, "If you love your neighbor as much as you love yourself, you will not want to harm or cheat him, or kill him or steal from him. And you won't sin with his wife or want what is his, or do anything else the Ten Commandments say is wrong. All ten are wrapped up in this one, to love your neighbor as you love yourself. Love does no wrong to anyone. That's why it fully satisfies all of God's requirements" (Romans 13:9, 10, Living Bible).

It is love for God and for men that results in righteousness, in fruit and in glory to Christ.

Love In Action

Also, we are commanded to love others because such love testifies to our relationship with the Father. We demonstrate by our love for others that we belong to Christ. The apostle John practically equates our salvation with the way we love others, when he tells us that if we do not love others, we do not know God, for He is love (I John 4:8).

John says, "But if someone who is supposed to be a Christian has money enough to live well, and sees a brother in need, and won't help him — how can God's love be within him? Little children, let us stop just saying we love people; let us really love them, and show it by our actions" (I John 3:17, 18, Living Bible).

Jesus said, "I demand that you love each other as much as I love you" (John 15:12, Living Bible). The Christian should love his neighbor because he is a creature of God made in the image of God; because God loves him; and because Christ died for him. Following the example of our Lord, we should love all people, even as Christ did. We should devote our lives to helping others experience His love and forgiveness.

Love Your Enemies

Jesus also said, "There is a saying, 'Love your friends and hate your enemies.' But I say: Love your enemies! Pray for those who persecute you! In that way you will be acting as true sons of your Father in heaven. For He gives His sunlight to both the evil and the good and sends rain on the just and on the unjust too. If you are friendly only to your friends, how are you different from anyone else?

Even the heathen do that" (Matthew 5:43-45, 47, Living Bible).

You may rightly ask how loving our neighbors relates to the problems of war, race, capital and labor? The answer is so obvious and simple that we have missed it in our frenzied quest for solutions. When Christians begin to act like Christians and love God, their neighbors, their enemies and especially their Christian brothers — regardless of color, race or class — we shall see in our time, as in the first century, a great transformation in the whole of society, in man's relationship with man. People will marvel, as they did in that first century, when they observe our attitudes and actions, "How they love one another."

Loving Ourselves

Some people have difficulty understanding God's command in Matthew 22:39 to love our neighbors as ourselves. They wonder what it means to love ourselves, since II Timothy 3:2-4 warns against those who in the last days will be lovers of themselves rather than lovers of God.

Obviously these two portions of Scripture are talking about different kinds of love. The love referred to in II Timothy applies to the natural and the carnal men — the fleshly men — who in arrogance and pride seek their own interests contrary to the will and way of God.

Agape love — God's love — enables the Christian to apply the truths of I Corinthians 13 to his own life, even as he applies them to his neighbors. Since God is patient toward, kind to and forgiving of us, we should also be patient toward, kind to and forgiving of ourselves and our neighbors, as we are enabled to be by His power.

I counsel with many students and older adults who are not able to accept themselves. Some are weighted down with guilt because of unconfessed sins; others are not reconciled to their physical handicaps or deformities. Still others feel inferior mentally or socially.

My counsel to one and all is, "God loves you and accepts you as you are. You must do the same. Get your eyes off yourself! Focus your love and attention on Christ and on others. Begin to lose yourself in service for Him and for your fellow man."

Love Unifies

God's kind of love is a unifying force among Christians. Paul admonishes us to "put on love, which is the perfect bond of unity" (Colossians 3:14), that our "hearts may be encouraged, having been welded together in love . . ." (Colossians 2:2). Only God's universal love can break through the troublesome barriers that are created by human differences. Only a common devotion to Christ — the source of love — can ease tension, erase mistrust, encourage openness, bring out the best in people and enable them to serve Christ together in a more fruitful way.

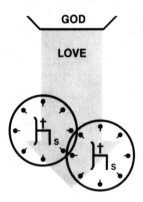

One mother shared how the discovery of how to love enabled her to be more patient and kind to her husband and children. "The children were driving me out of my mind with all of their childish demands. I was irritable with them, and because I was so miserable, I was a critical and nagging wife. No wonder my husband found excuses to work late at the office. It is all different now — God's love permeates our home."

A husband reported, "My wife and I have fallen in love all over again, and I am actually enjoying working in my office with men whom I couldn't stand before I learned how to love."

OUR INABILITY TO LOVE

Third, we cannot love in our own strength. Just as surely as "those who are in the flesh" (the carnal man) cannot please God" (Romans 8:8), so in our own strength we cannot love as we ought. This absence of the practice of God's love is widespread. Many of us refuse to love certain people. We love only those who are easy to love. Why can't we love the ones who are unattractive, or peculiar, or grouchy, or disagreeable or who don't love us? Because in our natural ability, we have neither the power nor the motivation to love them.

We cannot demonstrate *agape* love, God's unconditional love for others, through our own efforts. How many times have you resolved to love someone? How many times have you tried to manufacture some kind of positive, loving emotion toward someone for whom you felt nothing? It is impossible, isn't it?

In your own strength it is not possible to love with God's kind of love. By nature, we are not patient and kind. By nature, we are jealous, envious and boastful. We are proud, haughty, selfish and rude. We demand our own way. We could never love others the way God loves us. But when Christ comes into our lives and we become Christians, God gives us the equipment to be a different kind of person. With the motivation, He also gives us the ability. He provides us with a new kind of love altogether.

Review and Thought Questions

1. a) What are the basic elements of the command given believers in Matthew 22:36-40?

   _____

   _____

   _____

   b) What does each element mean to you?

   _____

   _____

   _____

2. a) Is the depth of God's love real to you?

   _____

   _____

   _____

   b) If so, what effect does that realization have on your life?

   _____

   _____

   _____

   _____

   c) If not, what can you do to increase your realization of His love?

   _____

   _____

   _____

   _____

3. How does the Bible define real love in I John 4:14-19?

   _____

   _____

4. How would you compare your initial zeal (or love) for Christ immediately after you became a Christian to your present love? (Give examples or a specific explanation.)

_____

_____

_____

_____

5. What part do the heart, soul, strength and mind play in love, as stated in Luke 10:25-28 (cf. Mark 12:28-34)?

_____

_____

_____

_____

6. a) Why is it important to love yourself?

_____

_____

_____

b) How do you do this?

_____

_____

_____

c) What often keeps a person from loving himself? How does this affect his love for others?

_____

_____

_____

_____

Discussion questions: 1, 2, 5, 6.

STUDY 3.

WE LOVE WITH GOD'S LOVE

Fourth, we can love with God's love.

It was God's kind of love that brought us to Christ. It is this kind of love that is able to sustain and encourage us each day. Through His love in us we can bring others to Christ and minister to fellow believers as God has commanded.

God's love was supremely expressed in the life of Jesus Christ. We have a perfect, complete picture of God's kind of love in the birth, personality, teachings, life, death and resurrection of His Son.

How does this love enter our own lives? It becomes ours when the Holy Spirit comes to indwell us the moment we receive Jesus Christ. The Scriptures say, "We feel this warm love everywhere within us because God has given us the Holy Spirit to fill our hearts with His love" (Romans 5:5, Living Bible). God is Spirit, and the "fruit of the Spirit is love . . ." (Galatians 5:22). When we are controlled by the Spirit, we can love with God's love.

But how do we make love a practical reality in our lives? How do we love? By resolutions? By self-imposed disciplines? No. The only way to love is explained in my final point.

WE LOVE BY FAITH

Fifth, we love by faith. Everything about the Christian life is based on faith. We love by faith just as we received Christ by faith, just as we walk by faith and just as we are filled with the Holy Spirit by faith.

If the fruit of the Spirit is love, we may logically ask if it is not enough to be filled with the Spirit. This will be true from God's point of view, but it will not always be true in our actual experience.

There are many Christians who have loved with God's love and have demonstrated the fruit of the Spirit in their lives without consciously or specifically claiming His love by faith. Yet, without being consciously aware of the fact,

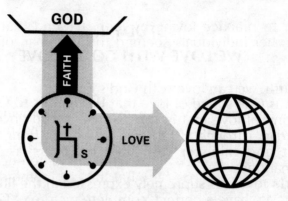

they were indeed loving by faith; therefore, they did not find it necessary to claim God's love by faith as a specific act. In Hebrews 11:6 we are reminded that "without faith it is impossible to please Him." Obviously there will be no demonstration of God's love where there is no faith.

Power To Love

I would remind those who have difficulty in loving others that Jesus has commanded us to "love each other as much as I love you" (John 15:12, Living Bible). Therefore, we know that it is God's will for us to love. We also know that He would not command us to do something that He will not enable us to do.

In I John 5:14, 15, God promises that if we ask anything according to His will, He hears and answers us. Relating this promise to God's command, we can claim by faith the privilege of loving with His love.

God has for us an unending supply of *agape* love — His divine, supernatural love. It is for us to claim, to grow on, to spread to others, and thus to reach hundreds and thousands with the love that counts, the love that will bring them to Jesus Christ. In order to experience and share this love, we must claim it by faith; that is, trust His promise that He will give us all that we need to do His will, on the basis of His command and promise.

This principle is not new — it is 2,000 years old. But it was a new discovery to me that early morning hour some years ago and, since that time, to many thousands of other Christians with whom I have shared it. When I began to practice loving by faith, I found that conflicts with other individuals seemed to disappear, often miraculously.

Claim God's Love

In one instance, I was having a problem loving a fellow staff member. It troubled me. I wanted to love him. I knew that I was commanded to love him; yet, because of certain areas of inconsistency and personality differences, it was difficult for me to love him. But the Lord reminded me of His command in I Peter 5:7 to cast this care on Him and love this man by *faith*. I did. When I claimed God's promise to take this care, and claimed God's love for the man by faith, my concern lifted. I knew the problem was in God's hands.

An hour later, I found under my door a letter from that very man who had no possible way of knowing what I had just experienced. In fact, his letter had been written the day before. The Lord had foreseen the change in me. This friend and I met together that afternoon and had the most wonderful time of prayer and fellowship we had ever experienced together. Loving with God's love by faith had changed our relationship.

Family Reunion

I could share many other illustrations of how God's love has overcome seemingly impossible conflicts. A special assistant to a former governor of California once visited our headquarters at Arrowhead Springs, and during his visit he received Jesus Christ as Savior and Lord. He began to discover how to love by faith. Recently, his son had left home after an argument with the father. In contemplating the problem, this new Christian realized that he had never told his son that he loved him. On his way home from Arrowhead Springs he asked the Lord to bring his son home so he could make things right. He wanted to express his love for his son. As he neared his own house, his heart quickened. The upstairs light was on, indicating that the son had come home! Soon, father and son embraced, became reconciled and established a new relationship, founded on God's forgiving love.

Racial Harmony

A young college football player, who had been raised in a community where blacks are resented, had always found it impossible to love blacks. One evening he heard me talk to a group of racially mixed students about loving by faith, especially in reference to loving those of other races.

"As you prayed," he told me later, "I claimed God's love for the black man. Then, as I left the amphitheater, the first person I saw was a black man, and he was talking to a white girl. Now that is about as explosive a situation as you can imagine for a man who hates blacks. But suddenly I felt a compassion for that black man! At one time, I would have hated him and probably would have been rude and angry with him. But God heard my prayer."

That same evening a young black couple approached me in the lobby of the Arrowhead Springs hotel. They were radiant. "Something wonderful happened to me tonight," the young woman said. "I was liberated from my hatred for the white man. I have hated the white man since I was a little girl. I have known that as a Christian I should love the white man, but I couldn't help myself. I hated the whites and wanted to get revenge. Tonight I have begun to love the whites by faith, and it really works." The young man added, "It worked for me, too; now my hatred for whites is gone. Thank you for telling us how to love by faith."

Whites who have hated blacks, and blacks who have hated whites have discovered God's supernatural love for each other. Christian husbands and wives who were living in conflict have claimed God's love by faith, and miracles have resulted. Parent-child conflicts have been resolved, and generation gaps have been bridged through loving by faith. Conflicts in working situations have been resolved. Enemies cease to be enemies when we love them by faith. God's love has a way of dissolving prejudice and breaking down barriers.

Power Of Love

Love is the greatest power known to man. It changed

the course of the first-century world, and God is using it to bring a great revolution in the 20th century. Love never fails. Nothing can overcome God's love. In the first century there was a wedding of love and faith, and then both were lost during the Dark Ages. The realization of Martin Luther and his colleagues that the "just shall live by faith" resulted in the Reformation, but there was little love. In fact, there was often conflict.

A missionary friend who had spent more than 20 years on a difficult field assignment responded to my message on loving by faith saying, "I have never spoken on the subject of love since my ordination. I am a conservative, and my emphasis has been on faith. I have left the love message to the liberal theologians."

How sad! The message of God's love and forgiveness and loving by faith is for every true believer to proclaim. We dare not continue to preach a partial message.

Today, God is bringing back to our remembrance the wedding of the two — faith and love. Through faith, that supernatural, divine love of God will reach out where nothing else can go to capture men and women for Christ. The love which results from that faith will engulf people everywhere, so that, as we live and love by faith, we shall spread God's love throughout the world. This love is contagious, attractive and aggressive. It creates hunger for God. It is active — constantly looking for things to do, people to uplift and lives to change.

Begin To Love

Begin to love by faith. Make a list of people whom you do not like, and begin to love them by faith. Maybe you yourself will be on the list. Have you thought of applying the truths of I Corinthians 13 to yourself by faith? Ask God to enable you to see yourself as He sees you. You have no reason to dislike yourself when your creator has already forgiven you and has demonstrated His unconditional love by dying for you!

If Christ is in you, you are complete, because Christ Himself *is* perfect love, perfect peace, perfect patience, perfect kindness. He is all goodness, and He is in you! Whenever Satan tries to attack you by reminding you of sins which you have already confessed or by magnifying your weaknesses and shortcomings, claim in faith the forgiveness and righteousness of God and thank Him that on the authority of His Word, you do not have to be intimidated by Satan's accusations. Thank Him that you are a child of God and that your sins are forgiven. Thank God that Satan has no control over you except that which is allowed by God (Acts 4:28). Then cast this care on the Lord as we are commanded to do in I Peter 5:7.

Pray For Others

Perhaps your boss, a fellow employee, your children or your father or mother is on the list. Pray for each person on your list. Ask the Holy Spirit to fill you with Christ's love for all of them. The next time you meet with them, draw upon God's limitless, inexhaustible, overwhelming love for them by faith. Watch God work through you! Watch Him use your smile, your words, your patience to express His love for each individual.

Try it on every one of your "enemies" — on everyone who angers you, ignores you, bores you, or frustrates you. People are waiting to be loved with God's love.

A housewife who, through a long, cold winter, had seen her family through mumps, measles, a broken nose, three new teeth for the baby and countless other difficulties, reached the point where those pressures and demands become too much for her. Finally, on her knees, she began to protest, "Oh Lord! I have so much to do!" But imagine her surprise when she heard herself say, "Oh Lord! I have so much to love!" We will never run out of opportunities to love by faith.

Problems Resolved

One day, after I had spoken at a large conference of hundreds of pastors and laymen, a pastor shared with me how a serious personality problem in his church had been solved since he had heard my lecture on "How to Love by Faith" and had applied this concept in his own life and ministry.

Remember that we love by *faith*. By faith, we can claim God's love step by step, person by person. "The fruit of the Spirit is love . . ." Like fruit, love grows. To produce fruit requires a seed, then a flower, then pollination, then some warm sun and refreshing rains, and even some contrary winds. Similarly, in daily life, your love will be warmed by joy, watered by tears, spread by the winds of circumstances.

God uses all that we experience to work His will in our lives. He is the one who makes our love grow. It is a continual, ever-increasing thing. As Paul says, "May the Lord make your love to grow and overflow to each other and to everyone else . . ." (I Thessalonians 3:12, Living Bible).

Love And Evangelism

Now, how does loving by faith motivate us to engage in aggressive personal evangelism and contribute to the fulfillment of the Great Commission?

The answer is obvious. When we begin to truly love God -- by faith — with all of our heart, soul, mind and strength and to love our neighbors as ourselves, we shall begin to see men as God sees them — individuals of great worth, as those for whom Christ died. As a result, we shall be motivated by the same love which constrained the apostle Paul, who said, "Everywhere we go we talk about Christ to all who will listen" (Colossians 1:28, Living Bible).

Love, God's kind of love, causes the Great Commission to become a personal responsbility and privilege. Furthermore, when non-Christians observe that Christians are not only saying that they love one another, but are also proving it by their actions, they, like their first-century counterparts, will marvel at "how they love one another" and will be drawn to receive and worship our Savior with us.

How exciting it is to have such a dynamic, joyful force available to us! And it all comes from our loving Savior, Jesus Christ, who explicitly promises in His Word all that we need. We need not guess, nor hope, nor wish. We can claim this love by faith, right now.

Why not make this prayer your own: "Lord, You never would have commanded me to love had You not intended to enable me to love and, on the authority of Your promise to answer if I ask anything according to your will, I appropriate Your love — the I Corinthians 13 kind of love — for You, for all people, and for myself."

One of the things that God impressed upon me the morning that I learned to love by faith was that I should share this truth everywhere I go and encourage others to do the same. As you practice loving by faith, you also will want to share this concept with others.

Review and Thought Questions

1. Why is faith important in love?

_____

_____

_____

2. Why do we feel love? (See Romans 5:5)

_____

_____

_____

3. How can you claim God's love?

_____

_____

_____

4. Why is love powerful enough to overcome prejudice, hatred, rebellion, anger, fear or jealousy?

_____

_____

_____

5. What resources do you have to cling to when you find it difficult to love someone?

I Peter 5:7 _____

_____

Philippians 4:13 _____

_____

Colossians 3:2, 13 _____

_____

I Thessalonians 3:12, 13 _____

_____

6. Is there anyone you find less than lovable?

_____

If so, what will you do this week to overcome that situation?

_____

_____

_____

7. How is love expressed in Colossians 1:28?

_____

_____

_____

8. a) How can you relate the promise in I John 5:14, 15, to claiming God's power to love others by faith?

_____

_____

_____

b) How does it relate to your own involvement in personal evangelism?

_____

_____

_____

_____

_____

Discussion questions: 3, 4, 6, 8.

CHAPTER STUDY GUIDE

1. The application of the principles outlined in the Concept will enable you to claim God's love by faith, so that, in time, loving others will become a way of life for you.

2. Memorize the following verses and references:

John 13:35: "By this all men will know that you are My disciples, if you have love for one another."

Matthew 22:37-39: "And he said to him, 'You shall love the Lord God with all your heart, and with all your soul, and with all your mind. This is the great and foremost commandment.' And a second is like it, 'You shall love your neighbor as yourself.'"

3. Make this Concept, "How to Love by Faith," a way of life by practicing the following:

   a. Make a thorough study of the basic passage on love, I Corinthians 13. Make a written list of the characteristics of love found in the passage. Ask God to show you which of these characteristics are lacking in your life. Confess these lacks and by faith ask for and claim these characteristics in your life.

   Then expect God to begin to make these characteristics increasingly evident in your life. Realize that the results may be gradual as you grow toward maturity in love. (For supplementary study, consult your Bible concordance for additional passages on the subject of love.)

   b. Make a list of people who tend to irritate you or for whom you are aware of a definite lack of love. Confess your past failures and claim God's forgiveness. Claim God's love by faith for these individuals. Ask God for ways in which you can begin to express His love for them. Pray for these people. Ask God to bless them. When situations arise that would normally cause you to respond in your former unloving way, claim God's love afresh. Remember Christ's reactions toward those who hated and abused Him. Thank Him that He lives in you.

AMPLIFIED OUTLINE

Study 1.

Introduction

A. The greatest power in all the world is love (I Corinthians 13:8).

B. There are three Greek words translated into the one English word "love."

1. *Eros* means sensual desire.

2. *Phileo* is used for friendship.

3. *Agape* love is God's supernatural love for us revealed through Christ's death on the cross for our sins (John 3:16).

C. The Lord Jesus gave His disciples a new commandment "to love one another as much as I have loved you" (John 13:34).

1. At Pentecost, through the outpouring of the Holy Spirit, the disciples were given this promised love.

2. This same divine love — *agape* love — is available to us today.

D. God emphasized this love through the apostle Paul in I Corinthians 13.

I. God loves us unconditionally.

A. He loves us with *agape* love — the love described in I Corinthians 13.

1. He loves us so much that He sent His Son to die for us (John 3:16).

2. Christ loves us so much that while we were yet sinners, He died for us (Romans 5:8).

B. The parable of the prodigal son illustrates God's love for those who are His children (Luke 15: 11-32).

C. God loves those who believe in Christ as much as He loves the Lord Jesus (John 17:23).

D. We need not fear God (I John 4:18).

E. Because of His love God chastens us when we are disobedient (Hebrews 12:6).

F. God's love never fails regardless of the circumstances (Romans 8:35-39).

Study 2.

II. We are commanded to love.

    A. We are commanded to love God (Matthew 22:37).

        1. The Holy Spirit supplies the love we need (Romans 5:5).

        2. We respond to God's love for us (I John 4:19).

    B. We are commanded to love our neighbors (Matthew 22:39).

        1. Love for our neighbor fulfills God's law (Romans 13:9).

        2. It also demonstrates our relationship to God (I John 4:8).

    C. We are also commanded to love our enemies (Matthew 5:43-47).

    D. God expects us to have a proper love for ourselves and to accept ourselves as He accepts us (Matthew 22:39).

III. We cannot love in our own strength.

    A. Most people love only those who are easy to love.

    B. By nature we are not patient and kind nor free of jealousy.

Study 3.

IV. We can love with God's love.

    A. Since God is love, everything said in I Corinthians 13 applies to God.

    B. It was the I Corinthians 13 kind of love which brought us to Christ and will bring others to Christ.

    C. This kind of love was demonstrated in the life of Jesus Christ.

    D. This love entered our lives when the Holy Spirit came to indwell us the moment we received Jesus Christ (Romans 5:5).

V. We love by faith.

A. Everything about the Christian life is based on faith.

B. If the fruit of the Spirit is love, is it not enough to be filled with the Spirit?

1. This is true from God's point of view.

2. It is not always true in our experience.

3. We are reminded in Hebrews 11:6 that without faith there can be no real demonstration of God's love.

C. The principle of loving by faith is based on a command and a promise.

1. God *commands* us to love (John 15:12).

2. God *promises* that He will hear and answer when we pray according to His will (I John 5:14, 15).

D. God has an unending supply of *agape* love from which we can draw by faith.

E. Loving by faith can resolve conflicts of race, marriage, family, etc.

F. We need a wedding of faith and love like that in the first century.

G. A practical way to begin is to make a list of people whom you do not like and begin loving them by faith with the I Corinthians 13 kind of love.

H. Loving by faith is a continually growing, ever-increasing process.

I. Loving by faith motivates us to engage in aggressive, personal evangelism.

CHAPTER 9

HOW TO PRAY

Study 1. What is Prayer?
         Who Can Pray?

Study 2. Why Are We To Pray?
         To Whom Do We Pray?

Study 3. When Should We Pray?
         What Should Be Included In Prayer?
         How Can We Pray With Confidence?

STUDY 1.

WHAT IS PRAYER?

Has it ever occurred to you as you kneel in your place of prayer that you have been given the privilege of being used of God to help change the lives of men and nations? God has literally made available to you a vast reservoir of power, wisdom and grace, if only you are willing to believe Him.

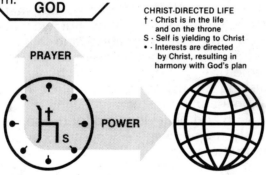

GOD

PRAYER

POWER

CHRIST-DIRECTED LIFE
† - Christ is in the life
  and on the throne
S - Self is yielding to Christ
• - Interests are directed
  by Christ, resulting in
  harmony with God's plan

God said to Jeremiah, "Call Me, and I will answer you, and I will tell you great and mighty things, which you do not know" (Jeremiah 33:3).

Resources Of God

Remember, the one who made that statement is the one who is the mighty risen Son of God in whom dwells all the fullness of the Godhead bodily (Colossians 2:9); the one who has commissioned us to go into all the world and preach the gospel and make disciples of all nations;

the one who said, "All authority has been given to Me in heaven and on earth . . . I am with you always" (Matthew 28:18, 20). He is the one who said, "If you ask Me anything in My name, I will do it" (John 14:14). Consider well these promises of God, for the mighty resources of deity are available to you if you are His child.

Why, then, are the lives of so few Christians characterized by the supernatural and the miraculous? If we would take seriously these words of our Savior and begin to claim in prayer, by faith, the things that we have been promised, miracles would attend our ways; multitudes would be changed.

Problem Of Unbelief

Why are we so impotent and fruitless today compared to the first-century Christians? The answer is to be found in the word "unbelief." The Lord Jesus Christ has commissioned us, as a demonstration of His loving concern and compassion for the world, to go and share the good news of the gospel everywhere. But we huddle in unbelief in our little prayer meetings and talk of peripheral, superficial matters. We are content to see accomplished in the name of Christ only that which man is capable of accomplishing through his own intellect, eloquence and organizational ability. Instead of calling upon the mighty power of God and believing God for the supernatural, we go aimlessly on our way — impotent, unbelieving and therefore fruitless.

Power In Prayer

The disciples knew and prayed to the omnipotent God, who, in response to their prayers and dedicated lives, used them to turn a wicked Roman Empire upside down for God. Read their prayer, as recorded in Acts 4:24-30:

"O Lord, creator of heaven and earth and of the sea and everything in them — You spoke long ago by the Holy Spirit through our ancestor King David, Your servant, saying, 'Why do the heathen rage against the Lord, and the foolish nations plan their little plots against Almighty God? The kings of the earth unite to fight against Him, against the anointed Son of God!'

"That is what is happening here in this city today! For Herod the king, and Pontius Pilate the governor, and all the Romans — as well as the people of Israel — are united against Jesus, Your anointed Son, Your holy servant."

"They won't stop at anything that You in Your wise power will let them do. And now, O Lord, hear their threats, and grant to Your servants great boldness in their preaching, and send Your healing power, and may miracles and wonders be done by the name of Your holy servant Jesus" (Living Bible).

Is it any wonder that God used these first-century Christians to change the course of history? The God whom we worship and serve is the same all-wise, all-powerful, loving God and Father whom they loved and served. His power has not changed — He longs to do the same through us.

Fruitless Witness

For more than a year before Campus Crusade for Christ began, I led church deputation teams into college dormitories, fraternities and sororities in the Los Angeles area; yet, to my knowledge, not a single person committed his life to Christ at any of these meetings.

But when God called this ministry into being, in the spring of 1951, we immediately formed a 24-hour prayer chain, which we divided into 96 15-minute periods. Scores of Christians invested 15 minutes in prayer every day in behalf of our new ministry at the University of California at Los Angeles.

Prayer Chain

During the very first sorority meeting at UCLA after the prayer chain began, more than half of the 60 girls present expressed a desire to receive Christ. In the course of the next few months, more than 250 students at UCLA — including the president of the student body, the editor of the newspaper and a number of top athletes — committed their lives to Jesus Christ. So great was their influence for Christ that the campus chimes began to play Christian hymns at noon each day!

This unprecedented demonstration of God's blessing was not an accident. God was responding to the prayers of many of His children. His blessing continues to this day as He uses this ministry to introduce tens of thousands to our Savior and to build disciples in most of the major countries of the world. Prayer continues to be a major emphasis.

However, we have learned through the years that the average Christian does not know how to pray. A friend of mine who has been a Christian for more than 50 years told me, "I never pray in public, and I know very little about prayer or how to pray." Because so many Christians — new and old alike — know so little about prayer, I wish to share with you some very basic truths and answer some very important questions about prayer.

WHAT IS PRAYER?

Prayer is simply communicating with God, or, as someone has said, "Prayer is a dialogue between two people who love each other — God and man." We might compare it with the famous "hot line" installed between Washington and the Kremlin, which provides instant, direct communication between the United States and the Soviet Union.

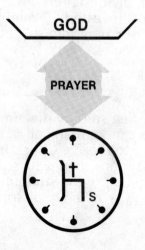

Every Christian has a "hot line" of direct communication with God, available to him at all times. But most Christians never lift the phone off the hook and often forget that the line exists until an emergency arises.

As children of God we are invited to "come boldly to the very throne of God and stay there to receive His mercy and to find grace to help us in our times of need" (Hebrews 4:14-16, Living Bible).

WHO CAN PRAY?

Those who belong to Christ can pray. Man instinctively prays — even if only to false gods built of sticks and stones. Whenever he is faced with tragedy, heartache, sorrow or danger, he prays.

However, there is a serious danger in "ignorant" prayer. It is a well-established fact of philosophy and history that man always assimilates the moral character of the object he worships. People who have worshipped gods of lust have become morally degenerate. When men have prayed to gods of blood, fire and war, they have become militaristic, ruthless and sadistic.

This same principle applies to the Christian. "As we behold His (Christ's) face, we are changed into the same image from glory to glory." This explains the scriptural emphasis on the worship of and prayer to the only true, righteous, holy and loving God.

The Only Way

Those who come to God in the authority and the name of Jesus can pray. According to the Scriptures, "There is one God, and one mediator also between God and men, the man Christ Jesus" (I Timothy 2:5). Jesus Himself claims to be the only way to God: "I am the way, and the truth, and the life; no one comes to the Father, but through me" (John 14:6).

Lest this sound too exclusive, let me remind you that Jesus Christ came to die for all people in all lands. He promises rest for all who are weary and heavy-laden. Many people who have ignored God for a lifetime come to a difficult situation near the end of life and are too embarrassed to pray. They reason, "I've ignored God all my life — it's too late now."

Do not feel this way. God proved His love for us by sending Christ to die for us while we were still in our sins. There is nothing that you can do that will cause God to cease to love you.

The fact still remains, however, that you cannot expect God to answer your prayers unless you come to Him in the name and authority of the Lord Jesus as your only mediator. Jesus promised six times on the eve of His crucifixion, "If you ask Me anything in My name, I will do it" (John 14:14).

Clean Hearts

Those who have clean hearts can pray. But there is a problem. We must not only ask in the name of Jesus. We must also come with clean hearts. As the psalmist says, "If I regard iniquity in my heart, the Lord will not hear me" (Psalm 66:18). Therefore, we cannot expect God to answer our prayers if there is any sin in our lives. Just as the omission of one ingredient can cause failure in baking a cake, so the omission of confessing any known sin can result in prayer failure.

Forgiving Spirit

Those who have a forgiving spirit can pray. One of the most frequent hindrances to prayer is an unforgiving spirit. Jesus said, "Whenever you stand praying, forgive, if you have anything against anyone; so that your Father also who is in heaven may forgive you your transgressions" (Mark 11:25). No prayer except the prayer of confession can be answered by God unless it comes from a heart that is free of bitterness.

In the Lord's prayer, the words "give" and "forgive" occur in the same sentence: "Give us this day our daily bread, and forgive us our debts, as we also have forgiven our debtors" (Matthew 6:11, 12). The well-worn compromise, "Well, I can forgive but I can't forget," only defeats our prayers.

What if that were God's attitude? His love has prompted a wonderful forgetfulness, in which He has pledged to put all of our sins behind His back and remember them against us no more. You and I must come to God with a forgiving heart, if we are to receive the Christian's legacy of power in prayer.

Pray In Faith

Those who pray in faith can pray. We must also have a believing heart if our prayers are to be answered. The same Lord who said, "All authority has been given to Me in heaven and on earth" (Matthew 28:18), and "Lo, I am with you always" (Matthew 28:20), also said, "If you ask Me anything in My name, I will do it" (John 14:14); "And everything you ask in prayer, believing, you shall receive" (Matthew 21:22); and "Be it done to you according to your faith" (Matthew 9:29). Yet few of us take seriously these words, and few dare to claim what God has so generously promised us.

Review and Thought Questions

1. a) What is prayer?

   We are Communicating to God

   b) Why is it important?

2. Whom does God hear when they pray?

   John 9:31 *That does his will*

   Psalm 66:18 *A person with heart*

   Mark 11:25 *A person that is able to forgive*

   Proverbs 15:29 *hears prayer of the righteous*

3. Why is faith important to success in prayer?

4. Why do some prayers seem to go unanswered?

5. What do these verses say about *how* to pray?

Psalm 145:18 *In truth*

_____

Matthew 6:5-7 *Pray to God in secret*
Be Specific

_____

Matthew 21:22 *Believing*

_____

Philippians 4:6 *Be thankful do not*
fret or have any anxiety But
pray about every thing and every thing

6. What vital elements of prayer can you see in Acts
   4:24-30?

_____

_____

_____

_____

**Questions 1 (especially part b), 3, 4 and 6 can be used to stimulate
effective group discussions.**

STUDY 2.
WHY ARE WE TO PRAY?

We pray *to glorify God*. Above all, the purpose of prayer is to glorify God. Jesus said, "Whatever you ask in My name that will I do, that the Father may be glorified in the Son" (John 14:13)

We pray *because God commands us to pray*. Our loving Father, who delights in our fellowship, has commanded us to pray without ceasing.

We pray *to communicate with God*. Prayer is not just an "escape hatch" for the Christian to get out of trouble, please himself and gain his own selfish ends. It is his line of communication with God. For this reason, God has commanded us to pray. "Call to Me and I will answer you, and I will tell you great and mighty things, which you do not know" (Jeremiah 33:3).

The New Testament commands are innumerable: "Pray without ceasing" (I Thessalonians 5:17), "Keep watching and praying" (Matthew 26:41), "Pray with thanksgiving" (Philippians 4:6), "Pray in the Spirit" (I Corinthians 14:15). "Always pray and not faint" (Luke 18:1). Pray for those in authority (I Timothy 2:2). Pray for utterance (Ephesians 6:19). Pray for boldness (Acts 4:29).

Fellowship With God

We pray to have *fellowship with God*. God waits anxiously for us to come to Him in prayer. This is the God who created us and loved us so much that He sent His only Son to die for us — the God who in spite of our sin and self-centeredness has done everything for us. It is incredible to me that God wants our fellowship!

We tend to think only of our own response during our quiet times with the Lord, rating the time unsatisfactory when our hearts are cold and we feel dry and unemotional. But the Bible says, "The prayer of the upright is His (God's) delight" (Proverbs 15:8), regardless of any emotional feelings which we may have. This very fact should motivate us to spend more time with the Lord because we wish to please and delight Him.

My own sons, when they were living at home, helped me to realize the importance of this fact. No matter how busy I was, when Zachary or Bradley wanted to talk with me, I gladly put aside everything else just to have fellowship with them. I longed and loved to be with them, and I liked to feel that they wanted to be with me. How much more God in His infinite love longs to fellowship with us.

Example of Christ

We pray *because of Christ's example.* Jesus Christ, the very Son of God, made prayer a priority, even though His day was filled from morning to night with many pressures and responsibilities — addressing crowds, healing the sick, granting private interviews, traveling and training His disciples. If Jesus was so dependent upon this fellowship in prayer alone with His Father, how much more should we be.

We pray *because of the examples of the disciples and others.* The lives of the disciples and the biographies of Christians who have done great things for God through the centuries all testify to the necessity of prayer. I do not suggest that we need to spend long hours each day in prayer, though some are called to this high privilege. But all of us are commanded by God to "pray without ceasing," bringing everything to God in prayer. We are commanded to pray for one another. Those who have prayed have been blessed and used of God.

Results Of Prayer

We pray *to obtain results.* Prayer does change things. Many people believe that prayer is only a psychological exercise in autosuggestion or positive thinking. Others believe that prayer so changes those who pray, that God is free to reveal His will. But Scripture clearly teaches that prayer can even change the course of nature.

For example, Jesus raised Lazarus from the dead (John 11:43); Elijah prayed that no rain would fall, and none did for three and one-half years. Then he prayed that it would rain, and soon the rain came pouring down (James 5:17, 18).

Talk To God First

Prayer is the major means of becoming a fruitful witness for Christ. The divine order is first to talk to God about men and then to talk to men about God. Witnessing is gathering the results of prayer, both the prayer of the one who is sharing Christ and the prayers of others. I am convinced that the most important factor in my becoming a Christian was the prayers of my godly mother.

We pray *to provide spiritual nurture.* Prayer, which involves our talking to God and God talking to us through His Word, the Holy Scriptures, is our major source of spiritual nurture. Just as a child needs food to grow physically, so we need food to grow spiritually. We can miss a meal and not feel any ill effects, but if we go without food for a week, we begin to weaken.

So it is in our spiritual lives. We can go through one day without feeding on God's Word or praying without any apparent ill effects, but if we continue this practice, we shall become undernourished, losing the strength to live a victorious life and to maintain the boldness necessary for a vital witness for Christ.

TO WHOM DO WE PRAY?

We pray to the Father in the name of the Lord Jesus Christ through the ministry of the Holy Spirit. Our prayers are validated by Jesus Christ and are interpreted to God the Father by the Holy Spirit. But since God is one God, manifested in three persons, it is also perfectly acceptable to pray to Jesus or to the Holy Spirit. There is no jealousy between the three persons of the Trinity. The scriptural pattern which Jesus taught addressed the Father.

It is meaningful and encouraging to realize that as we are praying, both the Lord Jesus and the Holy Spirit are interceding. Paul tells us in Romans 8:34, "Christ Jesus is He who died, yes, rather who was raised, who is at the right hand of God, who also intercedes for us."

The Spirit Intercedes

Earlier in Romans 8 we are told, "And in the same way

the Spirit also helps our weakness; for we do not know how to pray as we should, but the Spirit Himself intercedes for us with groanings too deep for words; and He who searches the hearts knows what the mind of the Spirit is, because He intercedes for the saints according to the will of God" (Romans 8:26, 27).

Because the one to whom we pray is the King of kings and the Lord of lords, the creator of heaven and earth, we come into His presence with reverence. But He is also our loving heavenly Father who cares for us and delights in having fellowship with us. Therefore, we can enter into His presence with relaxed, joyful hearts, knowing that God loves us more than anyone else has ever loved us or will ever love us.

Review and Thought Questions

1. a) Why do you pray?

   glorify God

   God Commands

   to Comm

   b) Why should you pray?

2. How does God look upon our prayers?

   II Chronicles 7:14, 15 _____

   Proverbs 15:8 *delight*

   Psalm 65:2 *hear us when we pray*

   I Peter 3:12 *ers are open*

   I Timothy 2:1-3 *our are pleasing*

3. What vital elements of prayer did Christ include in His prayer in John 17?

   ① *Glorify the father*

   ② *pray for believers*

   ③ *pray afor those closest to him*

4. What part does prayer have in witnessing?

_____

_____

_____

5. To whom do we pray? Why?

The father through Jesus.

_____

_____

6. How would you explain the elements of the model prayer Christ gave His disciples in Matthew 6:9-13?

_____

_____

_____

_____

_____

_____

_____

_____

_____

_____

Discussion questions: 1, 3, 6.

STUDY 3.
WHEN SHOULD WE PRAY?

There is a sense in which I pray without ceasing, talking to God hundreds of times in the course of the day about everything. I pray for wisdom about the numerous decisions I must make each day. I pray for the salvation of friends and strangers, the healing of the sick, and the spiritual and material needs of the Campus Crusade for Christ ministry, as well as the needs of various members of the staff and leaders of other Christian organizations.

I pray for our leaders and for those in authority over us. I even pray about the clothes I wear — that the way I dress, as well as my words and actions, will bring glory to God.

Quiet Time

But there is another sense in which there is a set-apart time each day for prayer — when I kneel quietly before the open Bible and talk with God as I read His Word. God speaks to us through His Word and through impressions as we meditate quietly in His presence.

Before I begin to read the Bible, I ask the Holy Spirit, who inspired its writing, to make my reading meaningful and edifying to me. Throughout the reading I pause to thank God for His loving salvation and provision, to confess the sins in my life that the Scriptures reveal, to ask Him for the boldness and faith His apostles displayed and to thank Him for new insights into His divine strategy for reaching the world with the good news of His love and forgiveness. To me, this is real prayer — asking God to talk to us as we talk to Him. There is more to prayer, but this is basic to true prayer.

Group Prayer

Group prayer is also a vital part of the Christian's prayer life, and yet few meetings are more dull, unattractive and boring than the average group prayer meeting. The reason is simple. The majority of individual Christians involved in the group have not spent time with God in private worship and prayer; consequently, they have nothing to say to Him in public except memorized prayers patterned after older Christians who have learned their way of praying from still others.

How much more exciting it is to teach the group to talk to God as though He were actually present, as indeed He is. This permits spontaneous, Spirit-directed prayer in which one area of praise or petition at a time is brought to Him as the Spirit brings subjects to mind.

Spontaneous Prayer

Following this vein, one person may begin, "Lord, I love You." Another follows, "Thank You that You are here today and that we can talk to You, knowing that You hear us." Another, "Thank You for Your love that sent the Lord Jesus to die for my sins." One quotes the psalmist, "Great is the Lord and greatly to be praised . . ."

Another may admit, "Lord I confess that I didn't want to come here tonight, but thank You that I am here and that You have already spoken to me." Another petitions, "I pray that You will draw my friend, Jim, to You, so that he may experience the new birth and become a vital witness and disciple for You." Another says, "I agree with this prayer, Father. Show us how we can approach him with the gospel soon."

In this type of spontaneous, Spirit-directed prayer — sometimes referred to as "conversational prayer," the same person may feel impressed to pray a number of times. However, each prayer should be short, to the point and based upon the Word of God.

Addressing God

There is a common practice which I personally find very objectionable, though I am sometimes guilty of it myself. It is the practice of using the name "Lord Jesus" or "Lord" again and again during a prayer. The fallacy of this becomes obvious when you think in terms of talking with a friend named "Tom."

Can you imagine the following conversation: "Tom, I'm so glad that you came. Tom, thanks so much for the gift. Tom, won't you come in? Tom, this — and Tom, that"? If you mentioned his name a dozen times within a two- or three-minute conversation, he would feel very uncomfortable and so would you.

Yet this is a frequent practice among Christians, who unconsciously punctuate their prayers with God's name. How much better to address God and state your prayer — whether it be praise, thanksgiving, petition, supplication or whatever — and then thank Him that on the basis of His Word He has heard you.

Avoid repeating the name of God or Jesus over and over again, as though you were a prophet of Baal trying to wake up God or gain His attention (I Kings 18:26, 27). Such praying is often offensive to others, especially non-believers and new Christians. Even worse, new Christians will begin to pattern their prayers after your example.

WHAT SHOULD BE INCLUDED
IN PRAYER?

There are certain basic elements which should be included in prayer. These elements can be easily remembered by the word "ACTS" which is composed of the first

GOD

ADORATION
CONFESSION
THANKSGIVING
SUPPLICATION

letter of the following words: Adoration, Confession, Thanksgiving and Supplication. However, the word

"ACTS" is merely a guideline and not a rigid sequence which you must follow.

Let us consider what each of these words means.

Worship God

Adoration: To adore God is to worship and praise Him, to honor and exalt Him in our hearts and our minds and with our lips. Prayer is often misunderstood as a vague, mystical element in one's relationship to a holy, awesome God. But the Word of God does not teach this. Rather, it teaches that God, our Father, desires the fellowship of His children.

Our relationship to our heavenly Father should be one of complete trust, faith and obedience. We approach Him in adoration and praise, with reverence and awe, with love and gratitude. Our prayer should be an expression of our complete trust in Him and of the confidence that He hears us. Prayer is much more than words — it is an expression of the heart toward God. It is an experience, not an action.

Reading aloud psalms of praise and other similar portions of Scripture can greatly enrich your prayer time. A cold, ungrateful heart will soon be warmed, and praising God will come easily.

Reverence For God

Personally, I cringe at such references to God as "the Man upstairs," for the God whom I worship is one whom I also honor and reverence. He is the omnipotent, holy God and creator of all things. Yet, I feel perfectly free to open my heart to Him — to share my deepest heartfelt needs, knowing that He is not only the omnipotent, holy God, but He is also my loving heavenly Father. He loves me more, understands me better, and believes in me more than anyone else in all the world.

I happen to pray in just about every conceivable posture: with my eyes open or my eyes closed, while I am walking, while I am lying in bed, audibly and silently. But my favorite posture is on my knees. The first thing I do when I awaken in the morning is acknowledge that the

Lord Jesus is in control of my life and thank Him that He loves me and is living His life in and through me.

I invite Him to continue His ministry of "seeking and saving the lost" through me, to use me in whatever way is pleasing to Him. Then I like to kneel before Him as a formal act of worship and adoration, acknowledging that I am His servant as well as His son.

Deal With Sin

Confession: For the Christian who needs to be restored to fellowship with Christ, the scriptural procedure for prayer should begin with confession (I John 1:9) on the basis of Psalm 66:18, "If I regard iniquity in my heart, the Lord will not hear me," and Isaiah 59:2, "But your iniquities have made a separation between you and your God, and your sins have hidden His face from you, so that He does not hear."

Confessing sin prepares the heart for adoration, thanksgiving and supplication.

If our discipline of prayer begins with worshipful adoration of God, any sin in our lives will be revealed by the Holy Spirit. For as we see God in His holiness and love, we become aware of our own sin and unworthiness. As the Holy Spirit makes us aware of presumptuous sins, we shall want to confess them, as well as "secret sins" which we have not consciously committed. Thus a daily waiting upon God is needed to expose our sins.

Just as a man wearing a beautiful white suit in a dark coal mine is unaware of what is happening to his suit until he sees himself in the bright light of day, so most people are unaware of their sin until they expose themselves to Christ, the Light of the world.

Totally Transparent

Always be totally transparent with God. Do not wear a facade or put on an act. Tell God exactly how you feel at all times. If you do not feel spiritual, tell Him so. If your heart is cold, confess it. If you have been disobedient, confess it and receive His forgiveness and cleansing, which will restore you to fellowship with Him.

The Greek word for confession means simply to "say the same thing with," or to agree with God about your sins, as taught in I John 1:9. Thus, when you confess your sins, you agree that what you have done is wrong. You acknowledge that all your sins — past, present and future — were forgiven at the cross, and you repent — turn in faith from doing what displeases God to doing what He wants you to do in the power of the Spirit.

We do not need to feel "spiritual" in order to confess our sins; the time to confess is the moment we realize that we have sinned.

Avoid Introspection

Confession should be real and honest, but beware of unhealthy extremes of introspection. Accept God's forgiveness and concentrate on Christ and His love and acceptance of you.

The Christian should be willing to accept God's forgiveness and then change his behavior appropriately. Never confess the same act of disobedience twice. To do so suggests that you do not believe God and His promise to forgive and cleanse. Should sins which you have confessed come back to haunt you, ask yourself if you have truly confessed those sins and if you have made necessary restitution. If you have done both of these, your problem can be traced to Satan, the accuser of believers. In this case, claim God's promise that you are forgiven and cleansed and ask the Lord Jesus to take care of Satan.

Give Thanks

Thanksgiving: Nothing pleases God more than our consistent expression of faith, and there is no better way to demonstrate our faith than to say, "Thank You." The writer of Hebrews makes it clear that without faith it is impossible to please God! (Hebrews 11:6) We are commanded to "give thanks for all things," because "this is God's will for you in Christ Jesus" (I Thessalonians 5:18). To fail to give thanks is to disobey God.

If we are filled with God's Holy Spirit and recognize

that He controls all things, we can thank God not only for the many blessings of each day, but also for the problems and adversities.

May I suggest that you meditate quietly on all of your daily blessings, such as your salvation through knowing Christ, assurance of sins forgiven, the opportunity to serve Christ, the opportunity to go to school, good health, loved ones, a good job, food, clothing, etc. Then thank God for each one of them.

Then make a list of each problem, disappointment, heartache or adversity which concerns you, and thank God for each one of them as we are commanded to do. Giving thanks demonstrates that you really do trust God. Expressing your faith pleases God and enables Him to make Himself strong in your behalf; whereas a critical, unbelieving spirit displeases God and hinders His efforts to bless and enrich your life and to use you for His glory.

Pray For Everything

Supplication: For many Christians, prayer is like window shopping — they spend much time looking but never buy anything. We are to pray for everything and in specific terms. Paul admonishes us, "Be anxious for nothing, but in everything by prayer and supplication with thanksgiving let your requests be made known to God" (Philippians 4:6). Supplication includes intercession for others and petition for our own needs.

Christians often do not realize the importance of intercession. The apostle Paul continually prayed for his converts (Ephesians 1:15, 16), and he also asked them to pray for him (Ephesians 6:19). Every Christian should pray for other Christians and should encourage other Christians to pray for him.

Petition

First of all, pray for yourself, that your inner person may be renewed and quickened — be made alert and alive, vital, refreshed, always sensitive to and empowered by the Holy Spirit. Pray about your problems, pray for wisdom and guidance, pray for strength to resist temptation, pray for comfort in time of sorrow — pray for everything. There is nothing too small or too great to bring before the Lord.

Intercession

Always pray daily for your husband or wife, for your children and for your parents. Then pray for your neighbors and friends.

Pray for your pastor and missionaries. Pray for various other Christians to whom God has given special responsibility. Pray for those in authority.

Pray especially for the salvation of souls, for a daily opportunity to introduce others to Christ and to the ministry of the Holy Spirit, and for the fulfillment of the Great Commission in our generation. Begin with your campus or your community. Pray for and seek to find one or more Christian friends with whom you can establish prayer partnerships.

Many who have discovered prayer to be a great adventure have kept a special book in which they record their prayers, accompanied by the date of each request and the date of the answer. You may want to use a similar method to encourage your faith when all of your prayers do not receive immediate answers. Sometimes God in His wisdom and sovereignty, may not answer your prayer as you expect.

HOW CAN WE PRAY
WITH CONFIDENCE?

How can we expect answers to our prayers? Four imperatives must be followed: First, *abide*. Second, *ask*. Third, *believe*. Fourth, *receive*.

Abide. Jesus revealed that abiding is the key to successful praying when He stated, "If you abide in Me, and My words abide in you, ask whatever you wish, and it shall be done for you" (John 15:7). In other words, if we are abiding in Christ — if our lives are totally yielded to Him and His Word is abiding in us so that we know His will — we can ask anything we wish, because our will is to do His will.

Abiding, then, is simply walking in the Spirit, with no

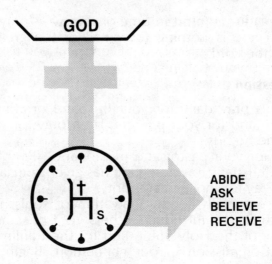

ABIDE
ASK
BELIEVE
RECEIVE

unconfessed sin and with a spirit of total availability to God. As we pray according to His will, we know He will answer us (John 15:7).

We Must Ask

Ask. If we expect answers to our prayers, we must ask. James says: "You do not have because you do not ask." Or, "You ask and do not receive, because you ask with wrong motives, so that you may spend it on your own pleasures" (James 4:2b, 3). There is tremendous authority invested in the Lord Jesus, and He said: "If you ask Me anything in My name, I will do it" (John 14:14).

"Until now you have asked for nothing in My name; ask, and you will receive, that your joy may be made full" (John 16:24). "Ask, and it shall be given to you; seek, and you shall find; knock and it shall be opened to you. For everyone who asks receives; and he who seeks finds; and to him who knocks it shall be opened" (Matthew 7:7, 8).

The problems in the world that remain unsolved are so great that they are almost without number. There are people who are still sick; souls yet unreached for Christ; evil men who still wield ungodly political and financial power; and many injustices that continue to be perpetuated — all because the children of God do not ask.

Ask In Faith

Believe. Jesus promised, "Everything you ask in prayer, believing, you shall receive" (Matthew 21:22). This is at the heart of answered prayer. But how do you get faith? Should you try to work up some kind of state of mind that will in some way equal faith? Of course not.

God does not require us to have a great faith. We simply are to have faith in a great God. Jesus said, "if you have faith as a mustard seed, you shall say to this mountain, 'Move from here to there' and it shall move; and nothing shall be impossible to you" (Matthew 17:20). We are further instructed to "ask in faith without any doubting" (James 1:6), for the double-minded man cannot expect God to answer His prayers.

You see, it is the quality, not the quantity, of the faith that is important.

Faith comes from God (Ephesians 2:8, 9). It is not something you try to have. It is something that the Holy Spirit produces in you as you continue to walk in faith and obedience. This is why it is important to be walking in the Spirit when you pray. You must be in tune with the Holy Spirit.

You cannot be on the throne of your own life and still pray in faith. A life of faith is experienced only by those who walk in obedience. You will never meet a person who has faith in a great God who refuses to obey the God in whom he is commanded to place his trust.

The Holy Spirit uses three basic means to produce faith in the one praying.

Word Of God

First, He uses the Word of God. As we study the Scriptures we learn more and more about the character of God — His love, His wisdom, His power, His works, His sovereignty. The more we know of God the more we trust Him. "Faith comes from hearing, and hearing by the Word of Christ" (Romans 10:17).

Second, the Holy Spirit uses fellowship with other Christians and various circumstances and experiences to encourage our faith. For example, our faith in God grows as we observe a friend being used of God to introduce others to Christ. When he shares his experience with us this encourages us to believe that God can use us, too.

Strong Impressions

The third way the Holy Spirit produces faith in the heart of the believer is through strong impressions or convictions which He gives. As Paul tells us in Philippians 2:13, "For it is God who is at work in you, both to will and to work for His good pleasure."

For example, if you receive an impression which you believe is of God, and that impression continues to grow, you should assume that God is leading, provided three things are true: you know that you are filled with and controlled by the Holy Spirit; the leading is scriptural; you have no fleshly or selfish motives, and your primary desire is to glorify God by introducing others to Christ and helping to fulfill the Great Commission.

Example Of Faith

Five young high school students began to sense their responsibility to God according to Matthew 28:18-20. Each of these students was impressed to make a list of three friends whom he wanted to claim for Christ. The first week they met daily to pray that these friends would sense their need of God. The second week they prayed for opportunities to speak to their friends about Christ. That week 15 students received the Savior.

With the promise that "nothing shall be impossible," we need not be limited to traditional methods of communicating the gospel. Do not be satisfied with impotence, fruitlessness and mediocrity. Believe God that "everything you ask in prayer, believing, you shall receive" (Matthew 21:22). This brings me to my final point.

Answered Prayer

Receive, by faith, the answer to your request. If you know that you are abiding in Christ, that you are controlled by the Holy Spirit and that you are praying according to the Word and will of God, you can expect God to answer your prayer, so be prepared to receive the answer. Imagine right now that you are receiving the answer to your request, and begin to thank God for answering your prayer.

In 1954, Roger Bannister broke the four-minute mile. It had never been broken in all the centuries of recorded history, but Roger Bannister believed it could be done. He developed a mental picture of himself breaking the four-minute mile record, and he did it. Since 1954, several hundred other athletes have broken the four-minute mile, simply because Roger Bannister proved that it could be done.

'Power Pills'

An experiment was conducted at Tulane University, in which two outstanding athletic groups were asked to perform an impossible gymnastic feat. Group A realized it had never been achieved before, and they expected that they too would fail — which they did.

But Group B was called aside and given special "power pills" which they were told would give them superhuman strength during the experiment, and with this confidence they proceeded to accomplish the feat. The pills were only common blackboard chalk and supplied no energy.

What I am suggesting is not dependent upon the power

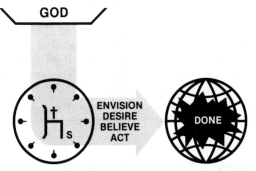

of autosuggestion or of positive thinking. Positive thinking is not enough. However, if an individual with only human resources is able to accomplish unusual feats of strength or other forms of outstanding success, how much more can we accomplish when we place our faith in the omnipotent God and draw upon His inexhaustible resources?

Scriptural Authority

It is a simple fact that whatever we vividly envision, ardently desire, sincerely believe and enthusiastically act upon must inevitably come to pass — assuming, of course, that there is scriptural authority for it.

Consider, for example, the Great Commission. For many years since that memorable moment when God gave me the vision for this ministry and for the world, I have been strongly impressed that the Holy Spirit wants the Great Commission fulfilled in our generation. In the beginning, there was little evidence from circumstances. But since that original deep impression, I have thought about little else.

Vivid Mental Picture

I have a vivid mental picture of what fulfilling the Great Commission will entail — saturating a world of more than four billion people; discipling millions; placing strategic representatives in every one of the 210 nations and protectorates of the world; and using every modern means of technology — science, radio, television, satellites, jet travel, high-speed presses and audio-visuals in all forms — to communicate God's love worldwide.

I see vividly with my mind's eye a day in the immediate future when millions on earth will become aware of the great truths concerning God's love and forgiveness in Jesus Christ and will crown Him Lord of lords. Inasmuch as I know that the fulfillment of the Great Commission is the will of God, because it is His command and the desire of His heart, I ardently long to have it come to pass.

Sincere Belief

Furthermore, I sincerely believe that the Great Commission will be fulfilled because it is God's idea, not man's. Therefore, it is inconceivable to me that the Lord would have given us the command without expecting us to seek to fulfill it and without giving us the needed resources with which to do it.

Can you imagine our Savior giving His life on the cross for us, sending us forth to fulfill the Great Commission, and then saying, "God bless you, and good luck! Do the best you can!" No! He claimed all authority in heaven and earth and promised to go with us to empower us to be His witnesses.

Enthusiastic Action

And finally, because I so vividly imagine, ardently desire and sincerely believe in the fulfillment of the Great Commission in my generation, I can enthusiastically act upon it by mobilizing myself and helping to mobilize millions of others toward its fulfillment.

We in the ministry of Campus Crusade for Christ have been impressed of God to believe that all of the nations of earth will be saturated with the gospel and that millions of people will be teaching what Jesus taught. Impossible, naive, presumptuous, audacious? Not at all. The strong impression of the Holy Spirit, the clear teaching of Scripture and the increasing evidence of circumstances have caused us to claim by faith that it will come to pass.

Personal Action

In your own life — your own home, community, state, nation and the world where you personally are concerned — determine, on a clearly scriptural basis, what God would have you vividly imagine, ardently desire, sincerely believe and enthusiastically act upon to help fulfill the Great Commission.

It may be that, in addition to your own personal ministry, God would have you pray for the personnel of a radio or television station or a newspaper to be an influence for righteousness. It may be that He would have you claim for Him a high school campus, a college campus, an office, or a community; or that every person within the radius of a mile of your home, or every home within the entire city, would be personally visited by trained workers who would lovingly, prayerfully and intelligently present the claims of Christ.

Even Greater Things

Remember that, as you bow in prayer, you are tapping a source of power that can change the course of history. God's mighty power, His love, His wisdom and His grace are available to you, if you will but believe Him and claim them. Jesus promised that we would do the same miracles which He did, and greater ones.

On the basis of the Lord's example while He was here on earth, and now as our intercessor at His place of authority and power with the Father, we can conclude that prayer is the greatest privilege of the Christian life and the most revolutionary source of power known to man.

If we were to take seriously the promises of God and begin to claim in prayer all that we have been promised, miracles would attend our way, multitudes would be introduced to the Lord Jesus Christ, the whole course of history would be changed, and we would see the Great Commission fulfilled in the United States and in the entire world during our lifetime.

Please join with me in prayer: "Father, we remember Your word of warning, 'You have not because you ask not.' We resolve at this time to claim in prayer the mighty victories which You have promised for Your glory to all who believe through Jesus Christ our Lord. We pray in His all-powerful name. Amen."

We are asking God for many thousands of prayer partners who will join with us in believing prayer for the fulfillment of the Great Commission in our generation. Will you join with us in praying for the Lord of the harvest to send forth millions of disciples to work with many local churches of all denominations and with various movements and organizations whose goals are the same as those of Campus Crusade for Christ?

Pray, too, for the mighty outpouring of God's Holy Spirit upon the entire world and for the money and materials needed to fulfill this God-given task.

Begin to pray daily that God will use you to bring special blessings to others and to introduce individuals to Christ, and thus help to fulfill the Great Commission in this generation.

Review and Thought Questions

1. a) When should you pray?

    _____

    _____

    b) Is one time better than another? Explain.

    _____

    _____

    _____

2. a) Why is a quiet time important?

    _____

    _____

    b) What should be included in a quiet time?

    _____

    _____

    _____

3. What are some of the promises Christ makes to us when we pray?

    Isaiah 65:24 _____

    _____

    Matthew 6:6 _____

    _____

    Matthew 18:20 _____

    _____

    Luke 11:9-13 _____

    _____

    _____

John 14:13, 14 _____

_____

4. What are the four parts of prayer in I Timothy 2:1? Explain briefly what each one means.

_____

_____

_____

_____

_____

5. Why would unconfessed sin hinder or halt your prayer life?

_____

_____

6. What important prerequisite to prayer do you find in these verses?

John 15:7 _____

_____

James 4:2b, 3 _____

_____

John 14:14 _____

_____

Matthew 21:22 _____

_____

James 1:6 _____

_____

7. What part does the Holy Spirit play in prayer?

_____

_____

8. What does it mean to be prepared to receive God's answers to your prayers?

_____

_____

_____

9. a) Why is prayer necessary in fulfilling the Great Commission?

_____

_____

_____

b) What (again) *is* the Great Commission?

_____

_____

10. What promise does James 5:16 give us?

_____

_____

11. How can you increase your prayer effectiveness?

_____

_____

12. a) What are some specific prayer requests you want to believe God for?

_____

_____

b) What are some promises from Scripture you can claim for each request?

_____

_____

Discussion questions: 1, 2, 4, 5, 8, 11.

CHAPTER STUDY GUIDE

1. The consistent application of the principles outlined in this Concept will transform your prayer life. it will enable you to be used by God to claim through prayer many blessings that God is waiting to bestow. This can have a great impact on your life and will enable you to share in a great spiritual awakening throughout the world.

2. Memorize the following verses and references:

Matthew 21:22: "And everything you ask in prayer, believing, you shall receive."

John 15:7: "If you abide in Me, and My words abide in you, ask whatever you wish, and it shall be done for you."

3. Finally, make this Concept, "How to Pray," a way of life by practicing the following:

a. Set aside a definite period of time each day for Bible study and prayer. Find the time that is best suited to you and your schedule. Many prefer to set aside time early in the morning. Others prefer different times in the day. Open with a brief prayer. Then spend some time in Bible study. Conclude with a longer period of prayer. Be sure to include the elements of adoration, confession, thanksgiving and supplications in your prayer.

b. Ask God to lead you as to the things for which you should pray. Be sensitive to the Holy Spirit's leading. Keep a prayer diary. List each request and indicate the date that you begin to pray for that particular item. Also list the date when the request is granted. Include in your list regular prayer for a great spiritual awakening to sweep the world and for the fulfillment of the Great Commission.

c. Seek to maintain an attitude of prayer wherever you are and in all you do.

AMPLIFIED OUTLINE

Study 1.

Introduction

    A. As you kneel in your place of prayer, you have the

power and privilege to be used of God to help change lives (Jeremiah 33:3).

B. We do not avail ourselves of this power today, primarily due to unbelief.

C. The disciples of the first century knew how to pray and claim in faith the power of the omnipotent God to help change the course of history, and we serve the same God today.

I. What is Prayer?

A. Prayer is simply communicating with God.

B. It is a channel for appropriating God's resources for our needs (Hebrews 4:14-16).

II. Who Can Pray?

A. Those who belong to Christ.

B. Those who come to God in the authority and the name of Jesus.

C. Those who come to God with a clean heart.

D. Those who have a forgiving spirit.

E. Those who come in faith.

Study 2.

III. Why Are We To Pray?

A. To glorify God.

B. Because God commands it.

C. To communicate with God.

D. To have fellowship with God.

E. Because of the example of the Lord.

F. Because of the examples of the disciples and others.

G. To achieve results for the glory of God.

H. To achieve spiritual growth.

IV. To Whom Do We Pray?

A. We pray to the Father in the name of the Lord Jesus Christ, through the ministry of the Holy Spirit.

B. Since God is one God, manifested in three persons, it is also acceptable to pray to Jesus or to the Holy Spirit.

C. We pray in the name of the one who is King of kings and Lord of lords, the creator of heaven and earth.

Study 3.

V. When Should We Pray?

A. There is a sense in which we pray without ceasing — talking to God hundreds of times in the course of the day about everything.

B. We should also set apart specific times each day for prayer.

  1. Reading and studying the Bible helps to prepare us for prayer. Therefore, pray with an open Bible.

  2. Talk to God, and allow Him to talk to you through His Word.

C. Group prayer should also be a vital part of the Christian's prayer life.

  1. Group prayer meetings are often dull and unattractive because Christians who participate do not have a vital personal prayer life.

  2. In spontaneous or conversational group prayer, each one prays briefly about only one area of praise or petition at a time. Each one may pray several times, as directed by the Spirit.

VI. What Should Be Included In Prayer?

A. *Adoration* should be the first act, to improve your attitude.

B. *Confession* is the next appropriate action as you dwell on God's righteousness.

C. *Thanksgiving* can then be offered in faith for "all things."

D. *Supplication* is your means of listing your prayer requests in specific ways.

VII. **How Can We Pray With Confidence?**

A. *Abiding* in Jesus and His Word will cause us to be in His will.

B. *Ask,* for Jesus said, "If you ask Me anything in My name, I will do it" (John 14:14).

C. *Believe* God: "Everything you ask in prayer, believing, you shall receive" (Matthew 21:22).

D. *Receive,* by faith and with thanksgiving, the answer to your request.

Whatever we vividly envision, ardently desire, sincerely believe and enthusiastically act upon must inevitably come to pass — assuming there is scriptural authority for it.

1. Imagine what will exist when your prayer is answered.

2. Ardently desire the actualization of that scene — ask God for it.

3. Sincerely believe that God will enable you to accomplish all that He has commanded you to do.

4. Enthusiastically act upon that for which God leads you to pray. Mobilize yourself and as many others as God gives you to help fulfill the Great Commission.

5. Claim as a part of the fulfillment of the Great Commission whatever sphere of influence God lays on your heart.

ADDENDUM

These Transferable Concepts are designed to make an important contribution toward your spiritual growth, but they are no substitute for the Word of God. If you do not already have a regular time when you study the Bible, I encourage you to begin one. To help you get started, a brief outline that you may want to use in your study follows. Simply select a short passage of Scripture and use the next four steps:

Observation. What do you see in this passage of Scripture? What does it tell you?

Interpretation. What does it mean?

Application. How can you use this in your life? What steps are needed to put this into practice?

Correlation. How does it fit in with other Scripture verses? (It is important to keep sections of Scripture in context with the entire scope of the chapter or book.)

More Books from Here's Life Publishers

The Holy Spirit: Key to Supernatural Living by Bill Bright. A clear explanation of what the Holy Spirit can do in your life now. Available in both quality paperback and hardback.

Vonette Bright's Prayer and Praise Diary by Vonette Bright. Excellent tool for developing an effective prayer life. Paperback.

Handbook for Christian Maturity. A Bible study series giving basic lessons on the exciting adventure of Christian living. Also available in a series of 11 individual booklets known as the Ten Basic Steps Toward Christian Maturity. Paperback.

Teacher's Manual for Ten Basic Steps. Bible study outlines for teaching complete series. Paperback.

Transferable Concepts by Bill Bright. Essentially the same material as that included in this Handbook of Concepts for Living, with each of the nine concepts available in an individual pocket-sized booklet.

Understanding Bible Truths. A systematic study of great biblical themes. Nine booklets with bright full color pictures. Endorsed by Bill Bright, Billy Graham and John Stott.

The Bible	The Holy Spirit	The Christian
God	Man	The Church
Jesus Christ	Salvation	Last Things

Available at your local Christian bookstore or from
Here's Life Publishers

Campus Crusade for Christ International
Arrowhead Springs
San Bernardino, CA 92414

☐ Please send me more information on how I can become a Christian.

☐ I have just received Jesus Christ as my Savior and would appreciate more information on how to experience the abundant Christian life.

☐ Please inform me of other materials for Christian growth.

Name _____

Street _____

City _____

State _____ Zip _____